THE LONGMAN COMPANION TO
SLAVERY, EMANCIPATION AND CIVIL RIGHTS

LONGMAN COMPANIONS TO HISTORY
General Editors: Chris Cook and John Stevenson

The following *Companions to History* are now available:

THE LONGMAN COMPANION TO
SLAVERY, EMANCIPATION AND CIVIL RIGHTS

Harry Harmer

An imprint of **Pearson Education**

Harlow, England · London · New York · Reading, Massachusetts · San Francisco · Toronto · Don Mills, Ontario · Sydney
Tokyo · Singapore · Hong Kong · Seoul · Taipei · Cape Town · Madrid · Mexico City · Amsterdam · Munich · Paris · Milan

Pearson Education Limited

Edinburgh Gate
Harlow
Essex CM20 2JE
United Kingdom

and Associated Companies throughout the world

Visit us on the World Wide Web at
www.pearsoneduc.com

———————————

First published in Great Britain in 2001

© Pearson Education Limited 2001

ISBN 0–582–40437–1 PPR

British Library Cataloguing in Publication Data
A CIP catalogue record for this book can be obtained from the British Library.

10 9 8 7 6 5 4 3 2 1
05 04 03 02 01 00

Typeset by 37
Set in 9½/12pt New Baskerville
Printed in Malaysia

Contents

Section 1: SLAVERY

Section 2: EMANCIPATION

Preface

This *Companion* attempts to provide, in a concise and accessible format, the essential information on the interlinked issues of slavery and the slave trade, resistance and emancipation, and civil rights. While, for reasons of space, the *Companion* concentrates on the experience of the Caribbean, colonial North America and the United States, I have included information on other areas which came under the control of European colonial powers, notably Brazil. The *Companion* also covers apartheid in South Africa, a central issue in racial oppression providing revealing comparisons.

Much of the information is presented in the form of chronologies but there are also – in addition to biographies and a glossary of terms – a number of tables illustrating some of the main themes. By its nature, the information provided on slavery can only be a series of relatively random snapshots of the institution and its contribution to the wealth of Europe and the United States. Similarly, the section on resistance to slavery cannot do justice to the extent of what must remain a largely hidden history. Fortunately, all these issues have become the subject of growing academic interest, as the reader who wants to look more deeply will find from the Bibliographies.

I should like to thank Dr Chris Cook for giving me the opportunity to contribute this *Companion* to the series and Hilary Shaw (formerly at Longmans) for her encouragement with both this title and with my previous book on the Labour Party. My thanks are due to Arianna Silvestri for tolerating my preoccupation and to Terry Tino Tigrottelli for his attempts to help.

Harry Harmer
January 2001

Abbreviations

ACMHR	Alabama Christian Movement for Human Rights
AFL	American Federation of Labor
ANC	African National Congress
CFA	Colored Farmers' Alliance
CIO	Congress of Industrial Organisations
CORE	Congress of Racial Equality
COSATU	Confederation of South African Trade Unions
MIA	Montgomery Improvement Association
NAACP	National Association for the Advancement of Colored People
PAC	Pan-Africanist Congress
RAC	Royal African Company
SCLC	Southern Christian Leadership Conference
SNCC	Student Nonviolent (later National) Co-ordinating Committee
SWAPO	South West African People's Organisation
UDF	United Democratic Front
UN	United Nations

Section 1

SLAVERY

1.1 Chronology of the Atlantic slave trade, 1441–1867

1441 The modern slave trade begins with the kidnapping of 12 Africans from a market on the Guinea coast by the explorer Antao Gonçalvez and their despatch to Portugal as a gift to Prince Henry 'the Navigator'; Portuguese explorers and traders have been operating in the Atlantic islands and on the West African coast from the early 15th century; Madeira is settled in 1419, the Azores from 1427, and exploration will move on to Senegal in 1435, Sierra Leone in 1446 and the Congo in 1481.

1442 Pope Eugenius IV grants Portugal exclusive rights in West Africa.

1444 Portugal has opened a direct trade with West African states in gold, ivory and slaves. Over 240 men, women and children are despatched from the Portuguese West African port of Lagos and 20% are given to the Regent of Portugal as domestic servants; African slaves are soon transported to labour on Madeira and Cape Verde in the Gulf of Guinea. By 1448 over a thousand slaves will be despatched to the Atlantic islands and in the next three decades 2,500 slaves will be carried there and a further 12,500 to Europe.

1452 The first sugar plantations are established on Madeira; the demand for the crop throughout Europe increases the need for slave labour.

1455 In the panic that follows the Ottoman capture of Constantinople, Pope Nicholas V issues the bull *Romanus Pontifex*, authorising King Afonso of Portugal to 'invade, search out, capture, vanquish, and subdue all Saracens and pagans whatsoever … and to reduce their persons to perpetual slavery'; Portugal interpret the bull as permission to conduct the trade in slaves from Africa.

1458 Prince Henry the Navigator's agents negotiate treaties with African rulers in which the Portuguese agree not to kidnap Africans but to purchase them.

1462 Pope Pius II writes to the bishop with authority over Portuguese Christians in West Africa, criticising traders who take African converts into captivity.

1480 The Portuguese slave trade is formalised with the establishment of a *Casa dos Escravos* in Lisbon under royal authority to organise shipments to the Atlantic islands and the Iberian peninsula; merchants purchase a contract to trade in slaves for a stipulated period and to sell them at public auctions in Lisbon. Portugal begins construction of a fortification at Elmina on the Gold Coast. In the next two decades 5,000 slaves will be taken to the Atlantic islands and 12,500 to Europe.

1486 The African kingdom of Benin begins trading with Portugal; slaves are transported from Benin to work in Portuguese sugar plantations on São Tomé in the Gulf of Guinea; by the end of the century a thousand slaves will have been taken to São Tomé. A further 12,500 will be transported to Europe and 5,000 to the Atlantic islands.

1492 Christopher Columbus conducts his first exploration of what will become known as the Caribbean, landing first in the Bahamas, Hispaniola and Cuba; in the following year Pope Alexander VI grants Ferdinand and Isabella of Spain all territories in the New World; this is followed by the Treaty of Tordesillas between Spain and Portugal which grants Portugal possession of the West African coast and what will later become Brazil in the Americas.

1498 Increasing numbers of slaves are being transported by Portugal to sugar plantations in Madeira and São Tomé; a total of 25,000 will be taken to the plantations over the next 30 years; another 12,500 will go to Europe.

1500 There is a major structural change in the slave trade as Portugal begins to meet the demand with slaves from the Spanish Caribbean islands; Spanish settlers in Hispaniola import the first African slaves into the Caribbean, initially as servants but increasingly as labourers in mines to replace the indigenous population; African slaves are reckoned to be four times as productive as local labour and more resistant to disease.

1506 The demand for slaves in the Caribbean increases as Spain begins sugar planting in the Greater Antilles; Portugal grants licences to Spanish settlers to import slaves direct from West Africa.

1502 Nicolas de Ovando, Spanish governor of Hispaniola, requests that no further shipments of African slaves are allowed to the colony because they encourage rebellion among the indigenous population.

1505 The first sugar plantation is established on Hispaniola; the majority of the slaves are from the indigenous population.

1510 The importing of slave labour into Portuguese Brazil begins as permission is given to transport 250 from Lisbon.

1513 A fee of two ducats is imposed for the importation of each slave into the Spanish Americas, a recognition of the growing importance of the trade. The first slaves are imported into Cuba from Hispaniola.

1514 Pope Leo X issues a bull condemning the slave trade and the institution of slavery.

1516 The West African kingdom of Benin prohibits the export of all male slaves, a ban it continues until the 18th century.

1517 The Bishop of Chiapa, Bartolomeo de las Casas, protests to Spain's King Charles V about the enslavement of indigenous peoples and asks that Spanish settlers in Haiti should be allowed to import 12 African slaves each to release indigenous slavery from forced labour; a licence is granted by Portugal for the importation of slaves into Spanish America.

1518 Charles V of Spain grants a licence to a favourite (which is then sold on to Genoese merchants) to transport 4,000 slaves annually for ten years to Hispaniola, Jamaica and Mexico; the licence passes to the Portuguese who continue to dominate the slave trade.

1520 São Tomé becomes a major centre of the Atlantic slave trade as its importance in sugar production begins to decline; 300 slaves are imported into Cuba as Spain introduces sugar plantations.

1523 The first sugar plantation is established in Puerto Rico; by the end of the decade 3,000 African slaves have been imported.

1524 The Spanish Crown gives permission for 300 African slaves to be imported into Cuba to work in gold mining.

1526 The Kongo king, Afonso I, who has declared his country to be Christian, complains about slave traders to João III of Portugal: 'They bring ruin to the country. Every day people are enslaved and kidnapped, even nobles, and even royal kinsmen.' His attempts to place limits on the trade are unsuccessful. In the course of the next two decades 12,500 slaves are taken to Spanish America.

1529 Spain begins the conquest of Peru, which is completed by 1537; the conquerors are granted at least 350 licences up to 1537 by the Council of the Indes to import African slaves and this soon develops into a flourishing trade; within 20 years there will be 3,000 slaves in the country, with demand increasing as silver mining intensifies.

1530 Portugal begins the conquest of Brazil; within seven years the first African slaves are landed in the north east of the country to work in sugar mills; importation is prompted by a papal bull forbidding the enslavement of the indigenous population and by its susceptibility to smallpox brought in by Europeans. The first slaving vessel sails directly from São Tomé to Hispaniola carrying 300 African slaves.

1531 The Spanish Crown allows loans at a reduced rate for settlers in the Caribbean to buy slaves for labour on sugar plantations.

1550 The intensification of the sugar plantation system by the Portuguese in Brazil increases the demand for slaves; by the end of the century the Bahia and Pernambuco regions are the world's sugar production centres; between 1500 and 1575 10,000 slaves are transported to Brazil.

1554 Three English ships return with ten African slaves from an expedition to Guinea and Benin financed by London merchants; the Dutch begin irregular slave trading on the Guinea coast.

1562 John Hawkins leads the first major English slave trading expedition, attacking a Portuguese ship and seizing 300 slaves whom he sells in the Spanish Caribbean colony of Hispaniola.

1564 Queen Elizabeth I – who originally declared, 'If any African were carried away without his free consent it would be detestable and call down the vengeance of Heaven upon the undertaking' – invests in Hawkins's second slaving expedition to Guinea; other prominent investors in the profitable mission include the Treasurer of the Navy, the Master of Ordinance to the Navy, a number of Privy Councillors and two future Lord Mayors of London.

1565 Spain transports slaves to St Augustine in what is now known as Florida, the first introduction of slavery in North America.

1570 Sugar plantation owners in Brazil are allowed to import up to 120 slaves at a reduced tax rate as investment in the industry is encouraged by growing profitability; there are now over 2,500 African slaves in the country.

1571 Portugal establishes a colony in the Luanda hinterland (now Angola) and a state is established in western Kimbundu devoted to supplying slaves; Portugal has a virtual monopoly of the slave trade and is now shipping over 10,000 directly across the Atlantic every year.

1576 Over the next two decades, an estimated 37,500 slaves are transported to Spanish America and 40,000 to Brazil.

1580 The crowns of Spain and Portugal are united under the Spanish king, Philip I.

1588 The Guinea Company is organised by English merchants to increase the effectiveness of their participation in the slave trade.

1595 Philip II of Spain grants Portuguese traders an *asiento* giving them the exclusive right to transport 38,250 slaves direct from Africa to South America at specified ports over a nine year period; over the next 45 years 268,000 slaves are imported into Spanish America.

1596 Dutch participation in the slave trade begins when a Dutch privateer takes slaves captured from a Portuguese ship to the Netherlands; they are freed.

1598 The Dutch establish their first trading posts on the West African Gold Coast and begin an attempt to dislodge Portugal from its dominance in the slave trade; they capture São Tomé in 1599 and within 30 years they will become the principal suppliers of slaves to the Spanish Caribbean.

1601 In the course of the next two decades, an estimated 100,000 slaves are carried to Brazil and 75,000 to Spanish America.

1609   The Virginia Company establishes an English colony in North America; the main source of labour for tobacco is initially white indentured labour contracted in England; the pattern is followed soon after in Maryland.

1619   The sale of 20 Africans (described as 'indentured servants') to the Virginia colony by a Dutch trader marks the introduction of slavery into non-Spanish North America; as white indentured labour becomes increasingly expensive it will be replaced by slave imports.

1625   The first consignment of slaves is landed in the Dutch North American colony of New Amsterdam; the numbers will remain low until the beginning of the 18th century.

1626   As the demand for labour intensifies, traders supply an estimated 100,000 slaves to Brazil and 52,500 to Spanish America over the next two decades. The first shipload of slaves is taken to the English Caribbean colony of St Kitts; in the next two decades an estimated 20,700 slaves will be taken to English Caribbean possessions and 2,500 to French possessions.

1630   A Dutch West India Company expedition captures the important Brazilian sugar production centres of Recife and Olina from Brazil; the capture of the Portuguese West African port of Elmina in 1637 and of Luanda allows the Dutch to end Portuguese influence in the area and to intensify their involvement in the slave trade. England establishes its first fortification on the Gold Coast and begins regular slave trading activity.

1634   The Dutch capture Curaçao from Spain and use the island as a centre for trading slaves throughout the Caribbean.

1636   Over the next eight years the Dutch West India Company will transport 2,500 slaves a year, marking a Dutch dominance in the trade that will last into the 1660s.

1637   The Dutch expand their area of control in north east Brazil and precipitate a revolution in sugar production that will further increase the demand for slaves. The first ship is built in Massachusetts specifically designed to transport slaves to North America.

1640   Sugar cane is introduced into the French Caribbean colonies of Martinique and Guadeloupe, opening up the 'sugar revolution' as the English follow suit and production develops in the Spanish colonies; as modern production techniques are introduced under Dutch influence, the demand for slaves increases. Portugal regains its independence from Spain.

1642   France begins its participation in the slave trade as Louis XIV grants authorisation.

1646   Sugar replaces the poor-quality tobacco grown in the English Caribbean colony of Barbados; the number of slaves on the island rises in ten years to 20,000 as the Dutch provide slaves they are unable to sell in Brazil.

1647 The Swedish African Company establishes a base on the West African coast to participate in the slave trade. Portugal grants Spanish traders direct access to purchase slaves in Guinea.

1648 Portugal recaptures Luanda from the Dutch, regaining access to a major source of slaves in Angola; within 50 years 70% of the slaves sold to Brazil will come from this area.

1650 Of 25,000 ships estimated to be involved in the Atlantic slave trade, 15,000 are owned by the Dutch.

1651 Over the next three decades, an estimated 185,000 slaves will be taken to Brazil and 62,500 to the Spanish Americas; a further 69,200 will be carried to the English Caribbean, 28,800 to the French and 20,000 to the Dutch possessions.

1654 The Dutch are ejected from north east Brazil by Portugal; the migration of Dutch planters to the Caribbean islands encourages the development of sugar production.

1663 The Company of Royal Adventurers Trading to Africa is established in England, financed by merchants in Bristol and London and including members of the Royal Family among its leading shareholders; the Company is granted a monopoly in slave trading to the English colonies but collapses through mismanagement.

1664 The French West Indies Company is organised with a monopoly in the slave trade to France's Caribbean colonies; it is wound up after a decade following opposition from independent traders and planters. The Portuguese king, Afonso VI, introduces measures to reduce overcrowding on ships transporting slaves to Brazil.

1670 Spain awards major contracts to the Dutch West India Company to carry slaves to Spanish America.

1671 The Danish West Indies Company, with members of the Royal Family among its leading shareholders, is granted a monopoly in Danish trade, including that in slaves.

1672 The Royal African Company is established with a monopoly in supplying slaves to English plantations in the Caribbean; over 40 years of trading the Company transports 125,000 slaves from Africa. As the demand for slaves intensifies, France offers a bounty for every slave transported to the French Caribbean; the monopoly on supplying slaves to French colonies is moved to the Senegal Company from the French West Indies Company.

1676 By the end of the century, an estimated 175,000 slaves will be carried to Brazil and 102,500 to the Spanish Americas; a further 173,800 will go to the British Caribbean, 124,500 to the French Caribbean and 20,000 to Dutch possessions.

1679   The Senegal Company undertakes to supply 2,000 slaves a year for eight years to the French Caribbean colonies.

1680   As the number of sugar plantations in the English Caribbean colony of Barbados rises to 350, over 1,300 slaves are imported every year. Over the next eight years, the Royal Africa Company supplies 46,396 slaves to English colonies in the Caribbean.

1682   The German kingdom of Brandenburg establishes its first trading post in West Africa and begins German involvement in the slave trade.

1684   The Portuguese king, Pedro II, issues further laws to reduce overcrowding on ships carrying slaves to Brazil in an attempt to reduce the high mortality rate.

1688   To meet the growing demands for labour in the English Caribbean, Jamaica requires the import of 10,000 slaves annually, the Leeward Islands 6,000 and the Bahamas 4,000.

1697   Denmark begins participating in the slave trade.

1698   The Royal African Company monopoly in the slave trade to English possessions is removed; private traders are allowed to send slave ships to and from Africa on payment of a 10% levy to the Company; in the following eight years, private traders carry 71,268 slaves to the Caribbean and the Royal African Company 17,760.

1700   The Asante Empire in West Africa begins to supply slaves to traders in exchange for firearms and will continue to do so until the early 19th century. Sugar production develops in the English Caribbean possessions of Antigua, Nevis, Jamaica and Montserrat; the fastest growth is in Jamaica, where 8,000 slaves are imported every year. The Dutch increasingly use Suriname as a staging point for the slave trade; 22,000 have passed through in the past three decades and 150,000 will be landed over the course of the next century.

1701   Between now and 1720 an estimated 292,000 slaves are imported into Brazil, with 90,400 to Spanish America; an estimated 160,000 are imported into the British Caribbean, 166,100 into the French Caribbean, 120,000 into the Dutch Caribbean and 19,800 into North America.

1702   As French participation in the slave trade grows with the capture of territories in West Africa, Spain awards the Royal French Guinea Company a concession to import 4,800 slaves a year into Spanish America for ten years; the Company goes into liquidation in 1710.

1713   Spain cedes the monopoly in supplying slaves to Spanish America to Britain under the Treaty of Utrecht; British traders are initially allowed to transport 4,800 slaves a year for 30 years and Britain becomes the largest slave trader; the contract continues (with one interruption during the war of 1739) to 1750 when the monopoly is relinquished for a payment by Spain of £100,000. Britain had already accepted a free trade in slavery for its subjects and through much of the 18th century wars between Britain and France are partly a struggle to control the slave trade.

1721 Over the next two decades, an estimated 312,400 slaves arrive in Brazil and 90,400 in Spanish America; 198,700 are transported to the British Caribbean, 195,500 to the French Caribbean, 80,000 to Dutch possessions and 50,400 to North America.

1730 In the British Caribbean, Jamaica begins to replace Barbados as a major sugar producer; the numbers of slaves in Jamaica rise from 74,000 to 173,000 in 1760 (half of all slaves in the British Caribbean); there is a similar pattern in the French Caribbean as Saint Domingue replaces Martinique.

1740 There are 117,000 slaves in the French caribbean possession of Saint Dominique, the leading sugar producer in the Caribbean and the area with the largest slave population; by the 1780s the slave population will be over 450,000. In the two decades after 1740, an estimated 345,000 slaves are carried to Brazil and 90,400 to Spanish America; 267,800 are transported to the British Caribbean, 297,800 to the French Caribbean, 80,000 to the Dutch Caribbean and 100,000 to North America.

1750 There are 145,000 slaves engaged in tobacco production in the British North American colonies of Virginia, Maryland and North Carolina, and 40,000 working in rice and indigo in Georgia and South Carolina.

1761 In the next two decades, 325,000 slaves are transported to Brazil and 121,900 to Spanish America; 335,300 are taken to the British Caribbean, 335,800 to the French Caribbean, 100,000 to the Dutch Caribbean and 85,800 to North America.

1762 Britain captures Cuba from Spain and opens Havana to a free trade in slaves; during the ten month occupation 10,000 slaves are imported into Cuba.

1763 Britain captures Grenada, St Vincent, Dominica and Tobago from France; sugar production is increased, leading to a greater demand for slaves.

1764 The agent for the British North American colony of Massachusetts in London reports that there are up to 60 absentee Caribbean plantation owners in Parliament who can hold the balance of power to protect their interests.

1778 Spain acquires two islands off Africa and the right of direct access to Portuguese territories in Africa to acquire slaves under a Treaty of Commerce and Friendship.

1780 British involvement in the slave trade reaches a peak with the transportation of 78,000 slaves a year (compared with an annual average over the 18th century of 45,000); half of all slaves transported are carried in British ships, with French and Portuguese ships accounting for a fifth. Over the next decade, an estimated 181,200 slaves are carried to Brazil and 42,200 to Spanish America; 100,200 are transported to the British Caribbean, 357,800 to the French Caribbean, 12,300 to Dutch possessions and 55,800 to North America.

1787 Freed slave Ottobah Cuguano – a Fante who was transported to Grenada – publishes his *Thoughts and Sentiments on the Evil and Wicked Traffic of the Slavery and Commerce of the Human Species in England* in which he writes, 'I was first kidnapped and betrayed by my own countrymen, who were the first cause of my exile and slavery; but if there were no buyers there would be no sellers.' A British government commission of enquiry into the slave trade reports that of the annual British export from Africa of 40,000 slaves, two thirds are sold on to Britain's economic competitors; this is viewed as detrimental to Britain's economic interests.

1789 Spain allows a free trade in slaves to its American and Caribbean possessions; there is a growth of slave trading centres in Colombia, Venezuela, Puerto Rico and Cuba.

1790 The number of slaves carried by Portuguese traders from Angola reaches 16,000 a year; this rises to 18,000 in the next two decades. British traders are carrying an annual 14,000 into Jamaica. Over the next decade 233,600 slaves are carried to Brazil and 77,400 to Spanish America; 194,300 are taken to the British Caribbean, 82,600 to the French Caribbean, 5,200 to the Dutch Caribbean and 79,000 to the United States.

1791 The trade in slaves to Cuba intensifies as virgin land is put under cultivation and the demand for labour on the sugar plantations rises; Spain reduces the import duty on slaves.

1792 As the abolition of the British slave trade is fiercely debated, the planter dominated Jamaican House of Assembly declares that 'the safety of the West Indies not only depends on the slave trade not being abolished, but on a speedy declaration of the House of Lords that they will not suffer the trade to be abolished'.

1793 The invention of the cotton gin by Eli Whitney will lead to an increased demand for slaves in the Southern United States as the cotton plantations expand.

1797 Spain authorises all subjects in its American possessions to engage directly in the slave trade.

1800 Brazil has a slave population of almost a million, with 23,000 being imported every year. In the course of the next decade an estimated 241,300 slaves are transported to Brazil and 85,700 to Spanish America; 105,400 are carried to the British Caribbean, 17,000 to the French Caribbean and 156,300 to the United States.

1807   Britain ends its participation in the slave trade but British banks continue to provide credit to assist foreign traders.

1811   Over the next decade, 327,000 slaves are transported to Brazil and 177,800 to Spanish America; there are few imports into the British Caribbean, but 18,800 are transported to the French Caribbean and 10,000 to the United States.

1817   Spain and Britain sign a treaty to end Spanish participation in the slave trade, with Spain to end slave trading north of the Equator immediately and south of the Equator in 1820; however, illegal slave trading to Cuba continues.

1821   Over the next decade, transportation of slaves to Brazil soars to an estimated 431,000; 103,500 are carried to Spanish America, 37,900 to the French Caribbean and 2,000 to the United States.

1822   Brazil declares independence from Portugal but Portugal continues to trade in slaves from Africa to Brazil; the trade intensifies between 1825 and 1850, with half the total number of Africans imported into Brazil arriving in this period.

1825   The British navy steps up anti-slave trading patrols off West Africa; over the course of the next 40 years they arrest 1,287 ships and free 130,000 slaves; however, despite this activity, an estimated 1.8 million slaves are transported to the Americas.

1831   In the course of the next decade, an estimated 334,300 slaves are transported to Brazil and 207,000 to Spanish America; in the run up to the abolition of slavery in British possessions, 10,200 are carried to the British Caribbean and 600 to the French Caribbean.

1841   Over the next decade, an estimated 378,400 slaves are transported to Brazil and 54,600 to Spanish America.

1844   A British representative on the Court of Mixed Commissions in Sierra Leone (a body established to prevent the slave trade) reports to the Foreign Office that the trade 'is increasing, and it continues more systematically than it has ever been before'.

1850   Despite the abolition of the slave trade by Brazil, an estimated 6,400 slaves are brought into the country over the next decade; 122,000 are carried to Spanish America and 12,500 to the French Caribbean.

1867   The last slave trading vessel crosses the Atlantic bound for Cuba. During the 1860s an estimated 31,600 slaves are transported to Spanish America and 5,900 to the French Caribbean.

1.1.1 Estimated numbers of Africans carried across the Atlantic as slaves, 1662–1867

1662–70	82,684
1671–80	89,316
1681–90	157,677
1691–1700	176,472
1701–09	359,940
1710–19	402,870
1720–29	516,650
1730–39	599,510
1740–49	551,060
1750–59	581,890
1760–69	783,200
1770–79	717,820
1780–89	793,860
1790–99	759,240
1800–10	605,770
1811–20	531,300
1821–30	593,100
1831–40	566,600
1841–51	455,400
1851–60	155,400
1861–67	49,900
Total	9,529,260

Source. Based on tables in Herbert S. Klein, *The Atlantic Slave Trade*, (Cambridge, 1999), pp. 208–9.

1.1.2 Destinations of Africans transported across the Atlantic, estimated numbers, 1451–1870

	British North America/ United States	Brazil	Spanish America	Caribbean*	Europe, the Atlantic islands & São Tomé
1451–75					15,000
1476–1500					18,500
1501–25					42,500
1526–50			12,500		31,300
1551–75		10,000		25,000	26,300
1576–1600	40,000	37,500	16,300		
1601–25	100,000	75,000	12,800		
1626–50	100,000	52,500	20,950	6,600	

1651–75	185,000	62,500	118,000	3,000	
1676–1700	175,000	102,500	322,300	2,700	
1701–20	19,800	292,700	90,400	352,300	
1721–40	50,400	312,400	90,400	373,100	
1741–60	100,400	354,500	90,400	651,900	
1761–80	85,800	325,900	121,900	816,100	
1781–90	55,800	181,200	42,200	474,900	
1791–1800	79,000	233,600	77,400	296,700	
1801–10	156,300	241,300	85,700	125,700	
1811–20	10,000	327,700	177,800	18,800	
1821–30	2,000	431,400	103,500	58,400	
1831–40	0	334,300	207,000	10,800	
1841–50	0	378,400	54,600	0	
1851–60	300	6,400	122,000	12,500	
1861–70	0	0	31,600	5,900	
Totals:	559,800	4,029,800	1,662,400	3,790,500	175,000

*Note: British, French, Dutch and Danish colonies in the Caribbean.
Source: Based on tables in Herbert S. Klein, *The Atlantic Slave Trade* (Cambridge, 1999), pp. 210–11.

1.1.3   Profits of the British slave trade, 1761–1807

	Numbers landed	Average individual gross sale price (£)	% profit
1761–70	284,834	29	8.2
1771–80	235,042	35	12.1
1781–90	294,865	36	10.7
1791–1800	393,404	50	13.0
1801–07	217,556	60	3.3
Total	930,642	42	9.5

Source: Based on table in Roger Anstey, *The British Slave Trade and British Abolition* (1975), p. 47.

1.2 Chronology of slavery in the Caribbean, 1492–1886

1492 Christopher Columbus reaches the Caribbean on his first voyage of exploration, landing first in the Bahamas, Hispaniola and Cuba; in the following year Pope Alexander VI grants Ferdinand and Isabella of Spain all territories in the New World. Hispaniola is the first island to be settled, followed by Jamaica in 1509, Cuba in 1511 and Puerto Rico in 1512. The colonists will initially use the indigenous population to meet their needs for labour.

1502 The Spanish king forbids the import of slaves 'suspect in the Faith' into the Caribbean; Nicolas de Ovando is appointed governor of Hispaniola to force the indigenous population to work in agriculture, as servants and later in extracting minerals. Ovando takes black slaves from Spain and Portugal but then asks that no more are introduced because they encourage the indigenous population to rebel and they themselves become fugitives.

1504 Five white slaves are taken to the Spanish colony of Puerto Rico and are joined a year later by a further two.

1505 Seventeen African slaves are taken to Hispaniola to work in copper mining; as the demand for labour increases, 100 more arrive during the year. The first sugar plantation is established on Hispaniola; the majority of the slaves working in cultivation of the crop are from the indigenous population.

1511 Dominican monks in Hispaniola write to the Spanish king informing him that 'as the labour of one Negro is more valuable than that of four Indians, every effort should be made to bring to Hispaniola many Negroes from Guinea'. The Spanish Crown authorises agents in Seville to despatch 250 slaves to work in mining in Hispaniola; this replacement of indigenous by black slaves will increasingly be the pattern in the Caribbean.

1512 The Law of Burgos declares an already declining indigenous population in the Spanish Caribbean to be free; it is to be converted to Christianity and forced to labour; the instruction is largely disregarded, as future events will show.

1513 The first African slaves arrive in Cuba as a landowner receives permission to import four from Hispaniola.

1516 The first mill to refine sugar is built in Hispaniola and the first cargo of sugar is shipped to Spain. Sugar mills are introduced in Jamaica (by 1523 there are 30), Puerto Rico (which has ten by 1533) and Cuba (where there will be 40 by 1540). Sugar will replace gold as the main economic activity within 20 years.

1517 Portugal is granted an *asiento* (a licence) to take 400 slaves to Spanish America, with a total to the Spanish Caribbean of 4,000 over the course of eight years. Requests mount for more African slaves to be imported into the Spanish Caribbean because of their superior qualities as workers.

1518 A smallpox epidemic throughout the western Caribbean kills much of the indigenous population.

1520 The first large group of slaves, totalling 300, arrive in Cuba.

1523 The first sugar mill is established in Puerto Rico; by the end of the decade there are 3,000 African slaves on the island. Authorisation is given for the import of a further 4,000 slaves into the Caribbean, 1,500 to be taken into Hispaniola, 500 to Puerto Rico and 300 each to Cuba and Jamaica.

1524 A further 300 slaves are taken to Cuba to work in the gold mines.

1528 Seven hundred slaves are imported into Cuba; a contract is given to German traders to bring 4,000 slaves to the Caribbean over the next four years.

1531 The Dominican friar Bartolomé de las Calas, who has been appointed Protector of the Indians, appeals to the Spanish government to allow the entry of more African slaves into the Caribbean colonies.

1532 Twenty Spanish colonists receive a licence to import white slaves into the Caribbean; the party includes women to marry the settlers.

1537 Pope Paul IV issues a bull demanding that the indigenous population should not be enslaved and those who have been taken into captivity should be released; the instruction continues to be ignored.

1542 King Charles V of Spain issues an instruction that slaves from the indigenous population are to be freed and to be well treated as labourers; following protests from their owners, the instruction is withdrawn the following year.

1552 As sugar production gains impetus as the main economic activity in Hispaniola, 2,000 slaves are imported into the colony in one year alone; each of the larger sugar mills is operated by over 200 slaves.

1571 There are 13,000 slaves in the Spanish Caribbean colony of Hispaniola out of a total population of 18,000; the average plantation has 200 slaves but there are now a number with up to 500.

1575 As competition from Brazil begins, sugar production in Hispaniola and Puerto Rico declines in importance and many mills are abandoned; slave imports into the area decline significantly. As Spanish Caribbean slavery becomes increasingly urbanised, the opportunities to secure manumission or to purchase freedom increase.

1610 Slaves make up half of Cuba's 20,000 population; many are working for the Spanish Crown constructing fortifications and in ship-building.

1619 The King of Spain decrees that it is not necessary to use the due process of law in dealing with fugitive slaves, a sign of the extent of flight among African slaves transported into the Spanish Caribbean.

1623 The English begin a long-term process of Caribbean colonisation when they land on St Kitts, which they divide with the French three years later; English colonists then occupy Barbados.

1634 The Dutch seize Curaçao, Bonaire and Aruba from Spain; Bonaire becomes a plantation colony owned by the Dutch West Indies Company while Curaçao becomes a transit centre in the growing Dutch slave trade.

1635 Guadeloupe is occupied by the French and slaves are soon moved into the colony.

1636 The English governor of Barbados declares that all Africans and Indians in the colony will be treated as slaves unless they have a written contract stating otherwise; there are 200 slaves who are initially used in the cultivation of tobacco and there are a further 2,000 white indentured servants. The tobacco is of inferior quality to that produced in the English North American colony of Virginia and is declining in importance as an export crop.

1640 Sugar cane is introduced into the French Antilles (St Christopher, Guadeloupe, Martinique, Marie Galante and St Lucia); there is a 'sugar revolution' as the English and Spanish follow in developing plantations and mills. The English colony of Barbados turns to sugar as sales of its poor quality tobacco fall away. There is a growth in the demand for slave labour throughout the Caribbean as indentured servants prove increasingly unsatisfactory; slaves are cheaper to maintain, are more resistant to disease and bring a greater knowledge of tropical agriculture.

1642 As sugar production takes off, France begins to introduce greater numbers of slaves into its Caribbean colonies; by the end of the 17th century over 10% of the slaves imported into the Americas are working on French sugar plantations; during the 17th century sugar plantation will prove to be among the most profitable of investments, with an average return of 10%, rising in some cases to 40%.

1645 With increasing sugar plantation activity in Barbados, there are 5,680 slaves; within a decade – as sugar production rivals that of Brazil, until now the leading producer in the Americas – numbers will grow to an estimated 20,000 and by the end of the 17th century to 42,000.

1654 A thousand Dutch expelled from Brazil as Portugal re-occupies the area move to Guadeloupe and 300 to Martinique; their introduction of advanced production techniques and access to new markets increases the importance of sugar production in the French colonies.

1655 England seizes Jamaica from Spain; there are 70 mills on the island producing 760 tons of sugar annually and 1,400 slaves; by the end of the 17th century there will be 40,000 slaves in Jamaica.

1660 There are 4,600 slaves in the French colony of Martinique and 2,500 in Guadeloupe; the English colony of Barbados has over 20,000 slaves.

1661 Barbados exports 15,000 tons of sugar, almost equalling the exports from Brazil; the colony brings in an 'Act for the Better Ordering and Governing of Negroes' which describes the slaves as 'heathenish', 'brutal' and a 'dangerous kind of people' to be suppressed at all times.

1663 A director of the newly established Company of Royal Adventurers Trading to Africa, which has a monopoly of the English slave trade, writes to King Charles II that the 'very being' of the Caribbean plantation system depends on the labour of African slaves.

1664 The French Senegal Company is established by Jean-Baptise Colbert (1619–83); one of its major activities is shipping slaves to Martinique via Guadeloupe to satisfy the need for labour on the sugar plantations; there are 2,700 slaves working in Martinique.

1667 Barbados has 80,000 slaves producing sugar on plantations operated by 745 owners; the colony's wealth has multiplied twenty-fold since the 1640s. The English Parliament passes an 'Act to Regulate the Negroes on the Plantations', the first of a series of codes setting out the treatment of slaves; it orders that slaves are to be controlled with 'strict severity', are not to work on Sundays and should be whipped and branded for striking 'a Christian' (which has effectively become a euphemism for 'white'). An English court rules that, 'Negroes being infidels, there could be property in them.'

1670 A decree of French King Louis XIV states, 'There is nothing which contributes more to the development of the colonies and the cultivation of their soil than the laborious toil of the Negroes.' The slave population of Jamaica has risen to 9,000.

1671 Jamaica, seized by England from Spain 15 years earlier, has 146 plantations; within 13 years this grows to 690, with sugar production predominating.

1672 The Royal African Company is established in England and granted a monopoly of trade with Africa; in its 40 year existence the Company will introduce 150,000 African slaves into the Caribbean.

1673 Denmark begins the import of slaves to work on the cultivation of tobacco and cotton in its Caribbean colony of St Thomas; within 15 years there will be almost 500 slaves on the island.

1674 The intensification of sugar production in the English Caribbean leads to a demand for greater imports of slaves; in Barbados the number of indentured servants falls to under 3,000 (compared with 13,000 in the 1650s) and the number of slaves rises to 35,000. As the work pattern is more intensive than that in Brazil, with an 18 hour working day, higher mortality and a lower birth rate, progressively higher supplies of slaves are necessary. Sugar production in Martinique rises to over 5,300 tons.

1680 As the numbers of fugitive slaves grow, the Spanish colonial authorities introduce more systematic laws for dealing with them; the expense of recapture is to be shared between the Crown and their owners; a slave who is absent for four days will receive 50 lashes, 100 lashes and two months in leg irons for eight days absence; a slave who has banded with other fugitives will receive 200 lashes; absence of over six months (together with a criminal offence) will receive the death penalty. Barbados has become a planter-dominated colony, with 200 large plantations working over 60 slaves each and a further 200 with 20–60 slaves.

1683 Sugar production in Martinique reaches over 7,000 tons and there are over 1,500 slaves in the colony; in Barbados, there are now over 350 sugar mills.

1685 The Spanish Council of the Indies reports that without African slaves it would be impossible to provide sufficient food for the kingdom. Plans by England to use the Caribbean island of Barbuda as a slave breeding colony are abandoned. France introduces the *Code Noir*, 'An Ordinance Concerning the Discipline of the Church, and the Condition of Slaves in the West Indian Colonies', the most systematic European attempt to regulate the conditions of slavery; all slaves are to be instructed and baptised in the Catholic faith, are to be under the control of a Catholic overseer and are not to work on Sundays and religious holidays; they are to be allowed to marry with the consent of their owner and to be allowed a weekly ration of two pounds of salt beef or three pounds of fish; they are not to carry arms except for hunting and are to be executed if they strike an owner and draw blood.

1688 To meet the demand for labour, Jamaica requires the import of an estimated 10,000 slaves annually, the Leeward Islands 6,000 and the Bahamas 4,000. In Barbados, legislation is introduced making the theft of even the smallest amount by a slave a capital offence.

1691 Bermuda introduces legislation forbidding slaves to cultivate tobacco, corn, potatoes or other provisions, to raise poultry and livestock, and to make clothes; the penalty for disobeying the instruction is whipping.

1700 There are an estimated 30,000 slaves working in the French Caribbean, 14,200 of whom are in Martinique (where sugar production is over 13,000 tons annually), 9,000 in Saint Domingue (where the sugar crop is beginning to grow in importance) and 6,700 in Guadeloupe. There are an estimated 100,000 slaves in the English Caribbean (where sugar has become the main and most profitable export crop) and in Spanish Cuba almost half the 50,000 population are slaves, working predominantly in sugar and tobacco production.

1706 Over 80% of female slaves and almost 60% of male slaves in the British colony of St Kitts are field slaves; the remainder of women are domestics, while men are engaged in other crafts and skills; this appears to be the general pattern throughout the Caribbean.

1711 Jamaica introduces legislation forbidding slaves to keep animals, to trade on their own account and to hire themselves out as workers without their owner's permission.

1715 As sugar production in the French Caribbean begins to rival that of Britain in importance, there are an estimated 26,000 slaves in Martinique and 24,000 in Saint Domingue; sugar production grows in Saint Domingue, where there are over 140 sugar mills, growing to over 300 in 1739 and almost 800 in 1790.

1721 Coffee is introduced to the British Caribbean colony of Jamaica; within a century there will be over 20,000 slaves working on coffee plantations.

1723 Marriage between slaves and Europeans is outlawed in the French Caribbean colonies.

1733 Denmark purchases St Croix from France and begins sugar production; within 50 years there are 20,000 slaves in the colony and annual sugar production rises to 8,000 tons.

1734 There are an estimated 46,000 slaves in Barbados. St Lucia introduces legislation forbidding slaves to sell coffee or cotton.

1736 There are 55,700 slaves in Martinique, an increase of over 50,000 in the past half century; in Guadeloupe, there are 33,400, a rise of almost 30,000.

1737 There is a mass suicide attempt on the British Caribbean island of St Christopher as 100 slaves being imported throw themselves overboard, 33 die immediately and others later.

1740 As dependence on sugar cane cultivation grows in Cuba, the Havana Company is established to intensify the import of slaves. Sugar produced by slaves has become the main export crop in Jamaica.

1744   France forbids slaves in its territories from trading in cattle; this is extended three years later to poultry, although slaves are allowed to sell fruit and vegetables with their owner's permission.

1745   The King's Council in France issues a decree stating that slaves fleeing into French colonies will become the property of the Crown after four slaves escape from English controlled Antigua to Guadeloupe.

1748   The Jamaican House of Assembly rejects a proposal that mutilation and dismemberment of slaves should not be allowed without the consent of a magistrate. The slave population of Barbados reaches over 47,000 and an estimated 90% of the Caribbean sugar producing islands' population are slaves.

1755   Denmark bans the separation of minors from slave families in its possessions.

1762   Britain occupies the Cuban capital of Havana for ten months during the Seven Years' War and declares a free trade in the importation of slaves; in this period over 10,000 slaves are introduced into the island.

1763   There are over 200,000 slaves in the French colony of Saint Domingue; over the next ten years a further 100,000 will be imported. In the same period Spanish Cuba imports an average of 1,000 slaves a year.

1764   There are 37,000 slaves in the British colony of Antigua, 25,000 of whom are working on 300 sugar plantations. Over 35,000 slaves will be imported into the British colony of Barbados over the next seven years, while the slave population will rise by only 5,000 as slaves succumb to the harsh work regime and inadequate food. As the numbers of slaves rise in Jamaica, the House of Assembly attempts to limit imports but is overruled by the governor. The agent for the British North American colony of Massachusetts in London reports that there are up to 60 absentee Caribbean plantation owners in Parliament who can hold the balance of power to protect their interests. There are 206,000 slaves in the French Caribbean, an increase of over 150,000 in the past 40 years.

1767   Slaves in the British Caribbean colony of St Vincent are forbidden to sell sugar, cotton or rum without their owner's written permission; growing unauthorised crops is deemed to be theft.

1774   Spanish Cuba's slave population reaches over 44,000; there are also over 30,000 free blacks on the island. Jamaica has 105,000 slaves working on 680 sugar plantations while a further 40,000 are engaged in producing other crops; a further attempt by the House of Assembly to restrict imports is overruled by the governor. Slave labour in the British Caribbean has pushed sugar production up to 100,000 tons annually.

1775 The slave population of the British colony of Barbados has risen to 60,000 and there are 190,000 slaves in Jamaica. Throughout the Caribbean, sugar plantations have an average of 240 slaves.

1776 The economist Adam Smith (1723–90) writes of the Caribbean, 'The profits of a sugar plantation in any of our West India colonies are generally much greater than those of any other cultivation that is known in either Europe or America.'

1780 There are 437,738 slaves in the French Caribbean out of a total population of 514,849. Despite a decline in sugar production on Barbados, there are over 57,000 slaves on the island. In the Dutch colony of Curaçao, where slaves are more important as a commodity than as a source of labour, there are an estimated 7,000 slaves. In the course of the 18th century the Dutch have brought almost 200,000 slaves to their Caribbean colonies for onward sale.

1784 The Consolidated Slave Act in Jamaica outlaws 'cruel and unusual' punishment for slaves and makes regulations governing their working hours, free time and clothing; separation of slave families is forbidden and female slaves who have borne six or more children are exempted from work. Other British colonies in the Caribbean pass similar legislation.

1787 There are 461,864 slaves and 7,706 free blacks in the British Caribbean out of a total population of 527,923. Spanish Cuba's slave population reaches over 50,000.

1788 With a slave population approaching 500,000 (two thirds of whom are African born and therefore recent imports), the French colony of Saint Domingue has 800 sugar plantations, 3,000 coffee plantations and almost 800 devoted to producing cotton. The quality of the soil makes the colony's sugar the most profitable in the Caribbean, with plantations making over 8% return on capital (and a third 12%); by comparison, sugar plantation profits in the British Caribbean are under 6% in Barbados, 5% in St Kitts, 4% in Jamaica, Grenada and Antigua and 3% in Montserrat; the French colony produces more sugar than the entire British Caribbean. In Cuba, where sugar has taken off as a crop since the 1770s, 14,000 tons of sugar are produced. The Jamaican House of Assembly notes 'the great proportion of deaths that happen among Negroes newly imported'; in the British Caribbean a third of imported slaves die within three years of import, largely succumbing to disease.

1789 There are 675,000 slaves in the French Caribbean and a white population of 54,000. Charles IV of Spain issues the Código Negro governing the treatment of slaves in Spanish possessions; slaves must receive religious instruction and punishments of over 25 lashes are forbidden; slaves are to be allowed to marry and to have holidays on feast days and priests are to check observance of the new regulations;

there are protests from slave owners, particularly in Cuba and Santo Domingo, and the rules are largely withdrawn in 1794, although some provisions remain.

1790   Spanish Cuba's sugar exports reach almost 14,000 tons; over the next 15 years the colony will import over 88,000 slaves at an annual rate of almost 6,000; by 1820 325,000 slaves will have been imported.

1791   There is a slave rising in the French colony of Saint Domingue (now Haiti) which eventually succeeds in overthrowing slavery; many French planters emigrate to Cuba with their slaves. Slaves in the Dutch Caribbean become the property of the King of the Netherlands as the Dutch West Indies Company begins liquidating its interests. Sugar production in Cuba rises as virgin land is put under cultivation, increasing the demand for slave labour; the Spanish government opens up Cuba to a free trade in slaves, reduces the import duty and allows slave traders to export rum and other commodities free of tax.

1792   As the abolition of the British slave trade is fiercely debated, the planter dominated Jamaican House of Assembly declares that 'the safety of the West Indies not only depends on the slave trade not being abolished, but on a speedy declaration of the House of Lords that they will not suffer the trade to be abolished'.

1794   Acknowledging the success of the revolution in Haiti, the Paris Convention outlaws slavery in French possessions; estate owners in Guadeloupe who remain loyal to the monarch are executed.

1802   Slavery is reinstated in the French colonies by Napoleon Bonaparte and resistance continues in Haiti. Cuban sugar exports reach over 37,000 tons.

1805   The acquisition by Britain of new colonies in the Caribbean threatens existing plantation owners with increased economic competition; in response they become more sympathetic to a restriction in the slave trade; the introduction of new slaves into British Guiana (later Guyana) and Trinidad is prohibited.

1806   The first African self-help organisation is established in the Spanish colony of Cuba to co-operate to purchase freedom for slaves.

1807   Britain ends its participation in the slave trade, although an illegal trade into the Caribbean continues.

1817   The first census in Spanish Cuba shows there are 239,000 slaves and 119,221 free blacks out of a total population of 630,000; the white population increasingly fears a slave rising following the example of Haiti and encourages an agreement with Britain for Spain to end its participation in the slave trade from 1820. However, some Cuban landowners regard this as a British attempt to stem competition and the illegal importation of slaves into Cuba continues. In the British

Caribbean colony of Jamaica, 37% of slaves are African born and in Trinidad and Guiana 53%.

1823 The Jamaica House of Assembly rejects instructions from Britain to improve the conditions of slaves, arguing that the existing codes 'render the slave population as happy and comfortable, in every respect, as the labouring classes in any part of the world'.

1825 Cuba has 2,000 plantations producing an annual 40,000 tons of sugar; the Spanish colony will soon be exporting more sugar than the rest of the Caribbean combined.

1826 The Spanish government declares that slaves able to demonstrate they have been illegally imported into Spanish possessions since Spain ended its participation in the slave trade in 1820 must be freed. Following the loss of Haiti, France has intensified sugar production in its remaining Caribbean colonies and Martinique and Guadeloupe now produce more than before Haiti's independence.

1827 A census in Cuba shows there are 287,000 slaves, most of whom are working on sugar plantations. In Puerto Rico the 34,240 slaves represent 10% of the population.

1832 France makes it simpler for individual owners to free their slaves by abolishing the tax levied on manumission and easing the procedure. In the following year the mutilation and branding of fugitive slaves is outlawed. The British colony of Jamaica has 527 sugar estates, with 117,670 slaves (almost half the island's slave population), with a further 22,562 engaged in coffee production.

1833 On the eve of emancipation of the slaves, production on plantations in the British Caribbean is declining, with sugar falling over the past 20 years by 1% (as competition increases from Brazil and British-controlled India), coffee by 14% and cotton – outstripped by the United States – by 88%; a House of Commons committee has reported on 'considerable distress' in the area.

1834 Slavery is abolished in the British Caribbean colonies. Of approximately 2,000,000 slaves imported into the British Caribbean over the past 180 years, the slave population now comprises less than 700,000, largely due to the climate, disease and a punitive plantation regime. Many slaves are forced to continue working for their former owners under the apprenticeship system. Slaves in Denmark's colonies are guaranteed a plot of land by royal decree and the right to manumission after a fixed period of service.

1840 As Cuban sugar production becomes the most mechanised in the Caribbean, over 45% of the Cuban population are slaves; there is continuing disappointment with the results of legislation allowing for the release of slaves illegally imported after Spain abandoned the slave trade in 1820.

1844   There is growing opposition to slave imports into Cuba following the ruthless suppression of rising at a sugar mill in which thousands of slaves are killed.

1846   There are 323,897 slaves in Cuba and 149,226 free blacks.

1848   France abolishes slavery in its Caribbean colonies; facing increased competition from domestic sugar beet, sugar production in Martinique has fallen by over 50% in the past ten years and has declined in Guadeloupe by over two thirds. Slaves are granted their freedom in the Dutch colony of St Maarten after threatening to move to the French section of the island. Denmark ends slavery in its possessions.

1851   Spain is urged by the British government to abolish slavery in its Caribbean colonies; Britain argues that this would act as a disincentive to the United States to annex Cuba.

1860   There are 1,318 sugar mills in Cuba producing 515,000 tons of sugar; the slave population has risen to over 370,000.

1863   The Dutch end slavery in their Caribbean possessions.

1867   There are no further slave imports into Cuba; a census shows there are 344,615 slaves on the island while the free black population has risen from 177,824 to 248,703 in the past ten years.

1868   There is a wave of slave liberations in Cuba following the declaration of independence from Spain by nationalist landowner Carlos Manuel de Céspesdes (1819–74); however, many slave owners and their slaves, particularly in the west of the island, fail to support the declarations and slavery is restored by Spain during the course of a ten year guerrilla war of independence.

1870   Spain announces emancipation for all slaves over 60 and those born after 1868 in Cuba (the latter under the 'law of the free stomach'). The number of slaves in Puerto Rico falls to 30,635 (5% of the total population), a dramatic decline over the past ten years from 41,736 (14%); planters have argued that the supply of labour for hire is adequate enough for slavery to be abolished.

1873   Spain abolishes slavery in its Caribbean colony of Puerto Rico. The black American activist Henry Highland Garnet (1815–82) calls for an invasion of Cuba to free the slaves. The Spanish First Republic announces a complete abolition of slavery in Cuba but it is restored in the west by the Bourbon monarchy in 1874.

1878   Spain promises the gradual emancipation of slaves in Cuba under the Treaty of Zanjón ending the first Cuban war of independence.

1880   Spain issues a decree gradually freeing the slaves without compensation to their owners.

1886   With the final emancipation of the slaves in Cuba, slavery ends in the Caribbean.

1.2.1 Slave population of the British and French Caribbean in the Eighteenth Century

	British	French
1690	95,000	27,000
1710	110,000	60,000
1730	219,000	169,000
1750	295,000	265,000
1770	428,000	379,000
1790	480,000	675,000

Source: Based on table in Robin Blackburn, *The Making of New World Slavery: From the Baroque to the Modern 1492–1800* (1997), p. 404.

1.3 Chronology of slavery in South America, 1500–1888

1500   The arrival on the coast of Brazil of a fleet commanded by Pedro Alvarez Cabral opens the European colonisation of South America; the Treaty of Tordesillas in 1494 has already delineated a division of territory between Portugal and Spain. Both powers find indigenous populations which they will use as conscripted labour, destroying many of their communities; some resist, others escape, while many die of diseases brought by the Europeans. In Peru, an estimated indigenous population of ten million in 1500 falls to eight million by the end of the century; in the Andes region, the indigenous population falls over the same period from nine million to under a million and there is a similar decline in Central America.

1501   The Spanish Crown's *Instrucciones* initially forbid the importation of anyone other than Christians born of Christian parents into the New World, partly in an attempt to prevent the import of Spanish born African slaves (*ladinos*) into the Americas.

1510   While little attempt is yet being made to colonise South America, Dominican friar Bartolomé de las Casas (1474–1566) protests at the treatment of the indigenous population and recommends imports of African slaves into the New World on the grounds that they are better suited to hard labour; as colonisation develops, this call will increasingly be heard from the Catholic church.

1517   Portuguese traders are granted a licence to import 400 slaves into Spanish America.

1518   The colonial administrator Alonso Zuazo writes to King Charles I of Spain proposing the granting of a licence to import further African slaves into the Americas as they are 'ideal for the work here, in contrast to the natives, who are so feeble that they are only suitable for light work'; Zuazo doubts the slaves will rebel and Charles I grants permission to carry slaves. In the course of the next 30 years, 12,500 slaves will be introduced into Spanish America as Spain begins to consolidate its occupation of Uruguay (1516), Panama and Costa Rica (1519), Nicaragua (1522), Guatemala (1523), Honduras (1524), Ecuador and Colombia (1525), Peru (1526) and Venezuela (1527).

1526   A decree of the Spanish Crown rules that the children of slaves are not to be granted their freedom, which has the effect of encouraging owners to force female slaves to breed; the terms of the decree are reiterated in 1541.

1529 The Spanish occupiers of Peru (the *conquistadores*) are given permission by the Crown and the Council of the Indies to import slaves to work in gangs of 10–15 in the gold and silver mines of Peru and Chile; their labour is so profitable that one year of work covers a slave's purchase price; over 350 licences to import slaves are granted by 1537. Within 30 years there will be 3,000 slaves in Peru, half in the main settlement, Lima, as mining increases the demand for ancillary labour.

1533 Portugal establishes its first settlement in Brazil at São Vicente and the territory is divided into 15 administrative districts known as 'captaincies'.

1537 Pope Paul IV issues a bull ordering an end to the enslavement of Brazil's indigenous population (the 'Indians') and declares that those who have been made slaves should be released; the bull is largely ignored.

1538 The first African slaves are landed in north east Brazil, encouraged by Portuguese experience in using African labour in sugar cultivation in Madeira, the Azores and São Tomé and in response to Pope Paul's bull against indigenous slavery.

1539 Duarte Coelho, the administrator of the Pernambuco in northern Brazil, seeks permission of King João III of Portugal to transport slaves from the Portuguese African colony of Guinea as sugar plantations are developed in Brazil; over the course of the next 30 years, the colonists will turn increasingly to Africa for slaves, as the indigenous population succumbs to disease and the Catholic church continues its opposition to its enslavement; sugar will become Brazil's dominant product, and the source of the main demand for slaves, for over two centuries.

1542 The 'New Laws' are introduced in Spanish America, partly in an attempt to suppress the slavery of the indigenous population (which, however, remains permissible if they are captured in war); this leads to an increased demand for African slaves.

1545 In an attempt to alleviate labour shortages in developing silver mines, Francisco de Toleda, the Viceroy of Peru, conscripts free blacks, mulattos and unemployed Europeans.

1549 Sugar plantations and mills are expanded in Brazil, building on Portuguese experience in the Atlantic islands; as world demand for sugar increases the demand for African slaves rises; sugar will produce greater revenue for the Portuguese Crown than gold; the first Portuguese governor-general for Brazil is appointed, with central government in the newly founded capital of San Salvador da Bahia, which soon becomes a centre for the import of slaves from Africa.

1550   Bahia receives its first significant import of slaves delivered directly from Africa for distribution to the sugar plantations of the Pernambuco region; over the next 25 years an estimated 10,000 slaves are introduced into Brazil; in Spanish America there are 15,000 slaves and over the next 25 years 25,000 slaves will be imported into this area (including Central America and the Caribbean).

1559   The Portuguese regent, Dona Catarine, orders her representative in São Tomé (off West Africa) to deliver slaves to every sugar producer in Brazil who has a licence from the colony's governor-general. Planters adopt a 'gang system' of working slaves; labour efficiency makes Brazilian sugar production cheaper than that of the Atlantic islands and slave labour is calculated to be a third more productive than free labour.

1570   There are 65 sugar mills in Brazil, worked by 3,000 African slaves. Portuguese King Sebastião I attempts to ban enslavement of the indigenous population, declaring that the local population can only be forced into slavery if captured in war or proved to be cannibals; there are, nevertheless, still an estimated 40,000 indigenous slaves and indigenous slavery will continue until the mid 18th century. A boom in silver production that will last for over 50 years begins in Peru, which, with the development of coastal sugar plantations, increases the demand for slave labour.

1572   The relative labour values of African slaves and the indigenous population in Brazil are demonstrated by their purchase prices, 25 dollars for an African and nine dollars for an indigenous slave.

1575   In the course of the next 25 years, 40,000 slaves are imported into Brazil and slightly fewer into Spanish America (including Central America and the Caribbean).

1580   Spain takes control of Portugal and its colonies, including Brazil; there are 2,000 African slaves in the Brazilian capital Bahia and this will rise in the next 50 years to 170,000 as the import of slaves undergoes a dramatic increase; two thirds of the population of the sugar producing areas of north east Brazil will be African slaves.

1582   There are 66 sugar plantations and 115 mills refining the crop; in 30 years there will be 192 plantations.

1590   There are an estimated 13,000 African slaves in Brazil working 118 sugar mills producing 8,000 tons of sugar annually. In Spanish-controlled New Granada (western Colombia) slaves are increasingly used in gold mining, working in gangs under the direction of a 'capitan'; a slave employed in mining has a life expectancy of less than eight years; in Colombia there is a growth in sugar cultivation.

1595   Spanish King Philip II renews the attempt to ban enslavement of Brazil's indigenous population.

1600   There are an estimated 15,000 slaves of African origin in Brazil and over the course of the next 25 years a further 100,000 will be imported; Spanish American imports over the same period (including Central America and the Caribbean) will total 75,000.

1605   Fugitive slaves in Brazil begin to establish the settlement (*quilombo*) of Palmares, away from areas of European occupation; the settlement will be described as 'Black Troy' and survives till the end of the century.

1608   In Spanish-controlled Peru, a royal official requests the import of up to 2,000 African slaves a year to work specifically in the silver mines and to gradually replace slaves from the indigenous population; there are already an estimated 20,000 African slaves working in agriculture (notably vineyards) and in sugar plantations on the northern coast.

1615   There are an estimated 2,000 slaves in Spanish Chile, working in agriculture and mining.

1621   The newly formed Dutch West India Company expands the trading post of Essequibo on the north eastern coast of Brazil and soon establishes the colony of Berbice; the area will develop into a major tobacco producer and by the 1660s will have a slave population of 2,500. The demand for slaves grows in Spanish Venezuela as cocoa production is developed; slaves are imported from the Caribbean rather than directly from Africa.

1626   There are over 150 sugar mills in Brazil producing over 20,000 tons of sugar annually (this will rise to over 30,000 tons by the end of the century); over the next 25 years an estimated 100,000 slaves are imported into Brazil and 52,500 into Spanish America (including Central America and the Caribbean).

1630   The Dutch seize the major Brazilian sugar-producing area of Pernambuco from Spanish–Portuguese control; this, together with the capture of the West African fort of Elmina and further expansion into north east Brazil, allows the Dutch to precipitate improvements in sugar production and a more intense use of imported slave labour. There are an estimated 60,000 slaves in Brazil and people of African origin make up half the population; in Spanish America the proportion is 2%.

1640   There are an estimated 330,000 slaves in Spanish America, with up to 150,000 slaves in Spanish Peru (20,000 in the capital, Lima) and the Andes region, 45,000 in Colombia and 12,000 in Venezuela. Portugal regains its independence from Spain and begins to re-assert control over Brazil; individual black slaves are offered freedom if they support Portugal in its attempt to oust the Dutch from Pernambuco; Portugal finally regains control over the area in 1654.

1650   A Portuguese cleric who preaches against the abuse of African slaves in Brazil, Father Antonio Viera says of the main sugar-producing area, 'without Negroes there is no Pernambuco, and without Angola there are no Negroes'. Three quarters of slaves in Brazil are engaged in sugar cultivation and refining. In the course of the next 25 years 185,000 slaves will be imported into Brazil and 62,500 into Spanish America (including Central America and the Caribbean).

1667 The Dutch establish the colony of Suriname in the north east of South America; within a decade there are 30,000 slaves, working predominantly in sugar; however, many slaves escape into the interior and sugar production proves unprofitable.

1675 By the end of the century, a further 175,000 slaves are imported into Brazil and 102,500 into Spanish America (including Central America and the Caribbean).

1680 As the numbers of fugitive slaves increase in Spanish America, the authorities introduce systematic laws for their treatment; the expense of recapture is to be shared between the Crown and their owners; slaves who are absent for four days are to be given 50 lashes, rising to 100 lashes and shackling for two months for an absence of eight days and 200 if they band together with other fugitives; the penalty for an absence of over six months is death.

1693 Gold is discovered in the Minas Gerais ('General Mines') region of Brazil and there is an influx of European colonists; the area becomes the centre of a large industry based on slave labour, with slaves experienced in West African gold mining being transported from the sugar plantations and directly imported from Africa.

1697 The fugitive slave settlement of Palmares in Brazil is destroyed following a series of Portuguese attacks throughout the century.

1700 Coffee is introduced into Brazil through the neighbouring French colony in Guiana; Brazil will develop into the world's major coffee producer using slave labour. There are an estimated 100,000 slaves in Brazil (a third of the population), 40,000 in Spanish Peru and 10,000 in Spanish Chile. Over the next 20 years 292,000 slaves will be imported into Brazil and 90,400 into Spanish America (including Central America and the Caribbean). The Spanish colonial authorities report that there are up to 20,000 fugitive slaves in settlements in Venezuela. Suriname is increasingly used by the Dutch as a staging point for slave sales, with 22,000 passing through in the past two decades and an estimated 150,000 being imported in the course of the 18th century; many will be retained to work on sugar and cotton plantations.

1721 In the course of the next 20 years 312,000 slaves will be imported into Brazil, while imports into Spanish America (including Central America and the Caribbean) remain at an estimated 90,400.

1728 Diamonds are discovered in Brazil; there is a particular demand in the harshly administered 'Diamond District' for slaves from the Gold Coast and Dahomey areas of West Africa with prospecting and extracting skills.

1741 An estimated 354,000 slaves will be imported into Brazil in the course of the next 20 years; imports into Spanish America (including Central America and the Caribbean) remain at an estimated 90,000.

1750 There are an estimated 500,000 slaves in Brazil (a third of the population); slaves working in sugar production have a maximum expected working life of 15 years and there is a 5% annual death rate.

1755 The importation of slaves into Portugal is banned but the direct shipment from Africa to Brazil continues.

1761 Over the next 20 years an estimated 325,000 slaves are introduced into Brazil while Spanish America (including Central America and the Caribbean) imports 121,900.

1770 The numbers of slaves in the Dutch colony of Suriname reach 50,000 (increasingly engaged in producing rice, bananas and citrus fruits); in the neighbouring Dutch colonies of Essequibo, Demerara and Berbice there are an estimated 14,000 slaves.

1775 Portugal re-asserts the ban on enslavement of the indigenous population of Brazil. In the next 20 years, an estimated 181,000 African slaves will be imported into Brazil while Spanish America (including Central America and the Caribbean) will import 42,900. There are 10,000 slaves in French Guiana.

1789 King Charles V issues the *Código Negro* (Black Code) on the treatment of slaves in Spanish America; planters are to ensure slaves receive religious instruction, have holidays on church feast days and are allowed to marry; floggings of over 25 lashes are banned and priests are authorised to check that owners are observing the Code; the Code is withdrawn in 1794 following protests from plantation owners but the general religious provisions remain in force.

1790 Cotton production begins to develop in the north of Brazil and there are 30,000 slaves working on plantations; however, Brazilian production as an export crop is soon threatened by developments in the United States. The slave population in Dutch-controlled Suriname peaks at 75,000; there are 90,000 slaves in Spanish Peru. By the end of the century, an estimated 233,000 slaves will be imported into Brazil and 77,400 into Spanish America (including Central America and the Caribbean).

1798 A census in Brazil shows there are 1,582,000 slaves in a total population of 3,248,000; this proportion will fall in the 19th century as European immigration into the country is encouraged.

1800 Almost a quarter of a million slaves will be imported into Brazil in the next decade; Spanish America (including Central America and the

Caribbean) will import a further 85,700. There are renewed reports of fugitive slave settlements up to 20,000 strong in Venezuela dating back to the early 18th century.

1803 Britain seizes the Dutch colonies of Berbice, Demerara and Essequibo (and is granted possession by treaty in 1814); the total number of slaves in the areas is estimated at 95,000.

1806 An African self-help and mutual aid organisation is established in the Matanzas area of Brazil to raise funds for the purchase of slaves' freedom.

1808 Prince Regent Dom João authorises the use of the indigenous population in Brazil as forced labour.

1810 The slave population in British Guiana is estimated at 100,000; Brazil will import 327,000 slaves over the next decade while Spanish America (including Central America and the Caribbean) will import 177,800. There are 5,000 slaves in Spanish-controlled Chile, but the indigenous population still makes up bulk of the labour force, as it does in Chile where slave numbers are similarly small. As wars of independence from Spain are waged in the next two decades in Argentina, Colombia and Venezuela, slaves are offered their freedom in return for service in the rebel armies.

1812 The government of Buenos Aires outlaws the sale of slaves in the area under its authority.

1819 There are over a million slaves in Brazil, representing almost a third of the population; they are employed on coffee and sugar plantations, as dockworkers, domestic servants and in a wide range of labouring work; Spanish America has 89,000 slaves in Peru (7% of the total population), 64,000 in Venezuela (8%), 54,000 in Colombia (5%), with the remaining 40,000 spread between Chile, Ecuador and the Rio de la Plata region.

1820 Productivity among slaves working in sugar plantations and refineries in Brazil has risen since 1750, while life expectancy has fallen and the death rate stands at 6%; Brazil will import an estimated 431,000 slaves in the next decade.

1821 Slavery is abolished in Venezuela; however, five years later over 30,000 slaves remain.

1823 Chile frees an estimated 4,000 slaves as the institution is abolished; Peru outlaws the sale of slaves.

1826 Emperor Pedro I of Brazil (which has become independent in 1822) agrees in a treaty with Britain to end participation in the slave trade within three years; the trade is outlawed in 1830; however, as the world demand for coffee continues to grow, over 60,000 slaves are imported every year; liberty is nominally granted to illegally imported slaves.

1831 Coffee passes sugar as Brazil's main export crop and accounts for half the world's supply. The slave trade, though now illegal, expands and in the course of the next ten years 334,300 slaves will be imported into the country. The general assembly bans enslavement of the indigenous population.

1835   A widespread revolt among slaves in the Brazilian province of Salvador da Bahia is suppressed.

1840   Despite British legislation authorising the seizure of ships transporting slaves to Brazil, 378,400 slaves are imported into the country over the next decade.

1841   Chile outlaws the sale of slaves followed by Uruguay in 1842 and Ecuador in 1847.

1850   The Brazilian general assembly, under British pressure, passes the Quierós Law abolishing the transportation of slaves from Africa; a further 6,400 slaves are imported, a dramatic fall; coffee planters now purchase their slaves from the cities and the north east of the country. Since the institution of slavery, Brazil has imported an estimated four million slaves, almost 90% of the total imports into South America.

1851   Bolivia and Colombia end the sale of slaves.

1853   Argentina frees its slaves; the slaves have worked predominantly as cattle herders and in sugar cultivation.

1854   Venezuela (which formally abolished slavery in 1821) frees the 12,000 remaining slaves and the 24,000 slaves in Peru are freed.

1866   Brazil frees government-owned slaves who volunteer to fight in the war against Uruguay.

1869   The Brazilian general assembly bans public slave auctions and prohibits the separation by sale of married couples and children under 15 from their parents; slave marriages are recognised by the Catholic church. With coffee playing an increasingly important part in the Brazilian economy, there are 245,000 slaves engaged in production in the Rio da Janeiro, São Paulo and Minas Gerais regions.

1870   The slaves in Paraguay are freed by Brazilian forces occupying the country.

1871   Children of slaves born on or after 28 September are declared free under the Rio Branco Law; among other reforms, the right of slaves to own personal possessions is recognised.

1881   The Assembly in Brazil's São Paulo province restricts the importation of slaves; there are demands in the north eastern province of Ceará for an end to the sale of slaves to the Southern plantations.

1884   Slavery is virtually abandoned in the northern Brazilian provinces of Ceará and Amazonas following intense abolitionist activity.

1885   All slaves over the age of 60 are freed in Brazil under the Saraiva-Cotegipe Law but are forced to work for their former owners without pay for five years or until they reach 65.

1886   Whipping as a punishment for government-owned slaves is outlawed in Brazil.

1887   Slavery collapses as an institution in Brazil's São Paulo province as thousands of slaves abandon plantations encouraged by abolitionists.

1888   Brazil's remaining 700,000 slaves are freed by the 'Golden Law', passed in response to the general abandonment of plantations by slaves.

1.4 Chronology of slavery in colonial North America and the United States, 1526–1860

1526   Slaves of African descent are first landed from Spain at San Miguel de Gualdape (present day Georgia); some later flee from captivity and live with the local indigenous population.

1565   Following the participation of slaves in a number of exploration expeditions, Spain establishes a settlement at St Augustine (in what is now Florida) which includes slaves.

1619   Twenty Africans captured from a Spanish slave trader are landed at Jamestown, in the English colony of Virginia, in exchange for supplies; four years later they are recorded as indentured servants (who have the right to freedom after a period of service and who are predominantly European) but it remains unclear whether or not they are slaves as the status of slavery as yet has no legal basis; they are, however, among the first involuntary African settlers in North America.

1626   There is the first recorded presence of black slaves in the Dutch West India Company colony of New Netherlands (later an English colony and the present day states of New York and New Jersey).

1628   The first recorded slave purchase takes place in the French North American colony of New France (later Canada).

1638   African slaves are landed at Boston in New England by the ship *Desire*; the slaves have been transported from the Caribbean.

1639   While their status remains uncodified, the English colony of Virginia passes its first legislation excluding what are described as 'Negroes' from the protection of the law, implying a shift from indentured service to slavery, and denying them the right to bear arms or purchase alcohol. Virginia exports an annual three million pounds of tobacco to England, a massive rise from the 1620s average of 65,000 pounds.

1640   Three indentured servants flee from a farmer in Virginia; the two white servants are sentenced to an additional three years of labour while the black servant's sentence is to 'serve his said master or his assigns for the time of his natural life here or elsewhere'.

1641   The English Massachusetts Bay Colony recognises the legal status of slavery and a Body of Liberties allows the enslavement of 'lawful captives taken in just wars, and such strangers as willingly sell themselves or are sold to us'. Slaves are increasingly used as labour to meet the demand for tobacco as exports rise.

1642 Virginia makes it an offence punishable by a fine to assist or harbour runaway slaves, although it has not settled the legal status of slavery.

1650 Slavery is legalised in the English colony of Connecticut.

1653 The daughter of a slave in Virginia successfully sues for her freedom on the grounds that she has been baptised as a Christian.

1660 The number of slaves in the English North American colonies reaches an estimated 300 out of a total population of 33,000; King Charles II urges the Council for Foreign Plantations to ensure that slaves are instructed in Christianity.

1661 Virginia recognises the legal status of slavery for both black and indigenous people; Slaves Codes are introduced governing the conditions under which slaves live; slaves are barred from leaving their plantation, cannot assemble together without their owners' permission and are denied the right to testify in court against a white person. Similar codes are soon adopted by other English colonies in North America.

1662 A Virginia court rules that all children born to slave mothers are slaves.

1663 The English colony of Maryland declares that any black person imported into the colony will automatically be considered to be a slave.

1664 Legislation in Maryland expresses concern at the number of marriages between slaves and white women and bans what it describes as 'such shameful matches'; similar legislation against what is called 'amalgamation' is soon adopted throughout the English colonies. A Maryland court rules that slaves are not freed by baptism to prevent 'the damage masters of such slaves may sustain'.

1665 The legal status of slavery is recognised in the English colony of New York.

1667 Virginia declares that a slave (whether black or a member of the indigenous population) cannot become free because of baptism as a Christian; an owner who kills a slave during punishment cannot be charged with murder 'since it cannot be presumed that prepensed malice … should induce any man to destroy his own estate'. The English colony of Carolina (where many Barbados slave owners have moved with their slaves), declares that, 'Every free man of Carolina shall have absolute power and authority over Negro slaves of whatever opinion or religion whatsoever.' Carolina will soon develop as a rice-cultivating colony (using the previous experience of slaves in

West Africa) and within 60 years will be exporting 20 million pounds of rice annually.

1670 Virginia – where tobacco exports to England have increased to 14 million pounds from three million pounds 30 years earlier (and will soon rise to 20 million) – has an estimated 2,000 slaves; slaves are also working in furs, hides, grain, as sailors and as domestic servants; slaves remain under 5% of the colony's total population.

1672 The Royal African Company is granted a charter by King Charles II to transport slaves to the North American colonies; in the last two decades of the 17th century, as slaves become increasingly important for the functioning of the economy, 20,000 slaves are imported into English North America, 4,000 of them going to Virginia.

1680 'Bacon's Rebellion' in Virginia reveals the depth of divisions between prosperous and poorer white colonists; the House of Burgesses responds by establishing a racial distinction between white indentured servants and slaves and institutes harsher punishments for slaves; slaves make up an estimated 7% of the population. To counter increasing slave escapes, the Massachusetts General Assembly bans blacks from being allowed on board shipping without the written permission of the governor.

1682 The legal status of slavery is recognised in the English colony of South Carolina; slaves will be predominantly employed in rice cultivation until the rise of cotton at the end of the 18th century.

1684 The recently established Quaker colony of Pennsylvania imports 150 slaves to clear woods and build houses.

1685 Virginia bans slaves from attending education classes which members of the Society of Friends (Quakers) have organised for them. Maryland begins the direct importation of slaves from Africa.

1691 As increasing numbers of slaves attempt to flee from their owners, Virginia introduces an 'Act for Suppressing of Outlaw Slaves' which makes it lawful to kill fugitives. Slaves freed by their owners must leave the colony within six months. The colony also declares that any white man or woman marrying a 'Negro, mulatto or Indian' is to be banished permanently.

1698 The English Parliament opens the slave trade to North America to all English merchants; the number of slaves in English North America reaches an estimated 28,000, of which over 20,000 are in the Southern colonies; almost half the imported slaves arrive in Charleston, South Carolina and remain in the colony to work in rice plantations, using their African experience in cultivation methods. The English colony of Massachusetts rules that all 'Indian, mulatto and Negro servants' are to be entered on tax returns as 'personal estate'.

1699 The direct importation of slaves from Africa into the Carolinas begins.

1700 The legal status of slavery is recognised in the English colony of Pennsylvania; there are an estimated 450 slaves in the colony and this will rise within two decades to 2,000 and by 1770 to 6,000 working in a wide variety of occupations and as domestic servants.

1701 In the course of the next 20 years, 19,800 slaves will be imported into British North America.

1702 The legal status of slavery is recognised in the English colony of New Jersey.

1703 The legal status of slavery is recognised in the English colony of Rhode Island; the colony will soon play a central part in the importation of slaves into North America. There are an estimated 4,000 African slaves in Carolina, with many engaged in the cultivation of rice.

1705 Virginia removes any possibility of black indentured servants securing their freedom when the General Assembly declares that all servants who were not Christians in their place of origin 'shall be held to be real estate'; the codes governing the lives of slaves are tightened; slaves who steal are to be placed in the stocks, to receive 60 lashes and have their ears cut off; slaves attempting to associate with whites will be whipped, branded or mutilated; slaves are not allowed to sue their owners. New York declares that slaves cannot become free because of baptism to Christianity.

1709 The legal status of slavery is recognised in the French colony of New France (Canada).

1710 There are an estimated 45,000 slaves in British North America as tobacco production reaches 30 million pounds annually.

1712 The categories of crimes for which slaves can be sentenced to death are extended in New York following a slave revolt in which nine whites are killed and 21 blacks executed.

1714 The legal status of slavery is recognised in the British colony of New Hampshire.

1715 An estimated 59,000 people in the British North American colonies are of African descent out of a population of 435,000; 24% of the population of Virginia are slaves.

1715 The population of the British North American colonies reaches 435,000, 59,000 of whom are of African descent. Maryland introduces a state constitution enforcing slavery. The legal status of slavery is recognised in the British colony of North Carolina.

1721 The legal status of slavery is recognised in the British colony of Delaware. In the course of the next 20 years an estimated 54,000 slaves are transported into British North America.

1723   The proportion of the population which is of African descent reaches 19% in Maryland and Virginia and 15% in New York.

1725   The total slave population in British North American colonies has reached 75,000.

1726   Pennsylvania adopts a comprehensive code setting out the treatment and rights of slaves; it is less rigorous than that of many Southern colonies and, because the code does not insist that freed slaves must leave the area, Pennsylvania will become a haven for escaping slaves from other colonies.

1730   There are 91,000 slaves in British North America, of which 17,000 are in the Northern colonies and 74,000 in the south (with 30,000 in Virginia alone); tobacco production – in which a significant proportion of slave labour is engaged – stands at 50 million pounds annually.

1732   There are 14,000 slaves engaged in rice cultivation in South Carolina and 6,000 in North Carolina.

1735   The English colony of Georgia – which has been established as a buffer colony against Spanish-controlled Florida – bans slavery under an 'Act for rendering the Colony of Georgia more defensible by Prohibiting the Importation and use of Black Slaves or Negroes into the same'; colonists hire slaves from neighbouring South Carolina.

1738   Spain establishes a town for freed slaves in Florida; the settlement is intended to act as a warning post in case of a British attack.

1739   The regulation of slaves in South Carolina is intensified under a 'Negro Act' following the Stono rebellion in which 25 whites are killed and 30 blacks later executed; slaves are barred from growing their own food, assembling in groups, earning money or learning to read. A Slave Code introduced the following year makes it legal to kill slaves found away from their plantation, even if they do not resist.

1740   The slave population of British North America reaches an estimated 150,000, with 126,000 in the south (40,000 in the rice-cultivating colony of South Carolina alone) and the remainder in the north; over the next two decades a further 100,400 slaves will be imported.

1750   Georgia – which banned slavery in 1735 – becomes the last colony to legalise slavery, at the insistence of colonists; by 1790 there will be over 29,000 slaves, 60,000 by 1800 and on the eve of the civil war in 1860, 462,198. The number of slaves in British North America totals 236,000 (a fifth of the population), of which 206,000 are in the Southern colonies.

1755   Georgia encourages the killing of fugitive slaves by offering a reward for the return of a dead male slave, double that for the return of a live woman or child.

1756   Over 40% of Virginia's population of a quarter of a million are slaves.

1760   There are 326,000 slaves in British North America, with 286,000 in the Southern colonies; Britain seizes Canada from France and acquires over a thousand black and 2,000 native American slaves. Over the next 20 years a further 85,800 slaves are imported into British North America. Slave labour dominates in the three major plantation products of tobacco, maize and indigo. There are 5,000 slaves in Spanish-controlled Louisiana and this will rise to 24,000 by the end of the century.

1766   A direct importation of slaves from Africa begins in Florida, a colony recently acquired by Britain.

1770   The slave population in British North America totals 462,000 and makes up 40% of the population in the Southern colonies, with concentrations in Virginia, Maryland, Georgia and South Carolina; most slaves are living on small and medium-sized plantations which have between five and 20 slaves; only about 20% are African born; 78% of exports to Britain are produced by slaves; Virginia alone exports 100 million pounds of tobacco to Britain annually.

1775   As the total slave population reaches an estimated half a million (with the majority in the Southern colonies of Maryland, Virginia, the Carolinas and Georgia) and tobacco production stands at 100 million pounds annually, the American colonists revolt against British rule; the British offer of freedom to slaves who desert their owners (which is repeated in 1779) encourages the support of slave owners for independence. The colony of Virginia threatens slaves who desert with execution or transportation to the Caribbean. An estimated 100,000 slaves take the opportunity of the upheaval of the war to escape (many to Canada and Florida), 30,000 from Virginia alone.

1777   Vermont abolishes slavery, followed three years later by Pennsylvania, beginning a process that sees the gradual abolition of slavery in all Northern states by the end of the century.

1780   There are 300,000 slaves in the Chesapeake region of Maryland and Virginia, where the first African slaves were landed in 1619; there are over 40,000 slaves in the Northern colonies of New York, New Jersey, Delaware and Pennsylvania, working as farm labourers, domestic servants, although a large minority are urban workers; the lower South has a black population of 210,000.

1783   As the North American colonies gain their independence from Britain, over 20% of the population are slaves, with more than half of these living in the tobacco-cultivating colonies of Maryland and Virginia. By 1790, a further 55,800 slaves are imported. Five thousand free and slave blacks who have fought for the British move to Canada; many later migrate to Sierra Leone when promises that they will be granted land for settlement are unfulfilled.

1785   General Charles Pinckney, an aide to George Washington, declares at a meeting in South Carolina, 'Negroes are to this country what raw materials are to another country... No planter can cultivate his land without slaves'; Pinckney is himself a plantation owner.

1787   The Continental Congress, the legislature of the newly independent British North American colonies, outlaws slavery in the North West Territory.

1789   The preservation of the slavery becomes a condition of the establishment of the United States; in negotiations over the Constitution, states in which slavery remains economically important have forced a compromise in which slaves are to be counted as three fifths of a person in calculating the population for representation and taxation; the import of slaves into the United States is to continue for a further 20 years and there is to be stringent action for the return of fugitive slaves.

1790   The first United States census shows there are 694,207 slaves out of a population of 3.9 million; over half the slaves are in the states of Maryland and Virginia and the majority of slaves have been born in the United States; free black people make up 8% of the population. By the end of the century, a further 79,000 slaves are imported into the United States.

1793   The Fugitive Slave Act ('An Act respecting fugitives from justice, and persons escaping from the service of their masters') makes it a crime to harbour escaped slaves or to place obstacles in the way of their recapture. The introduction of the cotton 'gin' (derived from 'engine') by Eli Whitney encourages an expansion of cotton as a crop in the Southern states that vastly increases the demand for slave labour, particularly female; the 500,000 pounds of cotton produced in 1793 will rise by 1800 to 18 million pounds; the slave population will rise from 694,000 in 1790 to 3,950,528 on the eve of the civil war in 1860; as this growing dependence on slave labour comes at a point when the Northern states are abandoning slavery, there will be increased tension between both sections of the United States over the question of slavery.

1797   The first black anti-slavery petition presented in the United States protests against a North Carolina law requiring the return of freed slaves to their owner; the petition is rejected.

1800   As the total slave population of the United States reaches 887,612, one in ten slaves work on cotton plantations (with cotton representing 7% of United States exports); within 60 years this will rise to one in three. The numbers of slaves introduced into the United States in the past two decades and the next eight years exceed the total imports since the 1620s. In Virginia, slaves are being bred for sale, a practice common in the Caribbean.

1801 Thomas Jefferson becomes President and takes slaves from his Virginia plantation to the White House to act as servants. As a ban on participation in the slave trade approaches, 156,300 slaves are imported into the United States over the next decade, particularly into Georgia and South Carolina.

1803 Cotton overtakes tobacco as the main export crop. The United States makes the Louisiana Purchase from France at a cost of $15 million (£3 million), doubling the country's territory and increasing the number of slaves by 12,000; there is an increase in the demand for slaves as the New South (Alabama, Louisiana, Mississippi and, later, Texas) is opened up for cotton and sugar cultivation.

1808 The import of slaves into the United States becomes illegal; the law is weakly enforced and widely evaded both by Southern planters and Northern business interests and an estimated 250,000 slaves are illegally imported into the United States from 1808 to 1860; the remainder of the soaring growth of the slave population will be as a result of the internal trade in slaves born in the country.

1806 Virginia makes manumission (the freeing of individual slaves by their owners) more difficult and orders all freed slaves to leave the state within a year; the practice is extended throughout the Southern states.

1809 James Madison becomes President and takes slaves from his plantation to the White House to act as servants; Madison writes of the undoubted 'moral, political, and economical, evil of slavery but nevertheless declares the evil can be ameliorated by 'good masters and managers'; in 1819 he proposes a gradual emancipation with compensation to owners.

1810 The census shows that there are 1,130,781 slaves in the United States; the number of slaves in the Louisiana territory rises from an original 12,000 to 35,000; troops are deployed to suppress two slave risings in Louisiana in the next year.

1812 The United States and Britain are at war; the British concentrate their offensive against the Southern states and offer freedom to any slaves who join them; a number participate in the British attack on Washington.

1816 As slavery takes on a renewed importance (the amount of cotton grown rises from 18 million pounds in 1800 to 83 million pounds in 1815), the American Colonisation Society is established to encourage the emigration of free blacks to Africa and declares it has no interest in the ending of slavery.

1818 The First Seminole War ends with the defeat of a combined force of fugitive slaves and native Americans in Florida.

1820 The slave population of the United States has risen to 1,529,012 and cotton exports stand at over 35 million pounds. Under the Missouri Compromise, slavery is banned in the north and west of the Louisiana territory; the number of slaves in the remainder of the territory rises to 69,000, a doubling in the past decade; Missouri (where there are 10,000 slaves, rising to 115,000 in 1860) enters the Union as a state in which slavery is legal and Maine as a free state. Manumission is banned in South Carolina; Mississippi follows in 1822, Arkansas in 1858, Alabama and Maryland in 1860.

1822 An attempted slave rising in South Carolina – the 'Denmark Vesey conspiracy' – is betrayed by one of its participants.

1824 Louisiana removes the right of slaves to marry.

1825 John Quincy Adams becomes President; he is quoted as having said that 'slavery in a moral sense is an evil, but in commerce it has its uses'; he will later become an opponent of the institution. A third of the slaves in the Americas are in the United States.

1829 The circulation of the anti-slavery pamphlet, *An Appeal to the Colored Citizens of the World,* in which the free black David Walker (1785–1830) calls on slaves to rise against their owners, arouses white alarm in many Southern states.

1830 The census shows there are 1,987,428 slaves in the United States. A Virginia legislator, Thomas Dew, describes his state as a 'Negro-raising state'; Virginia exports 300,000 slaves to other states over the course of the next three decades. Slave-produced cotton accounts for 41% of United States exports.

1837 President Martin Van Buren declares in his inaugural address that he is an 'inflexible and uncompromising opponent of every attempt on the part of Congress to abolish slavery in the District of Columbia … (and) in the States where it exists'.

1839 A slave owner is imprisoned in the case of *North Carolina* v *Hoover* for mistreating a slave while punishing him.

1840 The slave population of the United States has risen to 2,482,546.

1843 Black abolitionist and former slave Henry Highland Garnet (1815–82) advocates a slave rebellion and general strike to improve the conditions of slaves. A slave owner in Alabama is imprisoned for mistreating a slave while punishing him.

1845 James K. Polk becomes President and has the White House basement converted into quarters for ten slaves he has brought in as an economy measure.

1846 An attempt to prevent slavery in territories expected to be captured by the United States in the war with Mexico, the 'Wilmot Proviso' is defeated in the Senate; California and New Mexico are seized by the United States at the end of the war in 1848.

1847 Dred Scott, a slave who has been taken by his owner to the free areas of Louisiana and to the free state of Illinois, claims in the St Louis Circuit Court that this temporary residence has released him from slavery.

1848   As fears among Southern slave owners mount that a successful slave rising in Cuba would threaten their position, the United States government offers to purchase Cuba from Spain.

1850   There are 3,200,600 slaves in the United States, 1,815,000 engaged in cotton, 350,000 in tobacco, 150,000 in sugar, 125,000 in rice and 60,000 in hemp production. Under the 'Compromise of 1850', the sale of slaves is outlawed in Washington DC, California is admitted to the Union as a free state but slavery is allowed in New Mexico and Utah; there are to be more stringent measures against fugitive slaves, making it impossible for slaves to gain their liberty by escaping from a slave state to a free state.

1852   The Kansas–Nebraska Act repeals the 1820 Missouri Compromise and removes restrictions on slavery in the northern and western areas of the Louisiana territory; there is a protracted and violent struggle in Kansas (where there are already 400 slaves) between supporters and opponents of slavery; Kansas will not enter the Union, as a free state, until 1861.

1857   The Supreme Court rules in *Dred Scott* v *Sandford* that Congress has no power to prohibit slavery in any Federal territory and that black people are not citizens, a victory for pro-slavery forces that alarms abolitionists and is a milestone on the road to civil war between the South and the North. The largest ever sale of slaves in the United States is held at a race course in Georgia where 436 slaves are sold over two days for $303,850; the event is described as the 'weeping time'. An attack on slavery by a white Southerner, Hinton Helps, *The Impending Crisis of the South* is met with a defence of slavery entitled *Cannibals All.*

1859   The last slaves imported into the United States are landed at Mobile Bay, Alabama, by the *Clothilde*. The white abolitionist John Brown unsuccessfully attempts to encourage a general slave rising by attacking the arsenal at Harper's Ferry, Virginia.

1860   An Alabama court rules in *Cresswell's Executor* v *Walter* that slaves have 'no legal mind, no will which the law can recognise', adding that because they are slaves, 'they are incapable of performing civil acts'; Abraham Lincoln's election as President on a platform of opposition to the expansion of slavery into the Federal territories leads to the secession of the Southern states, the establishment of a Confederate States of America and a civil war that will ultimately revolve around the issue of slavery. On the eve of war the census shows there are 3,950,546 slaves in the United States, 47% in the lower South, 29% in the upper South and 13% in the border states; there are 350,000 slave owners, with 88% owning fewer than 20 and 50% fewer than five. Slave-produced cotton accounts for 57% of United States exports.

1.4.1 Estimated numbers of slaves in the British North American colonies in the Eighteenth Century

	1700	1770
New England	1,700	15,500
Middle colonies	3,500	35,000
Southern colonies	22,400	409,500
Total	27,600	460,000

Source. Based on table in United States Bureau of Census, *Historical Statistics from Colonial Times to 1790* (Washington DC, 1975), p. 1168.

1.4.2 Slavery and the United States Constitution, 1789

Slavery is only indirectly referred to in the United States Constitution which was drafted in 1787 and ratified in 1789. Clauses condemning slavery were removed from the draft Constitution at the insistence of representatives from South Carolina and Georgia as a condition of their joining the proposed Union. The sections of the Constitution which concern slavery, together with the Amendment which abolished slavery, are reproduced below.

Article 1, Section 2

Representatives and direct taxes shall be apportioned among the several states which may be included within this union, according to their respective numbers, which shall be determined by adding to the whole number of free persons, including those bound to service for a term of years, and excluding Indians not taxed, three fifths of all other persons.

Article 1, Section 9

The migration or importation of such persons as any of the states now existing shall think proper to admit, shall not be prohibited by the Congress prior to the year one thousand eight hundred and eight, but a tax or duty may be imposed on such importation, not exceeding ten dollars for each person.

Article IV, Section 2

No person held to service or labor in one state, under the laws thereof, escaping into another, shall, in consequence of any law or regulation therein, be discharged from such service or labor, but shall be delivered up on claim of the party to whom such service or labor may be due.

1.4.3 Thirteenth Amendment to the United States Constitution, 1865

1 Neither slavery nor involuntary servitude, except as a punishment for crime whereof the party shall have been duly convicted, shall exist within the United States, or any place subject to their jurisdiction.

2 Congress shall have power to enforce this article by appropriate legislation.

1.4.4 Slavery and the Constitution of the Confederate States of America, 1861

Abraham Lincoln was elected United States president in November 1860. Though a moderate abolitionist, Lincoln's platform showed him determined to prevent the spread of slavery into the western territories. A clash between the increasingly antagonistic free states and the slave states became inevitable. In December the slave state of South Carolina seceded from the Union, followed in January 1861 by Alabama, Florida, Georgia and Mississippi. They established a Confederate States of America in February. Texas joined the Confederacy in February, followed by Arkansas, North Carolina, Tennessee and Virginia. The American Civil War began in April with a Confederate attack on Fort Sumter. The sections of the Constitution of the Confederate States of America which refer to slavery are reproduced below.

Article 1, Section 9

(1) The importation of negroes of the African race from any foreign country other than the slaveholding States or Territories of the United States of America, is hereby forbidden; and Congress is required to pass such laws as shall effectively prevent the same.

(2) Congress shall also have power to prohibit the introduction of slaves from any State not a member of, or Territory not belonging to, this Confederacy.

(4) No bill of attainder, *ex post* facto law, or law denying or impairing the right of property in negro slaves shall be passed.

1.4.5 Slavery and cotton production in the United States, 1790–1860

Year	Number of slaves	Cotton production (in bales)
1790	694,207	3,000
1800	887,612	75,000
1810	1,130,781	178,000
1820	1,529,012	335,000
1830	1,987,428	732,000
1840	2,482,546	1,348,000
1850	3,200,600	2,136,000
1860	3,950,546	3,841,000

1.4.6 Average purchase price for the most efficient field hands in the Southern states, 1800–60

1800	$500
1805	$550
1810	$500
1815	$500
1820	$725
1825	$500
1830	$450
1835	$750
1840	$800
1845	$550
1850	$700
1855	$900
1860	$1,200

Source. Based on figures in W. Augustus Low and Virgil A. Clift (eds), *Encyclopaedia of Black America* (New York, 1984), p. 764.

EMANCIPATION

2.1 Outline chronology of the end to slavery, 1514–1980

1514 Pope Leo X issues a bull condemning slavery and the slave trade.

1542 Spain outlaws any further enslavement of the native population in its colonies, although existing slaves are not granted their freedom and the ban is widely ignored.

1543 Queen Elizabeth I of England declares slavery to be 'detestable' but this does not prevent her from taking a financial interest in slaving.

1569 A court declares in the Cartwright decision that England has 'too pure an air for slaves to breathe in'.

1735 The British North American colony of Georgia bans slavery, but later restores it.

1772 Lord Chief Justice Mansfield's ruling in the Somerset case that slavery has no basis in English law provides for the freedom of slaves brought to England.

1775 Slavery is abolished in Madeira.

1777 The constitution of the state of Vermont abolishes slavery.

1780 A judicial decision in Massachusetts interprets the state's constitution as outlawing slavery. The state of Pennsylvania introduces a gradual end to slavery.

1784 The states of Rhode Island and Connecticut pass laws to end slavery gradually.

1787 The Society for Effecting the Abolition of the Slave Trade is established in England.

1788 *Société des Amis des Noirs* (Society of the Friends of the Blacks) is established in France to campaign against the slave trade.

1792 Denmark begins a gradual abolition of engagement in the slave trade by Danish subjects. The Constituent Assembly abolishes slavery in France, though not in French colonies.

1793 The British territory of Upper Canada bans the import of slaves and grants freedom to slaves over the age of 25.

1794 The French National Convention abolishes slavery in all French possessions.

1799 The state of New York introduces a gradual end to slavery.

1802 Napoleon Bonaparte restores slavery in French possessions.

1804   Slavery is abolished in Haiti. The state of New Jersey introduces gradual emancipation.

1807   Britain and the United States prohibit trading in slaves.

1813   Sweden ends its participation in the slave trade. Argentina introduces a gradual end to slavery.

1814   Colombia introduces a gradual end to slavery. The Dutch end their participation in the slave trade.

1815   Napoleon abolishes the French slave trade, although it continues clandestinely. The Congress of Berlin criticises slavery but takes no action.

1818   France outlaws participation in the slave trade by its citizens.

1820   Britain begins using its navy to suppress the international slave trade.

1821   A gradual abolition of slavery begins in Venezuela.

1822   Slavery is abolished in the Dominican Republic.

1823   Slavery is abolished in Chile. The Society for the Mitigation and Gradual Abolition of Slavery Throughout the British Dominions is established.

1829   Slavery is abolished in Mexico.

1831   Slavery is abolished in Bolivia.

1834   Slavery is abolished throughout the British Empire, although a system of short-term apprenticeship remains.

1841   Britain, France, Russia, Prussia and Austria agree under the Quintuple Treaty to the mutual search of vessels on the high seas to suppress the slave trade.

1842   Slavery is abolished in Uruguay.

1843   British courts in India are prevented from allowing a claim for a slave.

1845   The slave trade is abolished in Zanzibar.

1848   Slavery is abolished in the French and Danish colonies.

1851   Slavery is abolished in Ecuador. The slave trade is ended in Brazil.

1854   Slavery is finally abolished in Peru and Venezuela.

1861   Slavery is finally abolished in Argentina. Holding a slave is made illegal in India.

1862   The slave trade is ended in Cuba.

1863   Slavery is abolished in all Dutch colonies.

1865   Slavery is abolished in the United States.

1868   Spain introduces legislation abolishing slavery in its remaining colonies but the law is not immediately enforced.

1870   Spain announces freedom of slaves over 60 in Cuba.

1871   A gradual end to slavery is introduced in Brazil.

1873 Slavery is abolished in Puerto Rico.

1878 Portugal makes a first attempt at abolishing slavery in its African colonies.

1886 Slavery is finally abolished in Cuba.

1888 Slavery is finally abolished in Brazil.

1894 Slavery is formally abolished in Korea but remains in existence until 1930.

1896 Slavery is abolished in Madagascar.

1897 Britain abolishes the legal status of slavery in Zanzibar.

1900 Britain abolishes slavery in the areas of Nigeria under its control.

1904 Italy outlaws slavery in Somaliland.

1910 Slavery is abolished in China and finally ended by Portugal in its African colonies.

1936 Britain abolishes the legal status of slavery in Bechuanaland.

1942 Slavery is abolished in Ethiopia.

1949 The United Nations Assembly requests the Economic and Social Council to undertake a study of continuing slavery.

1962 Saudi Arabia abolishes slavery.

1980 Mauritania abolishes slavery.

2.2 Chronology of the resistance against slavery, 1521–1888

1521   Within a few years of slaves first being transported into the Spanish Caribbean, there is a rebellion by 40 on an estate in south east Hispaniola owned by the son of explorer Christopher Columbus. Harsh measures had already been taken against slaves who fled into the mountains. There are ruthlessly suppressed slave risings in Hispaniola in 1533, 1537 and 1548. Spain prohibits the inclusion of African slaves on voyages of discovery because of increasing numbers of escapes from captivity.

1523   African slaves attempt to encourage the indigenous population in Mexico to revolt against Spanish rule.

1527   African slaves and the indigenous population ally in a revolt against Spanish rule in Puerto Rico.

1529   The port of Santa Maria in the Spanish South American colony of Colombia is burnt down by slaves.

1533   Slaves revolt in the gold-mining region of the Spanish Caribbean colony of Cuba. African slaves join the remaining indigenous population of Spanish Hispaniola in what becomes a ten year conflict.

1537   Slaves revolt in New Spain (Mexico), elect a king and are joined by the indigenous population in an attempt to kill the governor. There are attacks on pack trains by fugitive slaves.

1538   African slaves help French pirates to burn down the Cuban city of Havana; fugitive slaves attack convoys on the main roads.

1545   A series of slave revolts begin in Cartagena, the main trading port in Colombia.

1548   There is a slave revolt in the Spanish colony of Honduras.

1555   An escaped slave attempts to ally other runaway slaves (maroons) and Indians in a revolt in the Spanish South American colony of Venezuela. A slave rising in Panama ends only when the governor agrees to an armistice.

1570   Runaway slaves living in independent communities in Spanish Ecuador resist recapture.

1572   The English privateer Francis Drake captures and destroys the city of Nombre de Dios in Panama with the aid of fugitive slaves and raids the countryside.

1595 Slaves led by Amador destroy sugar plantations and besiege the city of São Paulo in Portuguese-controlled Brazil.

1598 There is a major rising involving thousands of slaves in the gold mines near Zaragoza in the Spanish South American colony of Colombia; the revolt follows a series of small rebellions.

1605 Escaped slaves living in an independent community in Palmares, Brazil, begin a resistance against the Portuguese that continues until the end of the century.

1612 There is a slave revolt in New Spain (Mexico).

1619 A slave plan to rise is discovered in Cartagena, Spanish Colombia.

1639 There is a slave revolt in the section of the Caribbean island of St Kitts controlled by France; 60 slaves flee and are killed by a force of 500 whites.

1642 The extent of slave escapes in the English North American colony of Virginia forces the authorities to introduce fines to deter assisting or harbouring them.

1649 Eighteen slaves are executed following the discovery of a plan to kill all whites on the Caribbean island of Barbados.

1656 A rebellion involving Angolan and Senegambian slaves on the Caribbean island of Guadeloupe is crushed by the French authorities; the rebels planned to establish two kingdoms.

1663 A planned rebellion by black slaves and white servants in Gloucester County, Virginia, is betrayed by one of the servants; this is the first major slave conspiracy recorded in English North America.

1673 The British Caribbean colony of Jamaica undergoes its first major slave revolt.

1675 A plot to revolt by slaves from the Gold Coast is discovered in the English Caribbean colony of Barbados.

1679 There is a slave revolt in the French Caribbean colony of Sainte Domingue led by a fugitive slave from the Spanish area of the island.

1686 Slaves and Irish indentured servants in Barbados are discovered to be planning a rising.

1688 Fugitive slaves attack a trading post on the Dutch Caribbean island of St Eustatius.

1690 Three hundred slaves in Jamaica seize their owner's house and weapons and kill an overseer on a neighbouring estate; 200 are killed by the militia and many survivors are hanged while others escape into the mountains.

1691 The extent of slave escapes encourages the English North American colony of Virginia to pass legislation making it lawful to kill fugitives.

1692 Skilled slaves in the British Caribbean colony of Barbados unsuccessfully plan a rising; over 90 slaves are tortured and then executed.

1693 There is a mass escape of slaves in the Dutch Caribbean colony of Surinam. A slave plan to rise is discovered in the port of Cartagena, Spanish Colombia.

1697 The fugitive slave settlement of Palmares, in Brazil's Alagoas province, is finally captured by the Portuguese following a series of attacks throughout the century.

1699 The French authorities in the Caribbean colony of Martinique discover plans for a slave rising; a further attempt is revealed in 1710.

1701 There is a slave rising in the British Caribbean colony of Antigua. The 18th century proves to be a period of almost continual slave revolt throughout the Caribbean.

1702 Forty slaves and two crew members are killed when slaves attempt to seize the British trader, the *Tiger* off the coast of Gambia.

1709 There is a mass attempt to escape by slaves in the British North American colony of Virginia.

1711 A slave conspiracy is discovered in Minas Gerais, Portuguese Brazil; there is an attempted slave rising in the British North American colony of South Carolina.

1712 Armed slaves burn houses in the British North American colony of New York, killing nine whites; 21 slaves are executed for participating and six commit suicide.

1719 A further conspiracy by slaves to revolt is discovered in Minas Gerais, Brazil; the attempt is repeated in 1729.

1725 There is a slave revolt in the British Caribbean colony of Nevis.

1728 Forty slaves rebel in the gold-mining area of Spanish Colombia; the revolt gathers support but is crushed.

1729 Slaves in the British Caribbean colony of Antigua mount a rebellion.

1730 A slave plot to resist is discovered in Norfolk and Princess Anne counties of the British North American colony of Virginia.

1731 Slaves in the Cuban copper mines of Santiago rise following a rumour that Spain has granted them their freedom but that this has been withheld by the colonial authorities.

1732 There is a slave rising in the Spanish South American colony of Venezuela. An estimated 30,000–40,000 slaves are involved in intermittent rebellion throughout the century.

1733 A slave rising begins on the Danish Caribbean island of St John; the revolt lasts into 1734 and is bloodily crushed by British, Dutch and French troops drafted in from across the Caribbean; many slaves commit suicide rather than surrender.

1734   Marie-Joseph Angelique, a slave in Montreal, French Canada, sets fire to her owner's house when she learns she is to be sold and attempts to escape, destroying over 40 buildings; she is captured, tortured and executed. There is renewed revolt in Jamaica.

1736   A plot is discovered on the British Caribbean island of Antigua in which slaves plan to kill the governor and planters at a ceremony to commemorate the coronation of King George II; over 90 slaves are executed, the majority by public burning.

1737   Over 30 slaves die when 100 throw themselves from the *Prince of Orange* in port on the British Caribbean island of St Kitts in a mass suicide attempt, with others dying later; there is a slave revolt on the island the following year.

1739   Over 80 slaves revolt in the British North American colony of South Carolina; they seize weapons and attempt to escape to Spanish Florida where they expect to be freed; 25 whites are killed in the rising and 30 slaves executed for their participation.

1740   The British slave trading vessel, the *Jolly Bachelor*, is attacked from the shore by Africans as it is sailing on the Sierra Leone River and the slaves on board are freed.

1741   Whites flee in panic following a series of fires in what is popularly believed to be a 'Negro Conspiracy' incited by Roman Catholic priests in the British North American colony of New York; the militia is deployed and 21 slaves are killed; other participants are later hanged or burnt at the stake. There is a slave rising in South Carolina in which over 40 slaves and 20 whites are killed.

1746   A slave conspiracy to revolt is discovered on the Danish Caribbean island of St Croix.

1748   There is a renewed attempt to revolt by slaves in the French Caribbean colony of Martinique.

1749   Free blacks and slaves are discovered to be planning a rising in the Spanish Venezuelan city of Caracas.

1750   Thirty plantation slaves (13 of whom are women) are executed following a rising in the Dutch Caribbean colony of Curaçao.

1751   A rebellion by fugitive slaves led by François Macandal begins in Saint Domingue (later Haiti); during the rebellion which lasts into 1757 an estimated 6,000 people die; it ends with the capture and burning of Macandal at the stake by the French in 1758.

1753   The British slave trading vessel the *Adventure* is taken over by slaves off West Africa, run aground and destroyed.

1756   The authorities discover a conspiracy to rebel by slaves in Minas Gerais, Brazil.

1757   There is a slave rebellion in logging camps along the Tempati River in the Dutch South American colony of Surinam.

1759   Slaves plotting a revolt in the Danish Caribbean colony of St Croix are discovered and punished.

1760   Tacky leads a rebellion of over 100 newly arrived slaves in two plantations in the British Caribbean colony of Jamaica; they seize weapons and, after killing 60 whites, most surrender to the militia; Tacky and 25 followers flee to the hills where they are killed by maroons (runaway slaves who have negotiated an agreement with the authorities); following the rising 400 slaves are murdered and 600 deported to Honduras in Central America.

1761   Slaves revolt in the British Caribbean colony of Nevis. A slave plot to rise is discovered in Bermuda.

1762   Slaves in the Dutch South American colony of Berbice burn their owner's house and flee to the forest, where most are recaptured; the events presage further resistance.

1763   Slaves protesting over increased exploitation because of falling logwood prices rise in two Berbice plantations, seizing weapons and establishing a base; the rebels request the colony's governor to divide the colony into a white area and a territory for freed slaves; the rising, which is known as 'Cuffy's rebellion', lasts for over a year and many of the colony's plantations are destroyed. Overwhelmed by Dutch forces and weakened by internal arguments, 3,000 rebels surrender and many are executed. There is a further but less extensive rebellion in 1768.

1765   There are slave rebellions in the British Caribbean colonies of Jamaica and Grenada.

1768   Slaves revolt in the British Caribbean colony of Montserrat.

1770   There is a slave rebellion in the British Caribbean colony of Tobago and a slave attack on the trading post in the Dutch Caribbean colony of St Eustatius.

1773   There is a six month slave rebellion in the British Central American colony of Belize in which six whites are killed and all trade in the area is brought to a halt; most surrender but some escape to freedom in Spanish territory to the north.

1775   The British North American colony of Virginia introduces legislation to deal with increasing slave escapes, including execution and transportation to the Caribbean.

1776   A Dutch slave trading vessel is seized by slaves off the Gold Coast; in the fighting that follows the ship explodes and 400 people are killed.

1779   Runaway slaves from the British Central American colony of Belize assist Spanish attacks on British settlers while others begin establishing free settlements.

1789   There is a slave rising in the French Caribbean colony of Martinique following rumours that the revolution in France has abolished slavery.

1791 What will become the Haitian revolution, and the establishment of the first independent black state in the Americas, opens with a slave revolt in the French Caribbean colony of Saint Domingue. There is a slave revolt in the Spanish North American colony of Louisiana.

1795 There is a major slave revolt in the province of Coro, Spanish Venezuela, led by a free black. A slave conspiracy is discovered in Spanish Louisiana. Two thousand slaves, encouraged by the French and Haitian revolutions, rise in the Dutch Caribbean colony of Curaçao. The Dutch are also faced with a slave rising in Demerara, in South America. In the British Caribbean colony of Grenada, slaves rise under the leadership of Julien Fédon; the island's governor is killed in the fighting which follows.

1798 A conspiracy of free blacks and slaves inspired by the French Revolution, the 'Tailors' Revolt', is discovered in Salvador, Brazil.

1799 A conspiracy by slaves and free blacks is discovered in Spanish Venezuela and a slave plan to rebel in the Spanish Colombian port of Cartagena.

1800 There is an extensive slave rising in Virginia led by Gabriel Prosser (c1775–1800), who intends that a thousand slaves should seize control of the state, but who is betrayed and then abandoned; Prosser and 34 others are later executed. Slave revolt in the Bahia region of Brazil opens a renewed period of rebellion that continues intermittently for the next three decades.

1801 Urban and rural slaves unite under creole leadership in an unsuccessful attempt to seize control of the British Caribbean colony of Tobago.

1802 Thousands are killed in the French Caribbean colony of Guadeloupe resisting the re-establishment of slavery by Napoleon; slavery had been abolished in the French colonies in 1794.

1805 The British Caribbean colony of Trinidad undergoes its largest ever slave revolt.

1811 There is panic among whites as United States troops put down two slave risings near New Orleans, Louisiana; numerically this is the most serious slave revolt so far in the United States.

1812 The colonial authorities discover plan by a free black Cuban militiamen Aronte to lead a revolt to overthrow slavery and Spanish rule.

1815 Slaves rebel in the British Caribbean colony of Jamaica. A plot for a revolt is discovered in the French Caribbean colony of Guadeloupe, and another in the following year.

1816 There is a slave rebellion led by Bussa in the British Caribbean colony of Barbados; the rising spreads across the south and centre of the island; one white is killed and over 200 slaves are executed, with others being deported to Sierra Leone. Fugitive slaves and native American allies seize and hold a fort in Florida until defeated by troops; the 'Black Seminole' leader Garcia is executed and the survivors are returned to slavery.

1820 Martial law is declared during a month-long slave rising in the British Central American colony of Belize; the rebels are offered a pardon by the authorities who agree that harsh treatment has provoked the rebellion.

1822 A plan for a 5,000-strong slave rising under the leadership of Denmark Vesey in Charleston, South Carolina, is betrayed; over 30 slaves, including Vesey, are executed. Fifty slaves escape from the salt mines in the British Caribbean Turks and Caicos Islands.

1823 There is a serious rising involving thousands of slaves in the British South American colony of Guiana in the Demerara sugar plantations; the rebels demand immediate emancipation and kill two overseers; martial law is declared and over 100 slaves are killed in the suppression of the rebellion. There is a rising by slaves in Jamaica who believe emancipation granted by the British Parliament is being withheld by the plantation owners.

1825 Hundreds of African and creole slaves kill six whites and destroy over 20 estates in a rising in the west of Spanish Cuba.

1829 Free black American David Walker (1785–1830) publishes an anti-slavery pamphlet entitled *An Appeal to the Colored Citizens of the World* in which he calls on slaves to rise against their owners; the pamphlet causes white alarm in many Southern states.

1831 Over 50 whites are killed in a slave revolt in Virginia led by Nat Turner (1800–31), the largest in United States history; 31 slaves, including Turner, are executed; the Southern states step up enforcement of the 'black codes' in response. Sam Sharpe (1801–32) is executed after leading a rising involving up to 60,000 slaves in the British Caribbean colony of Jamaica in which a dozen whites and over 200 slaves are killed; a further 344 slaves are executed after surrendering. There are risings in the French Caribbean colonies of Martinique and Guadeloupe, in response to news of the July revolution in France, and in the British Caribbean colonies of Barbados and Antigua.

1835 Five hundred slaves mount an unsuccessful rising in the Salvador da Batia area of Brazil.

1839 Slaves being transported from Cuba on the *Amistad* seize the ship under the leadership of Joseph Cinque (c1811–78) and attempt to force the crew to return them to Africa; they are ultimately granted their liberty by the Supreme Court after landing in the United States.

1841   Slaves being transported from Virginia to New Orleans seize the ship *Creole* and sail to the Bahamas where they are granted their liberty.

1843   Black American abolitionist Henry Highland Garnet (1815–82) calls for rebellion and a general strike to improve slaves' conditions but is condemned by Frederick Douglass (c1817–95) and other anti-slavery campaigners. Slaves led by a woman slave, Carolota, rise in the Matanzas region of Cuba over the Spanish authorities' failure to grant emancipation under an agreement with Britain to slaves illegally imported on to the island; the rising is violently put down but its effect is to encourage greater agitation among whites against the slave trade.

1844   The plan for a slave revolt is discovered in Cuba, the 'Staircase Conspiracy'; slaves conspire with free blacks and British abolitionists to rise; the plan is ruthlessly suppressed and thousands of slaves are killed.

1848   The governor of the Danish Caribbean colony of St Croix is forced to make a premature announcement of emancipation by a revolt of thousands of slaves. Slaves are granted their freedom in the Dutch colony of St Maarten after threatening to move to the French section of the island where slavery has been abolished. United States President James Polk offers to purchase Cuba from Spain for $100 million because of fears among slave owners in the Southern states that a successful slave rising in Cuba would threaten their control.

1851   There are unsuccessful slave risings on sugar plantations in the Chicama and Cañete valleys of Peru. There are successful black abolitionist actions in the United States to prevent the recapture of fugitive slaves.

1859   White American abolitionist John Brown (1800–59) leads five blacks and a dozen whites in an attack on the United States arsenal at Harper's Ferry, Virginia, in what was to be a preliminary to a general slave uprising; the attempt fails and Brown and his followers are executed.

1868   Slaves and their owners rise against Spanish rule in eastern Cuba; slavery is abolished by the radical government in Spain in 1873 but restored by the monarchy in 1874; the rising continues until 1880.

1882   As anti-slavery agitation intensifies throughout Brazil, there is a slave revolt in the city of Caminas in the province of São Paulo.

1887   Slavery is abandoned in Brazil's São Paulo province as thousands of slaves, encouraged by abolitionists, abandon the plantations; the government abolished slavery for slaves over 60 in 1885.

1888   Slavery collapses as an institution in Brazil as slaves throughout the country leave the plantations; slavery is then formally abolished.

2.3 Chronology of the abolition of the slave trade and of slavery in South America and the Caribbean, 1555–1888

1555   Fernão Oliveira, the director of a Portuguese university publishers, criticises the Portuguese slave trade in a book entitled *The Art of Sea War*, accusing traders of 'buying and selling peaceable free men, as one buys and sells animals'.

1569   Tomás de Mercado, a Spanish Dominican friar, denounces the slave trade and accuses anyone of buying a slave of committing a mortal sin.

1573   The Spanish writer Bartolomé de Albornos, who has worked in Mexico, attacks the slave trade for violating Africans' rights to liberty.

1639   Pope Urban VIII issues a bull condemning the slave trade for depriving its victims of their freedom.

1641   Pope Benedict XIV issues a bull repeating the condemnation of the slave trade.

1764   The agent for the British North American colony of Massachusetts in London reports that there are up to 60 absentee Caribbean plantation owners in Parliament who can hold the balance of power to protect their interests.

1774   A debating society in the British Caribbean colony of Jamaica votes that slavery is against the laws of nature and morality and that it is inconsistent with sound economic policy.

1792   As the abolition of British participation in the slave trade is fiercely debated, the planter dominated Jamaican House of Assembly declares that 'the safety of the West Indies not only depends on the slave trade not being abolished, but on a speedy declaration of the House of Lords that they will not suffer the trade to be abolished'.

1794   France abolishes slavery in the Caribbean. The institution is restored in 1802, except in Haiti where France has been ousted in a revolutionary rising.

1806   The first African *cabildo*, a self-help and mutual aid organisation, is established in the Matanzas area of the Portuguese colony of Brazil to raise funds for the purchase of slaves' freedom.

1807   Britain ends its participation in the slave trade.

1810 Portuguese Prince Regent Dom João agrees in a treaty with Britain to move towards abolition of the slave trade and to outlaw participation in the trade by his subjects outside Portuguese territories in Africa. In Spanish America, the Supreme Junta of Caracas and Hidalgo in Mexico abolish the slave trade. Planters in Cuba petition against any Spanish involvement in an anti-slavery policy (and repeat their petitions in 1822 and 1823). Slaves are offered their freedom in return for volunteering for rebel armies in wars of independence in Argentina, Colombia and Venezuela which are waged in the following two decades.

1811 The Spanish Constituent Assembly rejects a motion presented by a Mexican delegate to abolish the slave trade. The resulting constitution makes no reference to slavery.

1812 The Government of Buenos Aires abolishes the slave trade in the area under its authority.

1815 Britain secures a declaration against the slave trade at the Congress of Berlin but the King of Spain's representative privately opposes foreign intervention in the issue. Portugal agrees in a treaty with Britain to work towards making participation by Portuguese subjects in the slave trade north of the Equator illegal. Legislation abolishing the slave trade is to be enacted by Portugal and British and Portuguese will seize ships suspected of slave trading. The agreement results in little real action.

1816 Legislation in Jamaica requiring owners to pay £100 to the government for each slave freed is repealed, easing the process of manumission.

1817 Fears by whites in the Spanish colony of Cuba (with a population of 291,000 whites, 224,000 slaves and 115,000 free blacks) encourage the negotiation of an Anglo-Spanish agreement to end the slave trade. King João VI of Portugal reasserts the agreement with Britain to partially ban the slave trade but once again the agreement is not implemented.

1818 King João VI of Portugal introduces measures to protect free Africans in Brazil (*emancipados*) with the provision that they are placed in government or private employment for 14 years.

1820 The Anglo-Spanish treaty to end the transportation of slaves into Cuba formally negotiated in 1817 comes into force. British naval vessels are authorised to search ships suspected of participating in the slave trade and cases are investigated by mixed Anglo-Spanish commissions. Many Cuban landowners suspect this as a British attempt to ward off competition in the sugar industry, and the illegal import of slaves continues.

1821 Venezuela grants freedom to slaves; however, five years later over 30,000 slaves remain.

1822 Brazil declares its independence from Portugal as an Empire under Pedro I; the country's political dependence on Britain suggests the latter will have influence on Brazil's policies on slavery and the slave trade. Portugal continues to participate in the trade from Africa to Brazil and Cuba.

1823 Peru issues a decree abolishing the slave trade; Chile frees its remaining 4,000 slaves.

1824 The United Provinces of Central America abolish slavery.

1826 The Spanish government declares that slaves who can prove they were illegally imported after 1820 are to be set free and orders ships arriving in Spain's Caribbean colonies to provide log-books for inspection to check for possible slave trading. British officials on the mixed commission complain of lack of Spanish commitment to the rules but the British government fails to press the policy firmly. Emperor Pedro I of Brazil agrees in a treaty with Britain (a re-affirmation of the treaties negotiated with Portugal in 1815 and 1817) to end the slave trade three years after the treaty's ratification. However, as the world demand for coffee continues to grow, over 60,000 slaves are illegally imported every year.

1829 Mexico abolishes slavery; it is relatively unimportant economically and there are only 3,000 slaves, but illegal slave trading continues.

1830 The slave trade is outlawed in Brazil but nevertheless continues to expand. Liberty is formally granted to illegally imported slaves, with little effect. The subsequent deployment of British naval vessels off the Brazilian coast to intercept illegal slave traders strains relations between the two governments. France ends its participation in the slave trade.

1831 The Brazilian general assembly outlaws the enslavement of the indigenous population.

1832 France abolishes the tax on manumission (the freeing of individual slaves by their owners), eases the procedure in its Caribbean colonies and restores the practice of granting slaves freedom on their arrival in France.

1834 Britain abolishes slavery in its Caribbean possessions, although a system of apprenticeship is retained until 1838. A Society to Abolish Slavery is established in France. Denmark introduces compulsory manumission after a fixed period of service and the right for slaves to have a plot of land.

1835 Spain and Britain re-assert their joint commitment to end the slave trade in a new treaty. The British government instructs diplomatic representatives in Argentina, Chile, Colombia, Mexico, Peru, Uruguay and Venezuela to persuade governments of the territories to sign treaties against the slave trade based on the 1826 treaty with Brazil.

1836 Spain appoints a consul to the British colony of Jamaica to monitor abolitionist activity; he reports to the colonial administration in Cuba on largely fictitious plans by anti-slavery activists to foment slave rebellions in Cuba. Britain appoints a Superintendent of Liberated Africans in Havana to assist Africans rescued from illegal slave traders. France introduces legislation freeing all slaves who land in France.

1837 The Spanish administration in Cuba orders the detention of the black crews of foreign ships mooring in Havana; the authorities refuse to allow black British soldiers arriving to arrange the repatriation of freed slaves to land; Britain refuses to withdraw the ship and the Spanish authorities back down.

1838 Legislation to end slavery in the French colonies is defeated by owners' representatives in the National Assembly.

1839 Pope Gregory XVI issues a bull condemning the slave trade and threatening excommunication on any Roman Catholic engaged in the trade. The *Amistad* incident in which slaves being illegally imported into Cuba seize the ship in which they are being transported, attempt to take it to Africa but land in the United States. Despite Spanish demands for their return as 'assassins', they are eventually granted their freedom by the United States Supreme Court in 1841. Venezuela signs a treaty with Britain to end the slave trade. The 1823 decree abolishing the slave trade in Peru is annulled after Peruvian planters begin a campaign to retain slavery. Britain passes legislation (the 'Palmerston Act') authorising its naval vessels to seize Portuguese ships transporting slaves or equipped to do so. The French Chamber of Deputies appoints a committee to consider slavery in France's colonies.

1840 There are reports of increasing resentment among slaves in Cuba over the working of the 1826 Anglo-Spanish treaty guaranteeing their freedom if they can demonstrate they were illegally imported after 1820. In 1843–44 there is a series of ruthlessly suppressed slave risings.

1841 Chile signs a treaty with Britain to end the slave trade.

1842 Uruguay (where there are 300 slaves) and Mexico (where slavery was formally abolished in 1823) sign treaties with Britain to end slavery and the slave trade.

1843 A French Chamber of Deputies committee recommends a ten-year programme to emancipate the 250,000 slaves in France's colonies, with measures to protect the owners' interests. Over 90 planters in Matazas, Cuba's major sugar producing area, demand the abolition of the slave trade to the island.

1844 Workers in Paris petition the Chamber of Deputies demanding immediate emancipation in the French colonies, describing slavery as 'leprosy'.

1845 Britain passes legislation (the 'Aberdeen Act') authorising its naval vessels to seize Brazilian ships transporting slaves or equipped to do so. Admiralty courts are empowered to determine violations of the 1826 treaty.

1846 France frees all slaves who are the direct property of the state.

1847 Ecuador signs a treaty with Britain agreeing to end the slave trade. Sweden abolishes slavery in its Caribbean colonies. An 100,000 signature petition calling for an end of slavery in the French colonies is presented to the Chamber of Deputies.

1848 France abolishes slavery in its Caribbean colonies immediately after the triumph of revolutionary forces, with compensation for the former owners. Slaves are granted their freedom in the Dutch colony of St Maarten after threatening to move to the French section of the island. United States President James K. Polk offers to purchase Cuba from Spain to meet the fears of slave owners in the Southern states that a successful slave rising in Cuba would threaten their position. Denmark abolishes slavery in its Caribbean colonies but establishes a period of apprenticeship to last up to 30 years.

1849 Dutch workers demonstrate against King William III in Amsterdam calling for emancipation of the slaves in the country's possessions.

1850 The Brazilian general assembly (under pressure from Britain) passes the Quieróz Law outlawing the transportation of slaves from Africa and categorising the activity as piracy (150,000 slaves had been landed in the country in 1847–49). Slave trading within the country is allowed to continue. An illegal slave trade continues to provide labour to meet the world demand for coffee and raw materials. British warships enter Brazilian territorial waters in pursuit of suspected traders. Peru signs a commercial treaty with Britain including a clause agreeing to end the slave trade.

1851 British Prime Minister Lord Palmerston urges Spain to free the slaves in its Caribbean colonies on the grounds that this would remove any incentive the United States has to annex Cuba. Bolivia and Colombia sign treaties with Britain to end slavery and the slave trade.

1853 Argentina ends slavery and its participation in the slave trade.

1854 Venezuela (which formally abolished slavery in 1821) issues a decree freeing the remaining 12,000 slaves to prevent conservative rebels attempting to recruit them in a renewed civil war. A former president in rebellion against the government frees Peru's remaining 25,000 slaves and confirms the abolition of slavery and participation in the slave trade when he gains power.

1863 The Netherlands abolishes slavery in its Caribbean colonies following a decade of negotiations with the slave owners.

1864   The Brazilian government guarantees the liberty of free Africans (*emancipados*).

1865   The Spanish Anti-Slavery Society is established with a policy of campaigning for immediate emancipation in Spain's colonies.

1866   A Brazilian decree grants freedom to government-owned slaves who volunteer for the army to fight in the 1865–70 war with Uruguay; after the war, many remain in the army, instilling an anti-slavery consciousness. Planters in Puerto Rico – where the proportion of slaves in the population has fallen from 15% in 1860 to 5% – send a delegation to Spain demanding abolition of slavery on the grounds that, 'The general wealth of the island does not need it.'

1867   Emperor Pedro II of Brazil calls on the country's general assembly to introduce legislation to reform the institution of slavery; the Brazilian army presents an official petition requesting not to be deployed against slave rebels. Spain ends its participation in the slave trade through a treaty with Britain; the last slave trading vessel crosses the Atlantic to Cuba.

1868   Liberal Cuban landowner and lawyer Carlos Manuel de Céspedes issues the 'declaration of Yara', releasing his slaves and calling for independence from Spain. His action triggers a wave of slave liberations and he declares that, 'A free Cuba is incompatible with a slave Cuba.' Plantation owners who support the revolt are promised compensation for freed slaves; a ten year guerrilla war of independence opens; slavery is restored by the Spanish authorities in the course of the struggle; black Cubans play a significant part in the rebel forces, which include a black general – Antonio Maceo – as one of the leaders.

1869   The Brazilian general assembly bans public slave auctions and prohibits the separation of married couples and of children under 15 from their parents. A new Constitution in Spain encourages an increase in liberal and radical anti-slavery influence in the Cortes (parliament). There is also growing evidence from Spain's overseas provinces that production is rising as the slave trade diminishes.

1870   Spain passes the 'Moret Law' freeing slaves in Cuba at the age of 60. Children born to slaves are to become free at birth under the 'law of the free stomach' but will continue to work for their parent's owners as apprentices until they are 18. Slavery is abolished in Paraguay by Brazilian forces occupying the country following the War of the Triple Alliance.

1871   The 'Rio Branco Law' in Brazil frees children born to women slaves on or after 28 September. They will, however, be required to work for the owners as apprentices until they reach the age of 21. Other reforms in Brazil acknowledge the right of slaves to own personal possessions. The Cortes (parliament) passes a law abolishing the slave trade in Spanish possessions.

1873   Spain abolishes slavery in Puerto Rico with no compensation for owners. The black American activist Henry Highland Garnet (1815–82) calls for an invasion of Cuba to free the slaves. Following the nationalist rebellion by slaves and slave owners in eastern Cuba, the Spanish First Republic abolishes slavery in Cuba but it is restored in the west by the Bourbon monarchy in 1874.

1878   The Cuban war of independence ends with the Treaty of Zanjón, under which Spain promises a series of reforms, including the gradual emancipation of slaves throughout its Caribbean colonies.

1880   Spain issues a decree gradually freeing slaves in its Caribbean territories. The establishment of the Brazilian Anti-Slavery Society by Joaquim Nabuco, André Rebouças and the black abolitionist Luis Gonzaga Pinto da Gama is followed by the setting up of campaigning newspapers in Rio de Janeiro and other cities. Assemblies in the Brazilian provinces of Rio de Janeiro and Minas Gerais restrict the importation of slaves.

1881   The Assembly in Brazil's São Paulo province restricts the importation of slaves. Anti-slavery demonstrators in Fortaleza, in the north eastern Brazilian province of Ceará, demand an end to the export of slaves to southern plantations.

1883   Seventeen anti-slavery organisations from five Brazilian provinces unite to create an Abolitionist Confederation in Rio de Janeiro and issue a manifesto. Joaquim Nabuco agues in his book *O Abolicionismo* (Abolitionism) that the continuation of slavery is corrupting the life of Brazil.

1884   Abolitionist movements in the northern Brazilian provinces of Ceará and Amazonas force a virtual abandonment of slavery. The Liberal government of Manuel Pinto de Sousa Dantas proposes freeing all slaves when they reach the age of 60.

1885   The Brazilian general assembly frees all slaves aged 60 and over under the 'Saraiva-Cotegipe Law', with the proviso that they work for their former owners without pay for five years or until they reach 65.

1886   Slavery is finally ended in Spain's Caribbean territories as 60,000 slaves working to compensate their former owners are freed from all obligations.

1887   Slavery is virtually ended in Brazil's São Paulo province as thousands of slaves, encouraged by abolitionist activists, abandon plantations.

1888   Slavery collapses throughout Brazil as the abandonment of plantations by slaves intensifies. 'The Golden Law' (Lei Áurea) of 13 May formally abolishes slavery, emancipating approximately 700,000 people.

2.4 Chronology of the Haitian Revolution, 1789–1862

1789
July

The revolution begins in France; the Declaration of the Rights of Man by the Estates General brings the issue of slavery in France's colonies into prominence. In the French Caribbean colony of Saint Domingue there are 20,000 whites (divided between the planters and the less prosperous *petits blancs*); 30,000 free blacks and mulattos and 500,000 slaves; there are also large numbers of maroons (fugitive slaves) in mountain settlements.

1790
Mar.

The French General Assembly proclaims local autonomy in France's colonies; the *petits blancs* and the planters in Saint Domingue form rival assemblies.

Nov.

Saint Domingue mulattos Vincent Ogé and Jean-Baptist Chavannes lead a force to back their demand for citizenship rights for free blacks and mulattos but reject an alliance with the slaves; the force is defeated by the French.

1791
Aug.

A rising by maroons (fugitive slaves) led by Boukman begins in the north of Saint Domingue and spreads among slaves in the south and west; in the following two months 10,000 slaves and 2,000 whites are killed and a thousand plantations are destroyed; white soldiers are defeated at Port-au-Prince; free blacks and mulattos ally with whites against the rising.

Sept.

The *petits blancs* assembly recognises the citizenship rights of free blacks and mulattos; the French General Assembly votes to send three commissioners with troops to restore France's authority in Saint Domingue.

Oct.

François Domingue Toussaint (1746–1803) becomes commander of the slave forces; his tactical abilities lead him to be described as Toussaint L'Ouverture ('the opening').

Dec.

The French commissioners and 6,000 troops arrive in Saint Domingue but are unable to restore order as the alliance between whites, free blacks and mulattos breaks down.

1792
Apr.

The French General Assembly grants citizenship rights to free blacks and mulattos in Saint Domingue and appoints Léger Felicité Sonthonax as a commissioner to restore control.

1793
Jan.

Reactions to the execution of Louis XVI in France divides whites in Saint Domingue.

June

Slave forces massacre 3,000 whites in Le Cap, forcing 10,000 whites (half the white population) to flee to the United States.

Aug.	French Commissioner Sonthonax announces the abolition of slavery, securing the support of Toussaint in the restoration of France's authority; the abolition is recognised by the French government in February 1794.
Sept.	A 60,000–strong British army invades Saint Domingue from Jamaica and attempts to force the restoration of slavery.
1795 July	Following the defeat of a Spanish invasion in which Toussaint's forces support France, Spain cedes neighbouring Santo Domingo (later the Dominican Republic) to France but the territory remains under Spanish administration.
1796 Mar.	Toussaint is appointed Lieutenant Governor of Saint Domingue and then commander of French forces.
1797 Aug.	Toussaint orders Sonthonax to leave Saint Domingue and begins a campaign against British forces; fearing Toussaint's growing influence, France encourages conflict between his forces and mulattos led by André Rigaud; United States President John Adams agrees to provide Toussaint with arms.
1798 Feb.	The bulk of British-held territory is captured as 40,000 British soldiers die of disease.
1799	Britain agrees to withdraw; there is a division of areas of control in Saint Domingue between Toussaint's black forces and Rigaud's mulattos; civil war soon breaks out between the two and, because of its violence, is known as 'The War of the Knives'.
1800 Mar.	Rigaud's last stronghold of Jacmel falls.
Aug.	Toussaint's authority in Saint Domingue is complete and he begins preparations to invade Santo Domingo.
1801 Jan.	Santo Domingo is captured; Toussaint becomes Governor General for Hispaniola for life, the entire island.
July	Toussaint issues a new constitution abolishing slavery but insists that former slaves must remain on their plantations to preserve the island's economy; the constitution declares that Hispaniola remains a French territory.
Oct.	France and Britain make peace; Napoleon Bonaparte (who has seized power in France in a coup in 1799) prepares a force to invade Saint Domingue.
1802 Feb.	French invasion force arrives under the command of General Charles Leclerc; slave armies retreat and begin to wage a guerrilla war.
May	Toussaint surrenders to Leclerc with a promise that he will be allowed his liberty.
June	Toussaint is arrested and sent to France, where he dies in prison the following year. Leclerc begins an unsuccessful campaign to disarm the black forces which renew the rebellion.

Oct.	Black commanders Jean-Jacques Dessalines (c1758–1806), Henri Christophe (1767–1820) and Alexandre Pétion (1770–1818) withdraw their support from the French and ally with the black rebels as it becomes clear that Napoleon intends to restore slavery.
Nov.	Dessalines becomes rebel commander; a further 10,000 French troops land.
1803 May	As war is renewed between France and Britain, Dessalines becomes an ally of Britain.
Nov.	French forces evacuate Saint Domingue.
1804 Jan.	An independent republic of Haiti is proclaimed; the country's name ('the higher place') is that given it by the island's original inhabitants, the Arawak. Sugar production has fallen to a third of the 1791 level; Dessalines restores the plantation system with forced labour and imposes harsh penalties on fugitives.
Oct.	Dessalines is crowned Emperor Jacques.
1805 May	Slavery is declared illegal and it is proclaimed that all Haitians, regardless of colour, are to be described as black.
1808 Oct.	Emperor Jacques is killed while attempting to subdue a mulatto revolt; Henry Christophe takes power and appoints himself as King Henri; Pétion seizes control of the south as president for life and civil war ensues.
1809	Spanish rule is restored in neighbouring Santo Domingo with British aid and slavery is reimposed.
1818	Pétion, the southern president for life, dies without naming a successor; the commander of the Presidential Guard, General Jean-Pierre Boyer is appointed to the office.
1820 Oct.	Christophe, the northern ruler, commits suicide; Boyer becomes president of a reunited Haiti and promotes the rule of a mulatto elite.
1821	Santo Domingo declares independence from Spain.
1822	Boyer abolishes slavery in Santo Domingo following its conquest by Haiti; the area remains under Haitian control until 1844.
1825	Haitian independence is recognised by France.
1833	Britain recognises Haiti.
1862	The United States recognises Haiti following the secession of the slave-owning Confederate states.

2.5 Chronology of the campaign in Britain for the abolition of the slave trade and slavery, 1671–1838

1671   The Quaker George Fox (1624–91) calls on members of the Society of Friends to grant liberty to slaves who have served for a long period.

1690   Liberal philosopher John Locke (1632–1704) – who benefits from slavery as a shareholder in the Royal African Company – writes ambiguously on the subject of slavery in *Two Treatises on Government*, questioning the institution but implicitly supporting the expansion of colonies depending on slave labour.

1761   London Yearly Meeting of the Society of Friends (the Quakers) declares participation by its members in the slave trade is incompatible with the movement's beliefs.

1764   The agent for the British North American colony of Massachusetts in London reports that there are up to 60 absentee Caribbean plantation owners in Parliament who can hold the balance of power to protect their interests.

1765   Granville Sharp (1735–1813) begins his involvement in abolitionist activity when he attempts to prevent a fugitive slave, Jonathan Strong, from being forcibly returned to his owner. There is a two year legal struggle which Strong wins when the owner fails to take the case to court.

1767   Granville Sharp publishes *On the Injustice of Tolerating Slavery in Britain*, following his involvement in the Strong case. Sharp is called on to advise in similar cases involving John Hylas in 1768 and Thomas Lewis in 1770.

1772   Slavery is effectively outlawed in England as a result of Lord Chief Justice Mansfield's decision in the case of James Somerset, a slave brought to England from the British North American colony of Virginia. Mansfield reluctantly rules that Somerset should not be returned to bondage, declaring that no law in England allowed 'so high an act of dominion as slavery'. While not banning slavery directly, the ruling undermines claims that the institution had any legitimacy in England. The publicity surrounding the case, in which Granville Sharp plays an influential part, encourages growing opposition to slavery in the British colonies and Britain's role in the slave trade. As a result of Mansfield's ruling, liberty is restored to the 15,000 slaves (with an estimated value of £700,000) living in Britain.

1774 Methodist leader John Wesley (1703–91) publishes his influential *Thoughts upon Slavery*. Members of the Society of Friends (the Quakers) are threatened with expulsion if they associate with slave traders. A Member of Parliament introduces a bill against the slave trade on the grounds that it is 'contrary to the laws of God and the rights of man' but finds no-one to second him.

1776 As the campaign against slavery intensifies, members of the Society of Friends who own slaves are ordered to set them free or face expulsion from the movement. The economist Adam Smith criticises slavery as inefficient and provides an economic argument for abolition in his *Wealth of Nations* where he writes, 'It appears from the experience of all ages and nations, I believe, that the work done by free men comes cheaper than that performed by slaves.'

1780 William Wilberforce (1759–1833) is elected Tory Member of Parliament for Hull; he will for many years be the voice of abolitionism in the Commons.

1783 The Society of Friends begins an intensive campaign of anti-slavery propaganda, setting up a committee to publish information to encourage an end to the slave trade and presenting a petition to Parliament calling for abolition of the trade. The Prime Minister, Lord North, rejects the petition on the grounds that the slave trade is essential to every European nation. The *Zong* case has a strong effect on public opinion when it is revealed that 132 slaves were thrown overboard while the ship was sailing from Africa to Jamaica to enable the owners to make an insurance claim. Lord Chief Justice Mansfield reluctantly rules in favour of the owners, ordering the insurers to pay compensation for the loss of the slaves, and provokes widespread anger in Britain. Britain's first anti-slavery society – the London Meeting for Sufferings – is established in response to an appeal by Quakers in Philadelphia.

1785 Thomas Clarkson (1760–1846) writes a prize-winning essay *Anne liceat invites in servitutum dare* ('Is it right to make men slaves against their will?') as a student at Cambridge and opens his lifelong involvement in the campaign against the slave trade and then slavery.

1786 Granville Sharp becomes involved in the purchase of land in West Africa to establish the colony of Sierra Leone for the settlement of former slaves who had fought for the British during the American War of Independence and are refugees in London. He succeeds in securing funds and ships from the British government and buys a quarter of a million acres around St George's Bay.

1787 Four hundred former slaves and 60 Europeans leave England to settle in Sierra Leone. The Society for Effecting the Abolition of the

Slave Trade is formed by Thomas Clarkson, Granville Sharp and Josiah Wedgwood (1730–95). Nine of the 12 committee members are Quakers but the Society's establishment broadens the base of anti-slave trade activity. Sharp's call for the society to include the abolition of slavery in its programme is rejected by other members of the founding committee but he is elected chairman, with William Wilberforce as the body's main spokesman. This is necessary as the majority of the committee are Quakers and are debarred from becoming MPs. Wilberforce is an evangelical Anglican. The Society's seal – a kneeling black slave in chains with his hands lifted skywards and the motto 'Am I Not a Man and a Brother?' – is designed by Wedgwood. Women are excluded from the leadership but are estimated to account for 10% of financial support given to the organisation, rising to 25% in some areas. Clarkson is despatched to the two main trading ports of Bristol and Liverpool to gather evidence through interviews to provide background for a par-liamentary campaign. He conducts 20,000 interviews and obtains samples of equipment used in the ill-treatment of slaves during trans-portation. Clarkson's pamphlet *A Summary View of the Slave Trade and of the Probable Consequences of its Abolition* is published. A British government commission of enquiry into the slave trade reports that of an annual British export from Africa of 40,000 slaves, two thirds are sold on to Britain's economic competitors; this is viewed as detrimental to Britain's economic interests.

1788   An Act introduced by Sir William Dolben regulates the British slave trade, setting limits on the numbers of slaves that can be carried on slave trading vessels. In the course of the year, 102 petitions containing over 60,000 signatures of adult males against the slave trade and slavery are submitted to Parliament.

1789   Clarkson travels to France following the revolution and spends six months in Paris attempting to persuade the National Assembly to abolish slavery. A new French constitution promulgated in 1794 abolishes slavery but this is revoked by Napoleon in 1802. British Caribbean planters and merchants from Bristol present a petition against abolition of the slave trade, arguing that three fifths of Bristol's commerce depends on sugar; they are joined by merchants and ship owners from London in their appeal. Wilberforce presents a bill for the abolition of the slave trade but opponents win a post-ponement on the grounds that more information on the subject is required.

1790   A House of Commons select committee into the African slave trade is convened; it is estimated that abolition of the slave trade would cost the port of Liverpool alone over £7 million annually.

1791   The dying Methodist leader John Wesley writes to William Wilberforce calling on him to continue his opposition to slavery, despite the forces against him. 'Go on, in the name of God, in the power of his might, till even American slavery (the vilest that ever saw the sun) shall vanish away before it.' Wilberforce introduces his first anti-slavery motion in the House of Commons and makes a three and a half hour speech in which he denounces inadequate food and medical care in British Caribbean plantations and concludes, 'Sir, when we think of eternity and the future consequence of all human conduct, what is there in this life that shall make any man contradict the dictates of his conscience, the principles of justice and the law of God?' The motion is defeated by 163 votes to 88; leading opponents include King George III and the Duke of Clarence (the future William IV). The Prime Minister, William Pitt, declares that a slave would be twice as productive if he worked as a free labourer.

1792   The war against France which follows the French Revolution of 1789 proves an obstacle to the campaign to abolish the slave trade, which goes into virtual abeyance until 1805. However, in the course of the year, 519 anti-slavery petitions are presented to Parliament containing the signature of over 350,000 adult males. The Jamaican House of Assembly declares that 'the safety of the West Indies depends not only on the slave trade not being abolished, but on a speedy declaration of the House of Lords that they will not suffer the trade to be abolished'.

1793   Upper Canada becomes the first British colony to place limits on slavery when it bans the import of slaves and grants freedom to slaves over the age of 25. During the next half century over 30,000 slaves flee from the United States to Canada.

1804   There is a resurgence in abolitionist activity with Thomas Clarkson (1760–1846) prominent, largely through the press and pamphlets rather than agitation. Bills to abolish slavery achieve initial successes but fall as the government refuses to take up the issue.

1805   The acquisition by Britain of new colonies in the Caribbean threatens existing plantation owners with increased economic competition; in response they become more sympathetic to a restriction in the slave trade; the import of slaves into the newly acquired territories of British Guiana and Trinidad is prohibited. The House of Commons passes legislation outlawing the involvement of any British subject in the capture and transportation of slaves but the measure is defeated in the House of Lords.

1806   The formation of a Whig administration under Lord Grenville who, with his Foreign Secretary Charles James Fox, is an opponent of the slave trade, increases the possibility of legislation being passed. While Fox and Wilberforce argue the case in the Commons, Grenville leads the campaign in the Lords, denouncing the slave trade as 'contrary to the principles of justice, humanity and sound policy' and criticising the Lords for 'not having abolished the trade long ago'. Parliament passes legislation making it illegal for any British vessel to participate in the trade in slaves. The Commons vote in favour of the legislation is 114–15 while the House of Lords votes 41–20.

1807 The legislation against the slave trade receives Royal Assent after passing through the Commons by 283 votes to 16 and the Lords by 100 votes to 30.

1808 The last slave trading vessel sails from the port of Liverpool. The Royal Navy begins to blockade the West African coast. British captains convicted of involvement in the trade are to be fined £100. To reduce the danger when facing capture by Royal Navy, some captains order the slaves to be thrown overboard. British ships attempt to evade the law by flying 'flags of convenience' and this is met by the negotiation of treaties allowing reciprocal arrest on seizure of shipping. Wilberforce opposes the abolition of slavery, arguing in a pamphlet that to 'grant them freedom immediately, would be to ensure not only their masters' ruin, but their own'. He proposes initial training and education. Wilberforce is, however, eventually persuaded to support the emancipation campaign by Thomas Fowell Buxton. The Society for Effecting the Abolition of the Slave Trade is replaced by the African Institution, which attempts to persuade other states to follow Britain's lead and end participation in the trade.

1811 As fining slave traders proves ineffective, the British government declares any British subject engaging in the slave trade to be a pirate and institutes the death penalty.

1814 Britain and France declare in the Treaty of Paris which temporarily ends the war between them that the slave trade is 'repugnant to the principles of natural justice' and France agrees that it will place limits on its own participation in the trade and abolish it in five years. Seven hundred petitions containing a million signatures calling for an immediate end to slavery are presented to the House of Commons. Wilberforce rejects a proposal to free all slaves illegally imported into British possessions, saying that, 'Our object is... to produce by abolition a disposition to breed instead of buying.'

1815 With the end of the renewed war against Napoleon at Waterloo, Britain joins other participants at the Congress of Vienna in condemning slavery but no measures are taken to end it. The Duke of Wellington persuades delegates to sign a declaration that they will end the slave trade; the Dutch do so in 1814, the French in 1815 and the Portuguese gradually from 1815 to 1830.

1823 The Society for the Mitigation and Gradual Abolition of Slavery Throughout the British Dominions is formed by Thomas Fowell Buxton, William Wilberforce, Thomas Clarkson and Henry Brougham, with an initial aim of reforming slavery rather than forcing its immediate abolition. Fowell calls on the House of Commons to consider the conditions of the slaves in Britain's colonies.

1824 Elizabeth Heyrick's pamphlet *Immediate not Gradual Abolition* criticises the policy adopted by the predominantly male leadership of the Society opposing slavery. Heyrick declares that immediate abolition 'is the only solid foundation on which the reformation of the slave, and the still more needful reformation of his usurping master, can be built'. The Society's leaders attempt to suppress her views, which are supported by most women's abolitionist groups. Women's societies are formed in Birmingham, Leicester, Nottingham, Norwich, London, Darlington and by 1831 there are 73 women's organisations campaigning against slavery.

1825 With the retirement of William Wilberforce as an MP, Thomas Fowell Buxton (MP for Weymouth since 1818) becomes leader of the campaign against slavery in the House of Commons. The Royal Navy intensifies anti-slave trading patrols off West Africa; in the next 40 years they arrest 1,287 ships and free 130,000 slaves.

1830 The Female Society for Birmingham submits a motion to the Society for the Mitigation and Gradual Abolition of Slavery's national conference calling for a campaign for an immediate abolition of slavery in the British colonies and threatens to withdraw funding from the Society.

1831 Britain signs a treaty with France allowing for the mutual search of vessels suspected of engaging in the slave trade. The Society for the Mitigation and Gradual Abolition of Slavery submits a petition to Parliament calling for immediate freedom for the newborn children of slaves. The Agency Anti-Slavery Committee secedes from the Society for the Mitigation and Gradual Abolition of Slavery under Clarkson's leadership and demands an immediate and unconditional end to slavery. Professional organisers mount petitions and persuade voters to put pressure on Parliamentary candidates to support abolition. With women playing a prominent part in anti-slavery activity, there are now 40 women's abolitionist societies. Reports of the slave rebellion in Jamaica encourage abolitionist activity.

1832 In the first elections under the expanded franchise that follows the Reform Act, 104 of the returned Members of Parliament have pledged themselves to support the abolition of slavery.

1833 Five thousand petitions calling for an end to slavery containing a total of one and a half million signatures are submitted to Parliament. The Quaker abolitionist Joseph Sturge argues that emancipation and Parliamentary reform as interlinked: 'The people must emancipate the slaves, for the government never will.' The Abolition of Slavery Bill is presented to the Commons by Colonial Secretary

Edward Stanley; the 1832 Reform Act has changed the complexion of the Commons and eases passage of the legislation; the Bill initially proposes compensation of £15 million to slave owners and a 12 year period of 'apprenticeship' during which the free slaves will work for their former owners; during passage compensation is increased to £20 million and the apprenticeship period reduced to six years; the final legislation frees slaves in most British controlled territories. Wilberforce dies a month later.

1834   Over 800,000 slaves in the British Empire, predominantly in the Caribbean (but not in St Helena, India and Ceylon), are granted their freedom in July. All slaves under the age of six are freed immediately; those over six are to serve a period of apprenticeship for a further six years, undertaking compulsory paid work for their former owners. The British government allocates £20 million compensation to the owners, a sum amounting to half the annual budget.

1837   A Central Negro Emancipation Committee is formed to campaign for the abolition of apprenticeship.

1838   Apprenticeship in the British Caribbean colonies is abolished, two years earlier than originally intended.

2.5.1   Numbers of slaves in the British Caribbean and compensation paid to owners on emancipation in 1834

Island	Numbers of slaves	Compensation
Antigua	23,350	£415,173
Bahamas	7,734	£118,683
Barbados	66,638	£1,659,315
British Guiana	69,579	£4,068,809
British Virgin Islands	4,318	£70,177
Dominica	11,664	£265,071
Grenada	19,009	£570,733
Jamaica	255,290	£5,853,976
Montserrat	5,026	£100,654
Nevis	7,225	£145,976
St Kitts	15,667	£309,908
St Lucia	10,328	£309,658
St Vincent	18,114	£554,716
Tobago	9,078	£226,745
Trinidad	17,539	£973,442
Total	540,559	£15,787,869

Source. Based on table in Eric Williams, *From Columbus to Castro: The History of the Caribbean, 1492–1969* (1970), p. 332.

2.6 Chronology of the campaign for the abolition of the slave trade and slavery in colonial North America and the United States, 1643–1860

1643 The New England Confederation provides assistance to fleeing indentured servants and slaves.

1652 Rhode Island colony declares that slaves are entitled to their liberty after ten years service.

1641 Massachusetts formally outlaws slavery, declaring in its 'Body of Liberties' that 'there shall never be any bond slave, villeinage, or captivities among us unless it be lawful captives taken in just wars, and such strangers as willingly sell themselves or are sold to us'. However, the wording allows the institution to continue.

1676 Slavery is prohibited in west New Jersey.

1688 Members of the Society of Friends (Quakers) in Germanstown, Pennsylvania, adopt a resolution declaring that slavery is contrary to Christian teaching; this is the first unqualified attack on slavery as an institution. Many Quakers in England and the American colonies are slave owners and are involved in the slave trade.

1693 George Keith produces a pamphlet condemning slavery on the grounds that Christ died for liberty 'both inward and outward'.

1696 The Society of Friends in Germanstown, Pennsylvania, adopts a resolution calling for an end to the importation of slaves.

1700 Samuel Sewall, a judge in the 1692 Salem witch trial, publishes a pamphlet criticising slavery, *The Selling of Joseph: A Memory* in which he writes, 'It is most certain that all men, as they are the sons of Adam, are co-heirs, and have equal right unto liberty, and all other outward comforts of life.' He advocates that slaves presently in North America should remain slaves, believing that the majority 'can seldom use their freedom well', but that there should be no further imports.

1735 The English colony of Georgia – which has been established as a buffer state against Spanish-controlled Florida – bans slavery under an Act 'for rendering the Colony of Georgia more defensible by Prohibiting the Importation and use of Black Slaves or Negroes into the same'; colonists hire slaves from neighbouring South Carolina and at their insistence slavery is legalised in 1750.

1737 Controversy over the institution of slavery intensifies among Quakers with the publication by Benjamin Lay of a book in which he accuses Quaker slave owners of hypocrisy.

1754 Quakers are prominent in abolitionist activity in areas of their greatest strength – North Carolina, Pennsylvania, Rhode Island and west New Jersey. The Quaker abolitionist John Woolman circulates a letter in which he says, 'If we continually bear in mind the royal law of doing to others as we would be done by, we shall never think of bereaving our fellow-creatures of that valuable blessing liberty, nor grow rich by their bondage.'

1755 The Quakers declare the exclusion of any member who imports slaves.

1758 Quakers in Philadelphia declare that buying and selling slaves is inconsistent with Christian teachings and call on Quakers owning slaves to 'set them at liberty, making a Christian provision for them'.

1762 The Quaker abolitionist John Woolman's *Considerations on Keeping Negroes* provides further support for the campaign against slavery.

1767 The Quaker abolitionist Anthony Benezet's anti-slavery pamphlet *A Caution and Warning to Great Britain and Her Colonies* influences Benjamin Franklin and Benjamin Rush towards opposition to slavery.

1770 A fugitive slave, Crispus Attucks, is killed by British troops in the Boston Massacre, becoming one of the first people to die in the American struggle against colonial rule.

1772 The House of Burgesses, representing the colonists, drafts a petition to King George III calling for end to the import of slaves, which it calls a 'trade of great inhumanity'.

1773 An abolitionist cleric, the Rev Isaac Skillman, draws parallels between the growing struggle of the American colonists against Britain and the natural right of slaves to revolt against their owners. New England Quakers forbid members from owning slaves or engaging in the slave trade. Slaves living in Boston and other parts of the colony of Massachusetts submit a petition to the governor seeking their freedom, the first such petition presented in New England; although the petition was ineffective, it was later published as a pamphlet. The President of Yale College suggests that freed slaves should be returned to Africa.

1774 The representatives of 12 colonies meeting in a Continental Congress agree to suspend the import of slaves as part of wider sanctions against British trade. New Jersey Quakers are forbidden from owning slaves or engaging in the slave trade.

1775 The radical writer Thomas Paine (1737–1809) publishes an attack on
Mar. slavery in the *Pennsylvania Journal and the Weekly Advertiser*. 'That some wretches should be willing to steal and enslave men by violence and

murder for gain, is rather lamentable than strange', he writes. 'But that many civilised, nay, christianised people should approve, and be concerned in the savage practice, is surprising.'

Apr.   The American War of Independence begins (and ends with victory for the Americans in 1783). British writer Samuel Johnson asks in *Taxation No Tyranny*, 'How is it that we hear the loudest yelps for liberty among the drivers of negroes?' The Pennsylvania Society for the Abolition of Slavery, the first abolitionist organisation in America, is established in Philadelphia with Anthony Benezet and Paine prominent among its founding members; its initial activity is to assist fugitive slaves and to secure the release of illegally held free blacks. New York Quakers forbid members from owning and trading in slaves.

Nov.   Lord Dunmore, the British governor of Virginia, offers freedom to slaves who desert their owners to fight for the Crown against the colonists.

Dec.   After initial hesitation, and in the face of success of Dunmore's offer, the Continental Congress agrees to black recruitment to the colonists' army. However, an estimated 100,000 slaves take the opportunity of the upheaval of the war to escape, many to Canada and Florida.

1776
June   A clause in the draft Declaration of Independence denouncing slavery as a violation of the right to life and liberty and accusing King George III of forcing the institution on to the American colonies is deleted at the request of delegates from Georgia and South Carolina.

July   The Declaration of Independence is signed by the American colonies and avoids any reference to slavery in the interests of unity.

1777   Vermont abolishes slavery.

1780   The preamble to the Pennsylvania state constitution declares that as America has taken up arms for its freedom then slaves should be granted their liberty. A Gradual Emancipation Act is introduced, the first in the United States, limited to children born to slaves after the law comes into force and then only after they have worked for their owners until the age of 28. In 1780, there are 3,737 slaves in Pennsylvania; this falls to 64 in 1840 and to none in 1859.

1781   Two slaves successfully sue for their freedom in a Massachusetts court and one receives compensation for labour undertaken after the age of 21. The case intensifies the abolitionist campaign in the state. The Society of Friends in North America reiterates the exclusion of members engaging in the slave trade (though many continue to own slaves).

1782   Virginia passes legislation repealing the ban on the manumission of slaves, leading to the freedom of many slaves as the institution begins to weaken in the South; the number of free blacks in Virginia rises in a decade from 3,000 to 13,000. Manumission is granted provided the owners take responsibility for the support of the sick and those incapable of work, females between 18 and 45 males under 21 or over 45.

1783   A Massachusetts court declares that slavery violates a section of the state constitution holding that 'all men are born free and equal' and slavery is therefore unconstitutional. Maryland prohibits further imports of slaves.

1784   Connecticut and Rhode Island abolish slavery. The Methodist Church declares slavery to be against the will of God and orders members to free slaves within a year but the instruction meets intense resistance among Southern congregations and is withdrawn. The Continental Congress fails to ban slavery in all western territories by one vote.

1785   The New York Manumission Society is formed to campaign for abolition. The New York state legislature narrowly defeats a bill for gradual emancipation but accepts a ban on further imports of slaves.

1786   North Carolina increases the duty levied on imported slaves, forcing a reduction in the number brought into the state. The future United States President George Washington (1732–99) declares that he will not buy another slave and that he would like to see 'some plan adopted, by which slavery in this country may be abolished by slow, sure and imperceptible degrees'.

1787   The Continental Congress outlaws slavery in the North West Territory under the Ordinance of 1787. Benjamin Rush and Benjamin Franklin form the Pennsylvania Society for Promoting the Abolition of Slavery. Anti-slavery clauses in the draft United States Constitution are removed as South Carolina and Georgia insist on the continuation of slavery as a condition of joining the proposed Union. Delaware outlaws any further importation of slaves.

1789   The preservation of slavery becomes a condition of creating the United States; Article 1, Section 2 of the Constitution provides for a slave to be counted as three fifths of a person in calculating the population for representation; Article II, Section 9 says that the slave trade should continue for a further 20 years, and Article IV, Section 2 sets out stringent action on the return of fugitive slaves. The Maryland Abolition Society is established; its activities encourage the state legislature to enact legislation making it easier for slaves to purchase freedom and discouraging fresh imports of slaves.

1791   Pennsylvania passes legislation allowing freedom to any slave living in the state for more than six months. (When one of President George Washington's slaves escapes to Pennsylvania in 1795 he orders his apprehension but instructs his overseer to ensure his name is not mentioned in any proceedings.) Rev Jonathan Edwards Jr, a

Connecticut Congregationalist minister, publishes *Injustices and Impolicy of the Slave Trade and of Slavery of Africans.*

1794
Jan.

Delegates from abolitionist societies in Connecticut, Delaware, Maryland, New Jersey, New York and Pennsylvania meet in Philadelphia and agree to petition Congress to ban the slave trade and to appeal to state legislatures to abolish slavery in their territories. They produce an address calling on all American citizens to recognise 'the obligations of justice, humanity, and benevolence toward our African brethren, whether in bondage or free'.

Mar.

All United States citizens are forbidden to engage in the slave trade to foreign states and to manufacture or equip any vessel capable of doing so.

1797

A black petition protesting against a North Carolina state law requiring slaves freed by their Quaker owners to be returned to slavery is rejected by Congress. Former President Washington writes that he favours a gradual abolition of slavery in Virginia and provides in his will for the freeing of his slaves on his death.

1799

New York introduces the gradual abolition of slavery; all children born to a slave mother are free but males would be required to work for the owner until the age of 28 and females to 25; there are 12,000 slaves in the state.

1800

The government imposes penalties on any American citizen serving on ships undertaking slave trading between foreign countries. Future president Thomas Jefferson (1743–1826) declares that the Constitution gives the federal legislature no power to consider 'the question respecting the condition of property of slaves in any of the states, and that any attempt of that sort would be unconstitutional and a usurpation of rights Congress do not possess'.

1804

New Jersey introduces the gradual abolition of slavery.

1807

Congress passes legislation prohibiting the import of African slaves into the United States.

1808

The law forbidding the import of slaves into the United States comes into force on 1 January; penalties range from a $800 fine for knowingly purchasing an illegally imported slave to $20,000 for fitting out a slave vessel (both with our without imprisonment). The law is widely evaded both by Southern planters and Northern business interests and is weakly enforced by the responsible departments. An estimated 250,000 slaves are illegally imported into the United States from 1808 to 1860.

1815

Benjamin Lundy (1789–1839) – an abolitionist who advocates the emigration of freed slaves – establishes the Union Humane Society in Ohio.

1816

The American Colonisation Society is established to encourage and assist in the emigration of free blacks to West Africa; the society represents an uneasy alliance between pro- and anti-slavery elements.

1817 New York passes legislation ending slavery in ten years.

1819 Elhu Embree publishes a weekly newspaper in Tennessee, the first devoted to the abolition of slavery; by 1820 the *Manumission Intelligencer* will have, at 2,000, a larger circulation than the better known *Liberator*. Former president James Madison suggests the gradual emancipation of slaves at an estimated cost in compensation to owners of $600 million dollars, with an allocation of 200 million acres of land for settlement; no action is taken on the proposal.

1820
Mar. Under the Missouri Compromise, slavery is banned north and west of the 36°60' parallel in the Louisiana territory, and Missouri is allowed entry to the Union as a slave state and Maine as a free state.

May The Slave Trade Act makes participation by American citizens in the slave trade piracy, punishable by death. Only one person is executed, in 1862.

1821 Benjamin Lundy begins publishing the *Genius of Universal Emancipation*; William Lloyd Garrison becomes associate editor in 1829 but the paper ceases publication in 1835.

1822 Secretary of State John Quincy Adams refuses to accept the right of British naval vessels to search American ships suspected of engaging in slave trading, declaring that doing so 'would be making slaves of ourselves'.

1824 The United States negotiates a treaty to jointly suppress the slave trade but Britain withdraws after the Senate inserts conditions undermining the agreement's effectiveness.

1826 Pennsylvania passes legislation nullifying the 1793 Fugitive Slave Act and refuses to allow the return of fleeing slaves who seek refuge in the state; the law is declared unconstitutional by the Supreme Court in 1842.

1827
Mar. *Freedom's Journal*, the first black American newspaper, is established in New York City by John Russwurm and Samuel Cornish, publishing abolitionist propaganda during its two year existence.

Apr. Slavery is finally abolished in New York.

1829 David Walker's anti-slavery pamphlet *An Appeal to the Coloured Citizens of the World*, is published and its discovery in Southern states spreads alarm among slave owners with its call for a mass rising of slaves and violent attacks on their owners.

1830 Mexico forbids any further importation of slaves into the Texas Territory, an area of increasing American immigration. John Quincy Adams takes his seat in the Senate and presents 15 petitions from Pennsylvania calling for the abolition of slavery.

1831
Jan. William Lloyd Garrison publishes the first edition of the *Liberator*, an anti-slavery newspaper, with the support of many prominent black Americans, including James Forten, and 'declares war on slavery and colonisation'. Benjamin Lundy begins publishing the anti-slavery *The Genius of Universal Emancipation* in Washington.

Aug. Fears provoked by Nat Turner's slave rebellion in Virginia in which 55 whites are killed seriously weakens the abolitionist movement in the Southern states.

1832 The New England Anti-Slavery Society is established by William Lloyd Garrison and 11 white abolitionists. Legislation to abolish slavery in Virginia introduced by Thomas Jefferson's grandson is defeated by seven votes.

1833 The American Anti-Slavery Society, a loose confederation of abolitionists, is established in Philadelphia under the presidency of Arthur Tappen to conduct agitation; among others prominent in the Society are William Lloyd Garrison, Lewis Tappan, Wendell Philips and Theodore Dwight Weld. There are six members of the free black community on the board of managers; the majority of the estimated 160,000 supporters are middle class and generally committed to Christian denominations. The Society launches an intensive propaganda campaign, flooding the South with anti-slavery literature and Congress with petitions demanding abolition in the District of Columbia; Congress imposes the 'gag rule' to prevent consideration of petitions. A Female Anti-Slavery Society is established in Philadelphia by Lucretia Mott and others. Kentucky bans any further importation of slaves (this is repealed in 1850).

1835 The Kentucky Anti-Slavery Society is formed with James Gillespie (who had freed his own slaves the previous year) prominent among founding members. Abolitionist meetings are violently broken up in New York and Massachusetts in November; in Boston, William Lloyd Garrison is led through the streets by a rope until rescued by police. Gerrit Smith declares a war has broken out between North and South that cannot end until slavery is abolished. Abolitionists launch a postal campaign to flood the Southern states with anti-slavery pamphlets. Demonstrators burn abolitionist literature in Charleston.

1837 Anti-slavery women hold their first convention in New York but only allow black women to participate after a protracted discussion; there is growing black criticism that the majority of white abolitionists prefer all-white organisations. The United States rejects a British proposal for an international patrol to intercept slave traders. President Martin Van Buren declares in his inaugural address in March that he is the 'inflexible and uncompromising opponent of every attempt on the part of Congress to abolish slavery in the District of Columbia … (and) in the States where it exists'. Elijah Lovejoy, an abolitionist organiser in Illinois, is murdered in November by a mob that destroys the press he uses to print anti-slavery literature.

1838 An estimated 1,350 anti-slavery societies are in existence in the United States, with almost 250,000 members. The Underground Railroad to support escaping slaves to Northern states organised by abolitionists becomes increasingly active. There are anti-abolitionist riots in Philadelphia as new immigrants fear freed slaves will pose competition for jobs.

1839 The American Anti-Slavery Society splits over tactical differences; moderates led by Arthur and Lewis Tappan, Theodore Weld and James Birney leave to form the American and Foreign Anti-Slavery Society, with a programme of moral pressure and political action (through the newly formed Liberty Party). William Lloyd Garrison – whose followers (including Lucretia Mott and Wendell Phillips) denounce the United States Constitution as pro-slavery, favour increased agitation and are more sympathetic to the role of women in organisation – remains leader of the Anti-Slavery Society. With the national leadership divided, abolitionist activity has an increasingly local and state focus. Theodore Weld publishes *American Slavery As It Is*, a condemnation of slavery based on stories published in the Southern press.

1840 The American Anti-Slavery Society, the American and Foreign Anti-Slavery Society, the Pennsylvania Anti-Slavery Society and the New England Anti-Slavery Society send representatives to the first World Convention on Slavery held in London. William Lloyd Garrison walks out when American women representatives are refused admission. The abolitionist James Birney stands as presidential candidate for the Liberty Party, the first party to concentrate on abolitionism.

1842
Mar. The Supreme Court rules in *Prigg* v *Pennsylvania* that the Pennsylvania state law forbidding the return of fugitive slaves to their owners is unconstitutional.

Aug. The United States signs the Webster–Ashburton Treaty with Britain, part of which sets out agreement on co-operation between naval patrols off West Africa to suppress the slave trade.

1843 At a black convention in Buffalo, New York, black abolitionist Henry Highland Garnet advocates a general strike and rebellion to improve black conditions but is condemned by Frederick Douglass and other prominent anti-slavery campaigners.

1844 Southern Methodists withdraw from association with the Methodist Church in the North in protest against abolitionist activities and Georgia Bishop James O. Andrews refuses an instruction to free his slaves; the Baptists similarly divide in 1845. The abolitionist James Birney wins 62,000 votes when he stands for a second time as the Liberty Party's presidential candidate.

1845   An anti-slavery weekly, the *True American*, is established in Kentucky by the abolitionist Cassius Marcellus Clay.

1846   War begins with Mexico. Shortly after the outbreak, Democratic Representative David Wilmot of Pennsylvania introduces the 'Wilmot Proviso' to prohibit slavery in any territories that may be acquired in a United States victory. His proposal is passed in the House of Representatives but falls in the Senate and the bitterness of the argument intensifies antagonism between the Northern and Southern states.

1847
June   Dred Scott case begins as Scott claims in the St Louis Circuit Court that his temporary residence in the free area of the Louisiana territory and in the non-slave state of Illinois effectively releases him from slavery.

Dec.   Black abolitionist Frederick Douglass – arguing the need for more extensive black participation in the campaign against slavery – breaks his connection with Garrison's *Liberator* and begins publication of the *North Star* in association with Martin Delany; Douglass says his goals are to 'abolish slavery in all its forms and aspects, advocate universal emancipation, exalt the standard of public morality, and promote the moral and intellectual improvement of the colored people, and hasten the day of freedom to the three millions of our enslaved countrymen'.

1848   The war with Mexico ends in November with the Treaty of Guadeloupe Hidalgo under which California and New Mexico are ceded to the United States. The next two years are dominated by argument between abolitionists and supporters of slavery over the status of the new territories until the Compromise of 1850. The Free Soil Party is founded on a platform of denying the admission of slave states to the Union; the party's candidate, Martin Van Buren, wins 291,000 votes in the presidential elections. Slavery is abolished in Illinois.

1849   Harriet Tubman (c1821–1913), who will become the leading black woman abolitionist in the United States and a leading figure in the Underground Railroad, escapes from slavery in Maryland.

1850   The dispute over the status of territories captured from Mexico in the 1845–46 war is settled temporarily in September by the Compromise of 1850 under which California is to enter the Union as a free state, slavery is to be allowed in New Mexico and Utah, the slave trade is to be outlawed in Washington DC and a harsher fugitive slave law is to be enacted. Many Northern states refuse to enforce the law on fugitive slaves and where it is enforced demonstrators attempt to free those taken into custody.

1852   Harriet Beecher Stowe's *Uncle Tom's Cabin* is published in Boston and sells a million copies within a year of publication; the book's portrayal of slavery angers Southern slave owners and encourages abolitionist sympathy in the Northern states. The Republican Party is established by Whigs, disaffected Democrats opposed to any extension of slavery and members of the Free Soil Party.

1854   The Kansas-Nebraska Act repeals the 1820 Missouri Compromise, removing the restrictions on slavery in the Louisiana territory and leaving the decision on whether to enter the Union as slave states to Kansas and Nebraska themselves. Abraham Lincoln declares that future government policy should be on the basis of a restriction of slavery leading towards its abolition. Two thousand troops are deployed in Boston to force the return of a fugitive slave in the face of abolitionist demonstrations.

1855   Opponents and supporters of slavery clash in Kansas and each group drafts a state constitution.

1856   The sacking of the anti-slavery town of Lawrence, Kansas, by a pro-slavery force in May provokes retaliation by the white abolitionist John Brown (1800–59) who leads an attack at Pottawatomie Creek in which five slavery supporters are killed.

1857   The Supreme Court rules in *Dred Scott* v *Sandford* that black people
Mar.   are not citizens of the United States and that Congress has no authority to prohibit slavery in any Federal territory, a defeat for abolitionist supporters that alarms the Northern states, heartens the South and proves to be a milestone on the road to the Civil War that erupts in 1861. South Carolina governor James H. Adams calls for the repeal of the 1807 legislation banning the slave trade.

Dec.   The Leocompton Constitution allowing slavery is adopted in a Kansas referendum which is boycotted by opponents of slavery. President James Buchanan recommends the admission of Kansas to the Union as a slave state but Kansas remains a Territory following further confused referendums.

1858   Opening his unsuccessful Senate campaign against the Democrat Stephen Douglas, the future United States president Abraham Lincoln (1809–65) calls slavery 'an evil' and declares, 'A house divided against itself cannot stand. I believe this government cannot endure permanently half slave and half free.' Douglas says individual states must decide on slavery and wins the contest.

1859   White anti-slavery activist John Brown leads five blacks and a
Oct.   dozen whites in an attack on the army arsenal at Harper's Ferry, Virginia, in what he intends to be a preliminary to a general slave uprising but he fails to gain the support of any of the leading abolitionists.

Dec.   Brown and two black supporters are executed for their part in the Harper's Ferry attack. Georgia outlaws the freeing of slaves in wills.

1860
Nov.
The presidential election concentrates on the slavery issue. Abraham Lincoln is elected United States President as an anti-slavery moderate who opposes the expansion of slavery in the Federal territories.

Dec.
South Carolina secedes from the Union, beginning a wave of secessions by states which support slavery, leading to the establishment of the Confederacy and the outbreak of civil war in April 1861. At the last census, taken in 1860, there are 3,950,546 slaves in the United States and almost a third of all Southern families own slaves.

2.6.1 Numbers of slaves in the United States from 1790 to the eve of the 1861–65 civil war

1790	694,207
1800	887,612
1810	1,130,781
1820	1,529,012
1830	1,987,428
1840	2,482,546
1850	3,200,000
1860	3,950,546

2.7 Chronology of emancipation and the American Civil War, 1860–65

1860 Nov.	Lincoln elected President with 180 out of a possible 303 electoral college votes.
Dec.	South Carolina (where almost half the families own slaves) secedes from the Union; as the break-up of the Union approaches, there are 3,950,546 slaves in the United States.
1861 Jan.	Alabama, Florida, Georgia, Louisiana (in each of which almost a third of families own slaves) and Mississippi (where almost half the families own slaves) secede from the Union.
Feb.	The Confederate States of America is established by South Carolina, Alabama, Florida, Georgia, Louisiana and Mississippi at a convention in Montgomery, Alabama. Jefferson Davis is elected provisional President. Texas secedes from the Union.
Mar.	The United States Congress adopts a constitutional amendment which attempts to prevent any moves against slavery by forbidding amendments which 'abolish or interfere... with the domestic institutions' of the states 'including that of persons held to labor or service by the laws of the said State'; the amendment is never ratified. Lincoln is inaugurated as President of the United States. The Constitution adopted by the Confederate States bans the import of slaves but adds that, 'No bill of attainder, *ex post facto* law, or law denying or impairing the right of property in negro slaves shall be passed.'
Apr.	Confederate forces attack the Federal garrison at Fort Sumter, South Carolina; Lincoln declares a 'state of insurrection'; Virginia secedes from the Union.
May	Arkansas, Tennessee and North Carolina secede from the Union. Fugitive slaves at Fort Monroe, Virginia, are declared 'contraband of war' by the Union forces and put to work.
Aug.	Confiscation Act passed by United States Congress authorises the seizure of any property belonging to individuals aiding or abetting the Confederate rebellion, including slaves, who will be granted their freedom; this section of the legislation is not vigorously enforced. Union General John C. Fremont (Republican presidential candidate in 1856) places Missouri under martial law and issues a proclamation declaring all slaves 'forever free'.
Sept.	President Lincoln dismisses Fremont for exceeding his authority and revokes the proclamation. Union Navy accepts the enlistment of black Americans.

Dec.   President Lincoln orders Secretary of War, Simon Cameron, to remove sections from his annual report advocating the emancipation of fugitive slaves and their recruitment as soldiers and labourers; Cameron complies but resigns shortly after.

1862
Mar.   United States Congress adopts an order forbidding the return of fugitive slaves to their owners by the Union forces.

Apr.   Union commander in the South Carolina Sea Islands, General David Hunter, seeks permission from the War Department to recruit and arm black soldiers in the area; he begins recruiting a black regiment but is forced to disband it when the War Department refuses funds for pay and equipment. Acting on a proposal from President Lincoln, the United States Congress promises financial assistance to states beginning gradual emancipation of slaves and compensation for their owners 'for the inconveniences, public and private, produced by such a change of system'. District of Columbia Emancipation Act abolishes slavery in the area of the Federal capital, with compensation to owners of up to $300 for each slave; funds (up to $100 for each person) are made available for the migration of freed slaves to Haiti, Latin America and West Africa. In the next nine months over 3,000 slaves are freed at a cost of $1 million.

May   General Hunter, acting under martial law, declares all slaves in Florida, Georgia and South Carolina 'forever free'. President Lincoln attacks Hunter's order for causing 'some excitement, and misunderstanding', and declares it void, saying no commander has been authorised 'to make proclamations declaring the slaves of any State free' but repeats his request to the border states of Delaware, Kentucky, Maryland and Missouri to adopt 'a gradual abolishment of slavery', with compensation for owners.

June   President Lincoln signs a bill abolishing slavery in the United States territories, areas which have not yet become states.

July   Lincoln proclaims the conclusion of a treaty between the United States and Britain to suppress the slave trade more vigorously. President Lincoln urges Congress members from the border states of Delaware, Kentucky, Maryland and Missouri to support gradual emancipation with compensation but threatens that if they fail to agree slavery will be ended by 'the mere incidents of war'; his appeal is rejected by the majority of Congress two days later. A second Confiscation Act provides for greater sanctions on supporters of the Confederate rebellion, including 'the liberation of all his slaves, if any he have', forbids Union armed forces personnel from surrendering fugitive slaves to their owners and authorises the government to employ 'as many persons of African descent as he may deem necessary and proper for the suppression of this rebellion' under a new Militia Act, though at lower rates of pay than whites. (In the course of the war, 186,000 black soldiers serve with the Union forces, of whom 38,000 die, mainly as a result of inadequate medical treatment.) President Lincoln informs his cabinet of his determination to proclaim the emancipation of slaves in the Confederacy, but that he will do this only after Union forces gain a significant military success.

Aug.   President Lincoln is condemned by a black delegation when he urges them to encourage the emigration of freed slaves. Union General Benjamin F. Butler absorbs a number of free black units into his forces in New Orleans and commences recruitment of both free blacks and former slaves. Union War Department agrees to provide funds for black forces raised in South Carolina.

Sept.   Union forces' successful stand against a Confederate attack on Maryland is used by President Lincoln as the occasion to issue a preliminary Emancipation Proclamation. Slaves in all states or parts of states still in rebellion against the Union on 1 January 1863 will be declared free; financial assistance will be provided for the gradual emancipation of slaves in non-rebel states; freed slaves will be encouraged to move from the United States. The effect is to make slavery the central issue in the war and to prevent any possibility of the governments of Britain and France, where popular sympathies are abolitionist, supporting the Confederacy.

Dec.   Confederate President Davis responds to Lincoln's proclamation by describing it as 'the most execrable measure of guilty man' and ordering his forces to deny captured black Union soldiers and their officers the rights of prisoners of war and treat them as criminals.

1863 President Lincoln issues an Emancipation Proclamation declaring all
Jan.   slaves free in all states and territories in rebellion against the Union (except Tennessee, southern Louisiana and parts of Virginia) and announces the opening of enlistment in Union armed forces to black Americans. Women's Loyal League formed in the North by Susan Anthony to collect a million signatures on a petition in favour of amending the Constitution to outlaw slavery. By August 1864 the League has collected 40,000 signatures.

Mar.   Union Secretary of War Edwin Stanton appoints a Freedmen's Inquiry Commission to monitor the conditions of freed slaves and to make recommendations on improvements in welfare and employment.

May   The Confederate Congress passes a resolution declaring black Union soldiers and their officers criminals, implying they can be enslaved or executed. The Union War Department establishes a Bureau of Colored Troops to co-ordinate recruitment in the Northern states and in parts of the Confederacy under Union occupation. Black troops begin to play an increasingly significant part in the Union war effort.

July   Union forces have a run of military successes, including repelling a

Confederate invasion of Pennsylvania at Gettysburg and the seizure of Vicksburg. Blacks are attacked in riots in New York City against draft laws because they are ineligible for conscription into the armed forces. A thousand people, mainly black, die or are injured in the riots and there is $2 million damage. President Lincoln demands equal treatment of captured black and white Union soldiers by the Confederacy and threatens sanctions if black soldiers are forced into slavery.

Aug. Abolitionist Frederick Douglass meets President Lincoln to demand full equality for black soldiers in the Union forces.

Dec. President Lincoln issues an Amnesty and Reconstruction Proclamation promising the restoration of property, except slaves, to people living in the Confederate states willing to swear allegiance to the Union and to accept emancipation.

1864
Mar. A new constitution for Arkansas abolishing slavery is ratified by voters in the state.

Apr. The Senate approves the proposed Thirteenth Amendment to the Constitution abolishing slavery throughout the United States. Black Union soldiers captured at Fort Pillow, Tennessee, are massacred by Confederate forces under General Nathan B. Forrest, the future founder of the Ku Klux Klan.

June The House of Representatives rejects the proposed Thirteenth Amendment to the Constitution abolishing slavery. Congress provides for equal pay for black and white soldiers after a black regiment refuses to accept any pay as a protest against discrimination.

Sept. A new constitution for Louisiana abolishing slavery is ratified by voters in the state.

Nov. Slavery is abolished in Maryland following ratification of a new state constitution. Lincoln is re-elected President.

1865
Jan. A new constitution for Missouri abolishing slavery is ratified by voters in the state. General William Sherman and War Secretary Edwin Stanton met 20 black leaders in Savannah, Georgia, for discussions on the conditions of freed slaves. General Sherman issues Special Field Order No 15 reserving coastal areas of Florida, Georgia and South Carolina for black settlement, with each family entitled to a 40 acre plot, the payment of bounties for black soldiers, and the appointment of an Inspector of Settlements and Plantations. The House of Representatives approves the Thirteenth Amendment to the Constitution abolishing slavery and passes it to the separate states for ratification.

Feb. A petition in support of the amendment to the Constitution outlawing slavery is presented to the Senate by two black Americans. Slavery is abolished in Tennessee following ratification of a new state constitution.

Mar.   Congress establishes the Bureau of Refugees, Freedmen, and Abandoned Lands (Freedmen's Bureau) to encourage black recruitment and orders the emancipation of the wives and children of black Union soldiers. As the Confederacy faces certain defeat, recruitment of slaves to the armed forces begins, provided their owners agree. An estimated 65,000 free and slave Southern blacks were already serving unofficially in the Confederate forces, 13,000 of them in combat units.

Apr.   The civil war ends with the surrender of Confederate commander General Robert E. Lee at Appomattox Court House, Virginia. President Lincoln is assassinated and is succeeded by Andrew Johnson.

Dec.   The Thirteenth Amendment to the Constitution is ratified and slavery is abolished in the United States. The Amendment declares, 'Neither slavery nor involuntary servitude, except as a punishment for crime whereof the party shall have been duly convicted, shall exist within the United States, or any place subject to their jurisdiction.' In the last census, taken in 1860, there were 3,950,546 slaves in the United States.

2.8 Chronology of the involvement of Britain and the United States in the international campaign against the slave trade and slavery, 1807–89

1807   Britain ends its participation in the slave trade.

1808   The United States ends its participation in the slave trade. Following the designation of Sierra Leone as a Crown Colony, Britain deploys a naval squadron off West Africa to suppress the slave trade; recaptured slaves are released in the colony.

1810   Britain signs a treaty of co-operation with Portugal to achieve a gradual abolition of the slave trade across the South Atlantic.

1815   Britain places pressure on France, the Netherlands, Portugal and Spain at the Congress of Vienna to end their participation in the slave trade. Portugal agrees to end the slave trade to Brazil in return for a payment from Britain of £750,000 but the agreement is largely ineffective. The King of Spain's representative privately condemns foreign involvement in the issue of slavery. With the defeat of Napoleonic France, Britain increases activity to enforce abolition of the Atlantic slave trade through treaties with European and African states and through naval pressure.

1817   Britain signs a treaty with Spain under which Spain agrees to end its participation in the slave trade in return for a payment from Britain of £400,000; Spain is to end slave trading north of the equator immediately and south of the equator in 1820, and British naval vessels are authorised to stop and search Spanish ships. Britain negotiates a second treaty with Portugal for a partial ban on the slave trade but the agreement proves as ineffective as that of 1815.

1819   Britain intensifies naval patrols off the West African coast to combat illegal slave trading.

1820   Under British pressure, the United States agrees on joint naval patrols off the West African coast to combat the slave trade but the United States breaks co-operation and withdraws its vessels in 1823. The 1817 Anglo-Spanish treaty to end the transportation of slaves into Cuba comes into force. British naval vessels are authorised to search ships suspected of participating in the slave trade and cases are investigated by mixed Anglo-Spanish commissions.

1822   Brazil declares its independence from Portugal. The country's political dependence on Britain increases the latter's hopes of influencing Brazil's policy on slavery.

1824 Britain negotiates a treaty with the United States on joint suppression of the slave trade but refuses to sign when Senate amendments weaken the agreement's effectiveness.

1825 British colonial authorities in Sierra Leone initiate a campaign against slave traders operating in the region and force local chiefs to sign treaties to cede further territory to Britain. The Royal Navy intensifies anti-slave trading patrols off West Africa; over the course of the next 40 years they arrested 1,287 ships and free 130,000 slaves; however, despite this activity, an estimated 1.8 million slaves are transported to the Americas.

1826 Brazil agrees in a treaty with Britain to end the slave trade three years after the treaty's ratification. British officials complain that Spain is failing to implement its declaration that slaves illegally imported into its Caribbean territories after 1820 are to be set free but the British government fails to press the policy.

1830 The slave trade is outlawed in Brazil but nevertheless continues to expand. British diplomatic representatives condemn breaches of the law and the deployment of British warships off the Brazilian coast to intercept slave trades strains relations between the two governments. British authorities in the Bahamas free slaves being transported on an American ship from Virginia to New Orleans when the vessel is wrecked. Representatives of the British Caribbean planters in London call on the government to 'adopt more decisive measures than any that have hitherto been employed to stop the foreign slave trade' because it works against their economic interests.

1831 Britain and France agree on the right to mutual searching of suspected slave trading vessels.

1832 The Jamaica House of Assembly notes of the slave trade that the 'colonies were easily reconciled to the abolition of a barbarous commerce, which the advanced civilisation of the age no longer permitted to exist' and calls on the government to act more firmly against the continuation of the slave trade by other countries.

1833 Britain and France renew their agreement on the searching of ships suspected of being used by slave traders.

1835 Britain and Spain renew their joint commitment to end the slave trade in a new treaty. British naval vessels are authorised to take Spanish vessels suspected of engaging in the trade into custody and to present them to Courts of Mixed Commissions in Havana and Sierra Leone. Britain instructs its diplomatic representatives in Argentina, Chile, Colombia, Mexico, Peru, Uruguay and Venezuela to negotiate agreements against the slave trade based on the 1826 treaty with Brazil categorising the trade as piracy.

1836 A Court of Mixed Commissions opens in Sierra Leone under the terms of the 1835 treaty between Britain and Spain. Spain appoints a consul to the British colony of Jamaica to monitor abolitionist activity. He reports largely fictitious plans by anti-slavery activists to foment slave rebellions in Cuba. Britain appoints a Superintendent of Liberated Africans in Havana to assist Africans rescued from illegal slave traders.

1837 Britain proposes an international anti-slaving patrol to France and the United States but the latter declines to participate.

1839 British abolitionist Thomas Fowell Buxton publishes *The African Slave Trade and Its Remedy* in which he calls on the British government to negotiate treaties against slavery with African rulers. British and Foreign Anti-Slavery Society formed by Birmingham Quaker Joseph Sturge, with Thomas Clarkson as first president. The Society mounts a campaign to persuade other powers to follow Britain's lead in abolishing slavery and demands a ban on the import of slave-produced sugar. British naval vessels arrest two United States ships suspected of slave trading and escort them to New York to be tried for piracy. Following the arrest by Britain of further ships, United States officials arrest the owners and seize several vessels under construction. Britain and Venezuela sign a treaty to end the slave trade. Britain passes legislation (the 'Palmerston Act') authorising its naval vessels to seize Portuguese ships transporting slaves or equipped to do so.

1840 The first World Convention on Slavery is held in London, organised by the British and Foreign Anti-Slavery Society. The convention is attended by representatives of the French anti-slavery organisation, *Société des Amis des Noirs*, the American Anti-Slavery Society, the American and Foreign Anti-Slavery Society, the Pennsylvania Anti-Slavery Society and the New England Anti-Slavery Society. British naval squadron mounts land attacks on a slave trade centre off the Gallinas River in West Africa, freeing over 800 slaves and transporting them to Sierra Leone, and follows this with further raids inland.

1841 The British government, accepting Thomas Fowell Buxton's call for anti-slavery activity in Africa, sends an expedition to the Niger River Delta, establishing a missionary settlement and beginning negotiations. The attempt fails as the group suffers deaths through illness. The British Commissioners at the Court of Mixed Commission in Sierra Leone report to the Foreign Office that the slave trade is increasing, with large numbers being exported in particular to Cuba and Brazil. Britain and Chile sign a treaty to end the slave trade. The United States consul in Havana is dismissed for making no effort to prevent the involvement of American vessels in the slave trade in Cuba.

1842   Britain and the United States and Britain sign the Webster–Ashburton Treaty including an agreement on co-operation between naval patrols off West Africa to suppress the slave trade. Both countries are to supply ships carrying a total of 80 guns but Britain will have no authority to search American shipping. American vessels begin patrolling the following year. Mexico and Uruguay sign treaties with Britain to end the slave trade.

1844   A British representative on the Court of Mixed Commission, Sierra Leone, reports to the Foreign Office that 'the slave trade is increasing, and it continues more systematically than it has ever been before'.

1845   Britain passes legislation (the 'Aberdeen Act') authorising its naval vessels to seize Brazilian ships transporting slaves or equipped to do so. Admiralty courts are empowered to determine violations of the treaty negotiated in 1826.

1847   Britain and Ecuador sign a treaty to end the slave trade.

1849   British naval force attacks and destroys slave trade centres at Lomboko on the Gallinas River in West Africa.

1850   The Brazilian general assembly (under pressure from Britain) passes the Quierós Law outlawing the transportation of slaves from Africa. As the illegal trade continues, Britain begins sending naval vessels into Brazilian territorial waters in pursuit of suspected traders. Peru signs a commercial treaty with Britain including a clause agreeing to end the slave trade.

1851   British prime minister Lord Palmerston urges Spain to free the slaves in its Caribbean colonies on the grounds that this would act as a disincentive to the United States to annex Cuba. Britain and Colombia sign a treaty to end the slave trade.

1852   Britain and the Boers sign the Sand River Treaty which includes a clause forbidding slavery in South Africa.

1862   Britain and the United States (engaged in a civil war with the breakaway Confederate states) agree a treaty on the suppression of the slave trade.

1867   Under British pressure, Spain agrees a treaty to end its participation in the slave trade.

1873   Britain exerts pressure on Zanzibar to close public slave markets.

1884   Britain, the United States, Germany, France and the other leading European governments meet at the Congress of Berlin and agree on the division of Africa between the European powers and on the need to work actively to suppress the slave trade and slavery as a moral justification for seizing colonies.

1889   Berlin Act signatories meet to agree on further action against African slavery and the slave trade, largely to satisfy domestic demands, but the institution continues into the 20th century.

CIVIL RIGHTS

3.1 Chronology of black civil rights in the Caribbean and South America, 1766–2000

1766   Free blacks in French possessions are denied political and social equality with whites because, in the words of the ordinance, 'slavery has imprinted an ineffaceable brand on their posterity; and consequently, the descendants of slaves can never enter the class of whites'.

1767   Free blacks in the British Caribbean colony of St Vincent are barred from owning over eight acres of land and are prevented from becoming freeholders, which would allow the vote; all free blacks are ordered to live with a white to ensure that 'their lives and conversations may be known and observed'.

1771   Free blacks in the French Caribbean colonies are barred from the professions of law and medicine and from working in public service. Free blacks in the British Caribbean colony of Jamaica are required to carry a certificate proving their freedom and to wear a blue cross on their shoulders.

1778   The French government renews a ban on inter-racial marriage in its possessions.

1796   Free blacks in the Spanish colonies are granted the status of subjects of the Crown and become entitled to all rights and obligations; the law is strengthened in 1820 and 1824.

1802   The 4th Battalion of the British West India Regiment (which is largely made up of purchased Africans) mutinies over conditions in Dominica.

1806   The first black Cuban self-help organisation is established; members co-operate to raise the funds to purchase freedom for slaves.

1818   Freed slaves in Brazil (*emancipados*) are guaranteed their rights by the Crown.

1823   Free blacks are granted full rights as citizens in the British Caribbean colony of Grenada.

1830   Free blacks are granted full rights as citizens in the British Caribbean colonies of Barbados and Jamaica and in the French Antilles.

1831   Free blacks are granted full rights as citizens in the British Central

American colony of Belize (later British Honduras and then, once more, Belize).

1837 The Spanish governor of Cuba orders the imprisonment of all black sailors while their ships are docked in Havana; black British soldiers who arrive in Cuba to remove freed slaves are not allowed to land; Britain refuses to withdraw the sailors and the colony's governor relents after a year. The 1st battalion of the British West India Regiment mutinies in the British Caribbean colony of Trinidad in protest against conditions.

1838 The British Caribbean colonies end the system of apprenticeship which attempted to protect slave owners against the effects of emancipation but introduce vagrancy laws to preserve the plantation system.

1848 Universal adult suffrage is introduced in the French Caribbean colonies with the abolition of slavery but is removed four years later under the dictatorship of Napoleon III.

1849 Racial segregation in public places is formally introduced in the Spanish Caribbean colony of Cuba.

1853 The newly appointed governor of Jamaica institutes changes in the constitution allowing greater numbers of the black population on to the island's executive committee.

1865 There is a rebellion at Morant Bay in the British Caribbean colony of Jamaica over the imposition of new taxes and unpopularity of the magistracy; protestors kill over 20 militia members and magistrates, and burn and loot plantation houses. Troops deployed by the governor kill 580 people and burn a thousand black homes; the alleged leader of the rebellion, George Gordon, a black member of the island's Assembly, is publicly hanged following a court martial.

1864 The Brazilian government introduces legislation guaranteeing the rights of free Africans (*emancipados*).

1868 A ten year multi-racial guerrilla war of independence begins in the Spanish Caribbean colony of Cuba in which black Cubans play a significant part as members of the rebel forces; the rebels include a black general as one of their leaders.

1870 Universal suffrage and representation in the National Assembly in Paris is restored to the French Caribbean colonies.

1871 The 'Rio Branco Law' in Brazil acknowledges the right of slaves to own personal possessions.

1876 There are riots in the British Caribbean colony of Barbados over continuing dissatisfaction with conditions after the end of slavery, including chronic unemployment; eight people are killed by police and troops deployed by the island's governor.

1890 The Central Directory of Societies of Colour is established in Cuba;

members of the organisation will suffer severe repression in the early 20th century.

1891 The political influence of the landowners in British Guiana is weakened by the abolition of the College of Electors and a relaxation in the qualifications for suffrage.

1893 The Spanish colonial authorities in Cuba declare the equal civil status of black and white citizens.

1894 There is rioting by workers in British Honduras (later Belize) over pay and conditions; the police mutiny.

1895 A second war of independence begins in the Spanish Caribbean colony of Cuba, with black Cubans (*Los Mambises*) forming the core of the liberation forces.

1896 There are riots in the British Caribbean colony of St Christopher and Nevis during a strike for higher wages.

1897 The Trinidad Workingmen's Association is established, initially among the skilled, to protect the interests of black workers in the British Caribbean colony.

1898 Cuba gains independence from Spain as a result of the United States–Spanish war but remains under American occupation until 1902; Cuba's constitution includes the 'Platt Amendment' guaranteeing the United States a naval base and the right to intervene in Cuban affairs 'for the protection of life, property and individual liberty'.

1902 United States occupation forces leave Cuba; a Cuban government headed by Tomas Estrada Palima begins the repression of attempts by the black population to preserve an African cultural heritage.

1903 Riots in the British Caribbean colony of Trinidad over a government attempt to meter the water supply are put down by sailors after an attack on the governor's residence.

1905 The colonial authorities respond to rioting over dissatisfaction with living standards in British Guiana (the 'Rainveldt Riots') by granting concessions which increase the size of the electorate.

1908 The first independent black political party in the Western hemisphere, the *Partido Independiente de Color*, is founded in Cuba by Evaristo Estenoz, Gregorio Surín, and José Miguel Gómez, who is elected president. There is serious rioting in the British Caribbean colony of St Lucia.

1909 The black integrationist Martin Morúa Delgado is elected speaker of the Cuban Senate; he later helps make the *Partido Independiente de Color* illegal.

1910 The *Partido Independiente de Color* is outlawed in Cuba under a law proposed by the black Cuban Martin Morúa Delgado on the grounds that it is based solely on racial origins; he argues that the party is unconstitutional since black Cubans have full citizenship rights and there is no racial discrimination. There is growing repression of supporters of the party and other black movements and black members of the security forces are dismissed. Morúa dies shortly after his appointment as Minister of Agriculture and is given a state funeral to underline the government's integrationist policy.

1912 The purge of *Partido Independiente de Color* supporters intensifies in Cuba during the 'Little Black War' in which 6,000 party members and leaders are killed throughout the country; black culture and religion is suppressed. A third of Cuba's population is classified as black or of mixed race; white immigration is encouraged to reduce this proportion. Riots take place in Kingston, capital of the British Caribbean colony of Jamaica.

1915 United States troops occupy Haiti, forcing it to become a protectorate.

1917 United States forces Haiti to allow whites to own property for the first time since 1805. United States legislation guarantees universal male suffrage in Puerto Rico (annexed from Spain in 1898). Strikes by oil workers in the British Caribbean colony of Trinidad are suppressed by troops. The practice of indentured labour is outlawed in British Guiana; the British Guiana Labour Union is formed (and is legally recognised in 1921).

1918 British West Indies Regiment troops in Taranto, Italy, refuse to carry out duties in protest against the racism of their officers, send a petition of complaint to the Colonial Secretary and form an underground Caribbean League with political objectives. One soldier is executed, another sentenced to life imprisonment and the regiment is disbanded. Many veterans become active in anti-colonial agitation in the British Caribbean colonies when they are demobilised.

1919 British sailors are attacked in Port of Spain, Trinidad, following reports of casualties among black people during race riots in South Wales. A general strike by dock, plantation and oil workers breaks out over the employers' refusal to negotiate with the Trinidad Workingmen's Association; white vigilantes are deployed when the black police force appears to sympathise; black newspapers are banned by the colonial authorities and in 1920 strikes are made illegal. There is rioting in British Honduras (later Belize) by troops returning from service in World War One.

1921 The Jamaican Political Reform Association established as one of the first organisations to campaign for political change in the British Caribbean colony.

1922 British Junior Colonial Minister Edward Wood (later Lord Halifax) issues a report recommending a limited expansion in the franchise and in representative government through the local assemblies following a three month investigation during which he largely ignores the views of civil rights activists in the Caribbean.

1925 Black Cubans become active in the newly formed Communist Party and take leading positions in both the party and trade unions. Constitutional reform in the British colony of Trinidad adds seven elected members to the island's legislative council.

1931 The Brazilian Black Front (*Frente Negra Brasileria*) is established in São Paulo as the political voice of the black community but is repressed with all other parties under the Vargas dictatorship. The Puerto Rico Unionist Party, which has a policy of independence from the United States, is prevented from contesting elections.

1933 The Cuban revolutionary government passes the *Ley de Nacionalizacion del Trabajo* which increases employment opportunities for black Cubans in the commercial and service sector.

1934 Trinidad Workingmen's Association (a trade union formed in 1897) develops into the Trinidad Labour Party. There are protest demonstrations by workers in British Honduras (later Belize). United States troops are withdrawn from Haiti and the Dominican Republic.

1935 There are riots in the British Caribbean colony of St Christopher and Nevis during a general strike over the refusal of sugar plantation and factory owners to increase wages; the strike is broken by marines. Riots break out in the British Caribbean colony of St Vincent against the imposition of customs duties which increase the price of food and clothing; the police fire on rioters, troops are landed from a British warship and the governor declares a three week state of emergency.

1936 Legislation by the United States Congress abolishes property qualifications for suffrage in the Virgin Islands (purchased by the United States from Denmark in 1917) and guarantees civil liberties. Members of the Puerto Rico Nationalist Party (which calls for independence) are imprisoned after being found guilty of a seditious conspiracy to overthrow the United States government.

1937 Oil fields owned by a South African company in the British Caribbean colony of Trinidad are occupied by workers protesting against their employer's racism; strikes spread throughout the island and 14 people are killed and 59 wounded in clashes with British troops. There are riots in the British Caribbean colony of Barbados following attempts by the authorities to deport the radical Trinidadian activist Clement Payne (1904–47); 14 people are killed and 47 wounded by the police. Twenty people are killed during a demonstration in Puerto Rico demanding independence from the United States.

1938   A strike over pay on a sugar plantation in the British Caribbean colony of Jamaica in May develops into island-wide demonstrations and protests in which 12 civilians are killed, over 100 injured and over 500 arrested; the protests end when the government offers a £500,000 land settlement to alleviate unemployment. Bustamente Industrial Trade Union is established in Jamaica by the activist Alexander Bustamente (1884–1977) and the socialist People's National Party is founded by Norman Manley (1893–1969). The British government responds to three years of disorder by appointing a Royal Commission under Lord Moyne to investigate on conditions in the Caribbean colonies and to make recommendations on reform. The Labour Congress of the West Indies and British Guiana demands the formation of a West Indies Federation, universal suffrage, the nationalisation of the sugar industry and public utilities, social security, a minimum wage and trade union immunities.

1939   The Moyne Commission issues its report but this is not made public until 1944. The report criticises the colonial administration, attacking its economic competence and its handling of education, health, housing and labour relations. Moyne recommends greater funding of economic development, encouragement of trade unions, extension of the franchise to women and non-landowners, and greater self-government.

1940   A new constitution in Cuba formally outlaws discrimination on racial grounds.

1941   Following on the recommendations of the Moyne Report, the Colonial Development and Welfare Act provides for improved political and social conditions in the British Caribbean colonies, including greater popular participation in government.

1943   Colonial authorities in British Guiana reduce the property qualification for voting and for holding political office and give elected members a majority on the legislative council. Jamaican Labour Party formed as a wing of the Bustamente Industrial Trade Union (established in 1938).

1944   A constitution for the British Caribbean colony of Jamaica provides for a House of Representatives elected by universal adult suffrage. This is extended to Trinidad (1946), Barbados (1950), the Leeward and Windward Islands (1951) and British Guiana (1953).

1945   The Caribbean Labour Congress is formed to unite trade unions and political groups active in the struggle for independence from Britain, with T. Albert Marryshow (1887–1958) as its first President.

1946   General Councils of the French Caribbean colonies of Martinique, Guadeloupe and French Guiana vote to become overseas departments of France rather than become independent.

1948   Five sugar estate workers in British Guiana (later Guyana) are killed by police during a strike; the event is commemorated annually by trade unionists and a monument is erected to the dead after independence.

1951   Brazil passes the Afonso Arinos Law making racial discrimination in access to public facilities, education and employment a criminal offence. A bill to guarantee racial equality and imposing penalties for discrimination presented by the Cuban Communist Party is rejected by the House of Representatives.

1952   Fulgencio Batista, a mulatto active in United States appointed Cuban governments since 1933, seizes power in a coup. The six islands and one South American mainland territory of the Dutch Antilles are granted autonomy. There is a national strike in British Honduras (later Belize).

1953   New constitutions for the British Caribbean colonies of Jamaica, Trinidad, Barbados and British Guiana provide for a large measure of internal self-government, with control over foreign affairs and defence issues retained by the British.

1954   Universal suffrage is granted in British Honduras (later Belize).

1958   Batista attempts to ward off a revolutionary seizure of power led by Fidel Castro (born 1927) by warning, as a mulatto, that the rebels will worsen the position of black Cubans.

1959   Segregation on the basis of race in Cuba is formally outlawed by Castro's government.

1961   A referendum in Jamaica rejects continuing membership of the British-formed Federation of the West Indies.

1962   The British Caribbean colonies of Jamaica and Trinidad and Tobago become independent. Martinique, Guadeloupe and French Guiana vote to retain status as French overseas departments.

1964   British Honduras (Belize from 1973) is granted self-government.

1966   The British Caribbean colonies of Barbados and British Guiana (now Guyana) become independent.

1967   The first black government takes office in the British Caribbean colony of the Bahamas.

1969   The Caribbean colony of Anguilla is invaded by British troops and police in 'Operation Sheepskin' following its severing of links with St Christopher.

1973   The British Caribbean colony of the Bahamas becomes independent.

1974   The British Caribbean colony of Grenada becomes independent.

1975   The Institute for Research of Black Culture (*Instituto de Pesquias das Culturas Negras*) is established in Brazil as a black consciousness movement to combat racism and discrimination; by 1995 there are only four black members of the country's 500–strong Congress.

1976 Cuban president Fidel Castro declares, 'We are a Latin African people.'

1978 The British Caribbean colony of Dominica becomes independent. The first demonstration for many years against racism is mounted in Brazil by the Unified Black Movement Against Racial Discrimination.

1979 The British Caribbean colonies of St Lucia and St Vincent and the Grenadines become independent.

1981 The British Caribbean colony of Antigua and Barbuda becomes independent. Belize (formally British Honduras) becomes independent.

1983 The British Caribbean colony of St Christopher and Nevis becomes independent.

1986 Benedita da Silva is elected the first black woman member of the Brazilian House of Representatives, one of only nine people of colour among 500 members.

1991 The Brazilian state of Rio de Janeiro establishes an Extraordinary Secretariat for Defence and Promotion of Afro-Brazilian Populations to implement anti-discrimination policies.

1997 Benedita da Silva, the first black woman elected to the Brazilian Senate, declares that race remains a major source of social inequality in Brazil, with woman particularly facing major discrimination. She complains that Brazil has no black ambassadors, generals or bank managers.

2000 Cuban vice president Raúl Castro declares his dissatisfaction with the results of a drive to promote black and mixed race Cubans to leadership positions in the government and Communist Party and also calls for the closure of hotels which break the law by refusing entry to black people; the party has been in power for 40 years.

3.2 Chronology of black civil rights in colonial North America and the United States, 1664–1865

1664 The English colony of Maryland outlaws marriage between black men and white women. Virginia introduces similar legislation in 1691, Massachusetts in 1705, North Carolina in 1715, South Carolina in 1717, Delaware in 1721 and Pennsylvania in 1725.

1670 The English colony of Virginia repeals legislation that had allowed freed slaves and indentured servants to vote.

1705 The English colony of Massachusetts passed an 'Act for the Better Preventing of a Spurious and Mist Issue' banning mixed marriages.

1724 The English colony of Virginia passes legislation forbidding free blacks to carry arms or to meet slaves.

1740 Legislation in South Carolina deprives both slaves and free blacks of the right to trial by jury and to testify under oath in court.

1755 The first school in the British North American colonies for black children is established by Quakers in Philadelphia.

1770 Crispus Attucks, an escaped slave, is killed in a clash with British soldiers in Boston and becomes one of the first casualties in what will develop into a struggle for American independence.

1775
Apr. War for American independence from Britain begins (and ends with American victory in 1783). The British writer Samuel Johnson asks, 'How is it that we hear the loudest yelps for liberty among the drivers of negroes?'

Oct. Continental Congress of Americans resisting British rule prohibits black enlistment in the army fighting for independence.

Nov. Lord Dunmore, the British governor of Virginia, offers freedom to any slave who deserts his owner to fight for Britain against the colonists.

Dec. After initial hesitation, and in the face of the response to Dunmore's offer, the American commander General George Washington and the Continental Congress agree to accept black recruits. All colonies except South Carolina and Georgia recruit slaves, guaranteeing them freedom at the end of their military service, and over 5,000 (mainly from the North) join what is effectively an integrated Continental Army.

1776 June	A clause in the draft Declaration of Independence denouncing slavery as a violation of the right to life and liberty and accusing King George III of forcing slavery on to the American colonies is deleted at the request of delegates from Georgia and South Carolina.
July	The Declaration of Independence signed by the American colonies makes no reference to slavery.
1787 Apr.	The Free African Society, the first black American mutual aid organisation is formed in Philadelphia.
Oct.	Free blacks present a petition in Boston, Massachusetts, calling for equality in education.
1790	The Naturalisation Act rules that citizenship is open to 'all free white persons' who have lived in the United States for a year.
1791 Jan.	Free blacks in Charleston, South Carolina, present a petition to the state legislature protesting against the Act of 1740 depriving free blacks and slaves of the right to testify in court under oath and to trial by jury.
1794	Delegates from abolitionist societies in Connecticut, Delaware, Maryland, New Jersey, New York and Pennsylvania meet in Philadelphia and produce an address calling on all American citizens to recognise the 'obligations of justice, humanity, and benevolence toward our African brethren, whether in bondage or free'.
1797 Jan.	The United States Congress refuses to accept the first petition presented to it by black Americans; the petition protests against a South Carolina law requiring slaves freed by their Quaker owners to be returned to slavery.
1799	The United States Navy places restrictions on the recruitment of black Americans for service on fighting vessels and in the Marines.
1800	Following 'Gabriel's rising', an attempted slave revolt, Virginia rules that free blacks can only change residence with official permission and will be assumed to be slaves unless they can prove otherwise.
1803	Following the immigration of free blacks from Guadeloupe after the French restoration of slavery, the United States bans the entry of free blacks.
1804 Jan.	The Ohio legislature introduces 'Black Laws' removing the rights of free blacks to vote and hold public office, restricts the freedom of movement of free blacks.
1806	Virginia forces freed slaves to move out of the state within a year of their manumission as concerns grow over the rise in numbers of free blacks from 3,000 in 1780 to 30,000.
1807	New Jersey removes the right of black citizens to vote.
1810	North Carolina requires free blacks to wear shoulder patches with the word 'free' written on them; the practice is soon taken up in a number of states.

1814   Illinois restricts the rights of free blacks and requires a 'good behaviour' bond of up to a thousand dollars.

1816   Richard Allen (1769–1831) is appointed bishop of the African Methodist Episcopal Church, the first all-black denomination in the United States.

1817
Jan.   Free blacks mount protests against the American Colonisation Society's policy of encouraging them to migrate to Africa.

1818   Connecticut removes the right of black citizens to vote.

1821   New York removes the property qualification for voting from whites but retains it for blacks.

1824
Nov.   Northern and western states adopt measures to deny the vote to blacks after the removal of the property qualification by the Federal government, for voting opens the way to universal male suffrage in the United States.

1827
Mar.   The first black American newspaper, *Freedom's Journal*, is published in New York by Samuel E. Cornish (c.1795–1859) and John Brown Russwurm (1799–1851).

1828   Black workers in Baltimore – denied the right to participate in white labour organisations – establish one of the first black American trade unions, the Caulkers' Association.

1830
Sept.   The first National Negro Convention meets in Philadelphia with 49 delegates and calls for an improvement in the position of black Americans, including the establishment of a black college and the encouragement of black emigration to Canada; the establishment of the Convention movement prompts a cascade of black organisations that continues until emancipation.

1831   The Maryland General Assembly – in the wake of a slave uprising in Virginia – bans free blacks from owning weapons, buying alcohol, selling food or attending religious services at which no whites are present, and calls for the colonisation of free blacks in Liberia. The governor of Virginia calls for the establishment of a committee to raise funds to remove free blacks from the state.

1835   The National Negro Convention calls for the use of the word 'Negro' rather than 'African' or 'coloured'. Washington DC introduces legislation barring free blacks from a wide range of employment in the capital following rioting by anti-abolitionists.

1836   Washington DC legislation forces free blacks to carry identity passes.

1837   The Pennsylvania Reform Convention denies suffrage to free blacks on the basis of the state Supreme Court decision in *Foog* v *Hobbs* that as blacks are not free men only whites can vote.

1838
Mar.   There are black protests at the previous year's Pennsylvania Reform Convention which removed the right to vote from free blacks in the state.

111

1841   Maryland introduces legislation making it an offence punishable by up to 20 years' imprisonment for a free black to possess abolitionist literature.

1844   A black meeting held in Boston, Massachusetts, declares that
June   segregated schools violate the state constitution but schools in the state remain segregated until 1855.

1845   William A. Leidesdorff (1810–48) becomes the first black American
Oct.   diplomat when he is appointed a sub-consul in Mexico.

1847   Frederick Douglass (c1817–95) begins publishing the *North Star;*
Dec.   Douglass declares his aims to 'abolish slavery in all its forms and aspects, advocate universal emancipation, exalt the standard of public morality, and promote the moral and intellectual improvement of the colored people, and hasten the day of freedom to the three millions of our enslaved countrymen'.

1849   Benjamin Roberts, a black Bostonian, sues the city for refusing his
July   daughter a place at a white school; the Massachusetts Supreme Court rejects his claim, using what would later be called the doctrine of 'separate but equal' facilities for blacks and whites.

1853   A National Council of Colored People is established in Rochester,
July   New York, as a development from the Negro Convention Movement, with the aim of advancing the black cause in the United States; the Council's first proposal is to establish a co-educational industrial school.

1854   Lincoln University, the first black college, established in
Jan.   Pennsylvania.
July   Elizabeth Jennings, a black woman, refuses to give up her seat on a bus in New York City and is ejected; she sues the company and a Brooklyn judge declares, 'Colored persons, if sober, well behaved and free from disease, have the same rights as others' and could not be excluded.

1855   John Mercer Langston (1829–97) becomes the first black American to win election to political office when he becomes clerk of Brownhelm Township, Lorain County, Ohio.

1857   The Supreme Court rules in *Dred Scott* v *Sandford* that blacks that are
Mar.   not citizens; the court rejects Scott's claim that he had secured his emancipation as a result of periods of residence in a non-slave state. The decision, which heartens the Southern slave states and alarms Northern abolitionists, has repercussions for black civil rights as well as slavery. The California state legislature rejects an attempt to prevent black immigration into the state by 32 votes to 30.

1859   Legislation in Arkansas orders free blacks to leave the state or to face
Feb.   enslavement.
Mar.   The acting Commissioner for General Land for the United States,

	following the Supreme Court decision on Dred Scott, declares that as blacks are not citizens they are ineligible to claim lands allocated for settlement.
Nov.	In *Cresswell's Executor* v *Walter*, an Alabama court rules that slaves have 'no legal mind, no will which the law can recognise … Because they are slaves, they are incapable of performing civil acts'.

1861
Apr. The Civil War opens as Confederate forces attack the Federal garrison at Fort Sumter, South Carolina.

May Fugitive slaves captured by Union forces in Virginia are declared 'contraband of war' and used as labourers.

Sept. The Union Navy accepts the enlistment of black Americans.

Dec. President Lincoln orders the Secretary of War, Simon Cameron, to remove a section from his annual report proposing the emancipation of fugitive slaves and their recruitment as soldiers and labourers.

1862
Mar. The United States Congress forbids the return of fugitive slaves to their owners by the Union forces.

Apr. The Union commander in the South Carolina Sea Islands, General David Hunter, begins recruiting a black regiment in the area but is forced to disband it when the War Department refuses finance. District of Columbia Emancipation Act abolishes slavery in the area of the Federal capital; emigration is encouraged and funds of up to $100 for each person are allocated for the migration of freed slaves to Haiti, Latin America and West Africa.

July The Confiscation Act forbids Union forces from returning fugitive slaves to their owners, and authorises President Lincoln to employ 'as many persons of African descent as he may deem necessary and proper for the suppression of this rebellion', though at lower rates of pay than whites.

Aug. President Lincoln is condemned by a black delegation when he appeals to them to encourage freed slaves to emigrate. Union General Benjamin F. Butler begins recruiting free blacks and escaped slaves in New Orleans. The Union War Department agrees to finance black forces raised in South Carolina.

Dec. Confederate President Jefferson Davis orders his forces to deny captured black Union soldiers and their officers the rights of prisoners of war and treat them as criminals.

1863
Jan. President Lincoln issues the Emancipation Proclamation and formally opens enlistment in Union armed forces as volunteers to black Americans.

Mar. Union Secretary of War Edwin Stanton appoints a Freedmen's Inquiry Commission to monitor the conditions of freed slaves and to recommend measures to improve their welfare and employment.

May The Union War Department establishes a Bureau of Colored Troops to organise recruitment in the Northern states and parts of the Confederacy occupied by Union forces.

July   Blacks are attacked in riots in New York City against draft laws because they are ineligible for conscription into the armed forces; of the thousand people killed in clashes, the majority are black. President Lincoln demands equal treatment of captured black and white Union soldiers by the Confederate forces.

Aug.   Abolitionist Frederick Douglass (1818–95) meets President Lincoln to demand full equality for black soldiers in the Union forces.

1864
June   Congress introduces equal pay, arms and medical treatment for black and white soldiers after a black regiment refuses to accept any pay as a protest against discrimination.

1865
Jan.   General William Sherman issues Special Field Order No 15 reserving coastal areas of Florida, Georgia and South Carolina for black settlement, with each family entitled to a 40 acre plot and the payment of bounties for black soldiers.

Mar.   Congress establishes the Bureau of Refugees, Freedmen, and Abandoned Lands (Freedmen's Bureau) to provide assistance for freed slaves and poor whites. As the Confederacy faces defeat, it begins to recruit slaves into the armed forces.

Apr.   The civil war ends with the surrender of Confederate commander General Robert E. Lee.

May   President Andrew Johnson announces a Reconstruction Programme to begin reintegration of the former Confederate states into the Union. Meetings are convened by black Americans in Mississippi, North Carolina, Tennessee and Virginia to formulate demands for suffrage and equal rights. The black activist Frederick Douglass declares, 'Slavery is not abolished until the black man has the ballot.'

3.3 Chronology of black civil rights in the period of Reconstruction in the United States, 1865–77

1865
Mar.
Congress passes the Freedmen's Bureau Act establishing the Bureau of Freedmen, Refugees and Abandoned Lands as a section of the War Department to assist freed slaves and poor whites, initially for one year. During its existence the Bureau will issue over 20 million rations (five million to whites), resettle over 30,000 people, set up 4,330 schools (with 247,000 pupils) and assist in the establishment of black colleges. Congress also establishes a Freedmen's Bank which remains in operation until 1874. The Mails Act outlaws racial discrimination in Federal employment.

Apr.
As the civil war ends, President Lincoln declares that black veterans who served in the Union forces and 'very intelligent' blacks may be given the right to vote. He is assassinated three days later and succeeded by Andrew Johnson, a Democrat elected on a Republican ticket.

May
President Johnson announces a Reconstruction Programme to begin reintegration of the former Confederate states into the Union. Black Americans meet in Mississippi, North Carolina, Tennessee and Virginia to demand suffrage and equal rights.

Dec.
Congress meets for the first time since Lincoln's assassination and ratifies the Thirteenth Amendment to the Constitution prohibiting slavery. All former Confederate states except Mississippi have accepted reintegration into the Union but the House of Representatives refuses to allow Southern delegates to take their seats and establishes a Committee for Reconstruction. Mississippi enacts the first 'Black Code', legislation based on former slave codes, limiting the rights of freed slaves and placing restrictions on their movements; white-controlled legislatures throughout the former slave states gradually follow Mississippi's lead.

1866
Feb.
The powers of the Freedmen's Bureau are renewed and extended despite an attempt at veto by President Johnson. A proposal for the Bureau to distribute land to freed slaves is rejected in the House of Representatives by 128 votes to 37. Johnson informs the black activist Frederick Douglass (c1817–95) that he intends to block black voting to protect the interests of Southern whites.

Apr.   Congress passes the Civil Rights Act, again over a veto attempt by President Johnson; the Act, which provides the basis for the Fourteenth Amendment to the Constitution, declares that 'all persons born in the United States and not subject to any foreign power, excluding Indians not taxed, are hereby declared citizens of the United States' and is aimed at Black Codes being enacted by former slave states in an attempt to deny freed slaves their rights as citizens.

May   Congress passes the Prevention and Punishment of Kidnapping Act to counter any attempts to return blacks to slavery.

June   The Fourteenth Amendment is submitted to individual states for ratification.

Nov.   An anti-Johnson Republican majority is elected to the House of Representatives and the Senate, opening the way for deepening conflict between the President and Radical Republicans over his resistance to attempts to guarantee and extend black civil rights. The National Labor Union (NLU), a federation of skilled white workers, excludes black members but accepts the need for black workers to organise.

1867
Jan.   Congress begins a series of ultimately unsuccessful attempts to impeach President Johnson. Congress grants suffrage to black males in the District of Columbia despite a veto by President Johnson.

Feb.   Frederick Douglass (c1817–95) leads a black delegation to President Johnson to urge him to extend the franchise to all qualified black males.

Mar.   Congress begins passing a series of Acts to enforce Reconstruction and continues the legislative process until July. The South is divided into five military districts under Federal authority and individual states are refused readmission to the Union until they have ratified the Fourteenth Amendment. Military governors are given the power to take over the organisation of elections in the Southern states to ensure blacks are allowed to vote and take office. Black Virginians mount a sit-in on streetcars in Charleston and win the right to use them equally with whites.

Apr.   The first national convention of the racist Ku Klux Klan is held in Nashville, Tennessee.

May   The process of registering black voters begins in the Southern states; within six months almost 750,000 will have registered, forming a black majority in Mississippi, Louisiana, South Carolina, Tennessee, Alabama and Florida.

Aug.   Black electors voting in a Southern state for the first time give the Republican Party a majority in Tennessee.

Oct.   Monroe Baker is elected mayor of St Martin, Louisiana and becomes the first black town mayor.

1868
Apr.   The first black Americans become members of state governments when Francis L. Cardozo is elected as secretary of state in South

Carolina, Oscar J. Dunn as Louisiana Lieutenant Governor and Antoine Dubuclet as Louisiana state treasurer.

May Black Americans are allowed to participate in the Republican Party National Convention for the first time.

June The former slave states of Alabama, Arkansas, Florida, Georgia, Louisiana, North Carolina and South Carolina re-enter the Union.

July The South Carolina Legislature (with 87 black members and 40 whites) becomes the only state legislative assembly in the United States to have a black majority; whites recapture control in 1874.

Sept. As incidents of racial violence begin to rise in the Southern states, over 200 blacks are killed in Louisiana.

Nov. Ulysses S. Grant is elected President; John W. Menard is elected in Louisiana as the first black member of the Senate.

1869
Feb. With racial violence intensifying, Congress approves the Fifteenth Amendment guaranteeing black Americans the right to vote. The Amendment declares, 'The right of citizens of the United States to vote shall not be denied or abridged by the United States or by any State on account of race, color or previous condition of servitude.' However, Congress refuses to allow John Menard (elected in Nov. 1868) to take his seat in the Senate on the grounds that it is 'too early to admit a Negro'. A National Convention of Colored Men is formed in Washington DC under the leadership of Frederick Douglass.

Dec. Georgia's representatives are refused entry to Congress after black voters are obstructed from exercising their rights following the withdrawal of Federal troops from the state. The Colored National Labor Union is organised in Baltimore by Isaac Meyers in response to the exclusion of black workers from the white National Labor Union.

1870
Feb. Republican Hiram R. Revels (1822–1901) – returned to the Mississippi seat formerly held by Confederate President Jefferson Davis – becomes the first black American allowed to take his Senate seat.

May Congress passes the Enforcement Act guaranteeing black citizens the right to vote and imposing penalties for attempting to obstruct this right; the Act is partly aimed at the growing activities of the Ku Klux Klan.

Oct. Robert B. Elliott (1842–84), Robert C. DeLarge (1842–74) and Joseph H. Rainey (1832–87) are elected as the first black members of the House of Representatives; Rainey will remain a member until 1879.

1871
Oct. Federal troops are deployed in South Carolina to enforce a proclamation ordering the Ku Klux Klan in the state to disband and to surrender its weapons.

1872
June The Freedmen's Bureau ceases to function.

| Dec. | Pinckney Stewart Pinchback (1837–1921) becomes the first black governor of Louisiana. |

1873
Jan.   Pinckney Stewart Pinchback is elected to the Senate.

1875
Mar.   President Grant signs the Civil Rights Act, the last such legislation in the United States until 1957; the Act prohibits racial discrimination and declares that 'all persons within the jurisdiction of the United States shall be entitled to the full and equal enjoyment of the accommodations, advantages, facilities, and privileges of inns, public conveyances, on land or water, theaters, and other places of public amusement'. The Act will be ruled unconstitutional by the Supreme Court in 1883.

Sept.   Federal troops are deployed in Louisiana after 30 blacks are killed by whites attempting to prevent them voting.

Oct.   Federal troops are deployed in South Carolina following racial clashes in which one black and five whites are killed.

Dec.   One black senator and seven black congressmen are elected.

1876
Mar.   The Supreme Court rules in *United States* v *Cruikshank* that the Fourteenth Amendment is intended to protect black Americans against violations of rights by states and not by individuals, opening the way for organisations such as the Ku Klux Klan to continue their activities unhindered. The Senate refuses to allow Pinckney Stewart Pinchback to take his seat following his re-election.

Nov.   After allegations of irregularities in the presidential election, a Congressional committee is appointed to decide which candidate has won.

1877
Mar.   Following his agreement to withdraw the last of the Federal troops overseeing Reconstruction in the Southern states, the Republican Rutherford B. Hayes is declared president. Frederick Douglass is appointed marshal of the District of Columbia.

Apr.   The withdrawal of Federal troops from New Orleans effectively marks the end of Federal commitment to protect black civil rights in the former slave states; as the United States undergoes economic depression, civil rights decline in importance as a political issue to the majority of the population.

Sept.   The 'Exodusters' – freed slaves from the Southern states seeking an escape from continuing discrimination – begin moving to Kansas.

3.4 Chronology of black civil rights in the United States, from the end of Reconstruction in 1877 to 1954

1877
Apr.
The withdrawal of the last Federal troops from the South signifies the end of Federal commitment to protect black civil rights in the former slave states.

Sept.
The 'Exodusters' – freed slaves from the Southern states seeking an escape from continuing discrimination – begin moving to Kansas.

1881
Tennessee introduces racial segregation on the railways, opening a pattern of legalised discrimination in public facilities that will spread through the Southern states.

July
The black activist Booker T. Washington (1856–1915) opens the Tuskegee Institute in Alabama to provide agricultural and industrial education for black Americans to equip them for economic independence.

Dec.
Five thousand black Americans move to Arkansas from South Carolina in response to persistent discrimination and violence.

1883
Oct.
The Supreme Court prepares the ground for systematic racial segregation by declaring the 1875 Civil Rights Act unconstitutional on the grounds that the Reconstruction Acts do not extend to public facilities and are concerned with discrimination by states rather than individuals.

Nov.
A racially integrated local government in Danville, Mississippi is ousted by whites and four black people are killed.

1884
May
Black activist Ida Wells-Barnett (1862–1931) wins $500 damages after refusing to sit in an all-black railway coach; the result is overturned by the Tennessee Supreme Court in 1887; Timothy Thomas Fortune (1856–1928) establishes the influential black newspaper the *New York Age*.

1886
Mar.
The leading American union organisation, the Knights of Labor, allows a black delegate to address its national convention; he declares that one of the organisation's objects should be 'the abolition of those distinctions which are maintained by creed or color'. His appearance is criticised by segregationist delegates but the Knights go on to organise thousands of black workers, despite pressure to exclude them. However, many individual unions continue to hold out against black membership.

The Colored Farmers' Alliance is established; by 1890 it has a million members.

1887   Florida introduces legislation to enforce racial segregation in public facilities; Mississippi follows in 1888 and Texas in 1889.

1890   An attempt to secure Federal funds to combat illiteracy among freed
Mar.   slaves (at a time when literacy tests are being adopted as a condition of securing the right to vote) is defeated in the Senate by 37 votes to 31.

Nov.   A constitutional convention in Mississippi adopts literacy tests and the poll tax to disenfranchise what are described as 'unworthy' voters; a black appeal to President Benjamin Harrison to intervene on the grounds that this disproportionately affects black citizens is ignored.

1891   The Lodge Bill, an attempt to prevent infringements on black voting
Jan.   rights, is rejected by the Senate.
Sept.   Black cotton pickers in Texas establish a union and strike for increased pay.

1895   Booker T. Washington delivers the 'Atlanta Compromise' speech at
Sept.   the Cotton States International Exposition in Atlanta, calling on black Americans to concentrate on education, economic progress and the development of a 'high character' to advance in society rather than turning to political agitation.

Dec.   South Carolina attempts to exclude black citizens from voting by adopting an 'understanding' clause in its state constitution.

1896   The Supreme Court's decision in *Plessy* v *Ferguson* upholds the con-
May   stitutionality of providing 'separate but equal' facilities for blacks, providing the legal basis for segregation into the 20th century. The court upholds Plessy's conviction for refusing to travel in a black railway coach. In a dissenting statement, Justice John Harlan declares, 'The destinies of the two races in this country are indissolubly linked together, and the interests of both require that the common government of all shall not permit the seeds of race hate to be placed under the sanction of law.'

July   The National Association of Colored Women is established in Washington DC by Mary Church Terrell (1863–1954) and Ida Wells-Barnett (1862–1931).

1897   The American Federation of Labor issues a statement requiring all affiliated trade unions 'never to discriminate against a fellow worker on account of color, creed or nationalist', but discrimination in union organisation continues.

1898   Louisiana introduces a 'grandfather clause' into the state con-
May   stitution, excluding blacks from voting by restricting the ballot to descendants of people who had the vote in 1867, before Reconstruction began to have an impact on black civil rights. South

Carolina introduces legislation instituting segregation in public facilities.

July   The war against Spain begins; 20 segregated black regiments serve in the conflict.

Nov.   Following a press campaign to disenfranchise black voters in Wilmington, North Carolina, a white mob attacks the black section of the town, killing at least 30 people.

1899   North Carolina introduces legislation to institute segregation of the races in public facilities. The Supreme Court rules in *Cumming* v *Richmond County Board of Education* that separate schools for whites are constitutional, even where no comparable education is offered to blacks. The National Afro-American Council (formed in 1898) designates 4 June as a national day of fasting in protest against lynchings of black people.

1900   The National Negro Business League is launched by 400 delegates
Aug.   from 34 states at a convention in New York City; Booker T. Washington becomes the League's president. Within five years the organisation will have over 300 branches. Virginia begins systematic racial segregation in public facilities and, with North Carolina, introduces literacy tests to exclude black voters.

1901   The House of Representatives loses its last black member when
Mar.   George H. White fails to be re-elected in North Carolina; White, who was first elected in 1896, attacks 'Jim Crow' laws in his final speech and declares that black Americans will return to Congress.

Oct.   Booker T. Washington dines with President Theodore Roosevelt in the White House; although there is much criticism of the invitation, it marks Washington's acceptability to the American establishment. However, black journalist and activist William Monroe Trotter (1872–1934) begins publication of the militant *Boston Guardian* in which he condemns Washington's policy of compromising black interests and publishes what he calls 'propaganda against discrimination based on color'.

Nov.   Alabama adopts a 'grandfather clause' to exclude black voters.

1904   Maryland legislates to enforce racial segregation in public facilities.

1905   Black activists from 14 states form the Niagara Movement to conduct
July   a militant campaign for black civil rights with William Monroe Trotter (1872–1934) and W. E. B. Du Bois (1868–1963) as leading figures; the Movement opposes the accommodationist policies of Booker T. Washington. Robert S. Abbott (1870–1940) begins publishing the *Chicago Defender* which will become one of the most influential of black newspapers.

1906   Black soldiers who clash with white civilians in Brownsville,
Apr.   Texas, following racial insults, and in which three whites are killed, are dishonourably discharged from the armed forces by President

Roosevelt before they have an opportunity to state their case.

Sept. Following a press campaign to disenfranchise black voters in Atlanta, Georgia, there are race riots in which at least 12 people are killed.

1907 Oklahoma introduces legislation to institutionalise racial segregation in public facilities. By the end of the year, every Southern state enforces racial segregation in transport and all public places.

1908 Serious racial clashes close to Lincoln's birthplace in Illinois prompt
Aug. liberal whites to call a conference to establish what will become the National Association for the Advancement of Colored People (NAACP). Georgia introduces literacy tests to exclude black voters.

1909 The NAACP is established in New York City at a meeting of 47 whites
Feb. and six black intellectuals to work for black civil rights and integration through the courts rather than agitation. Although a number of black activists criticise the NAACP's initial white dominance, W. E. B. Du Bois becomes a leading figure in the organisation, editing its organ, *The Crisis*.

1910 The National Urban League is established in New York City to
Apr. provide assistance to the increasing numbers of blacks migrating from the Southern states in search of work and freedom from overt segregation.

Dec. Baltimore, Maryland, introduces the first legislation in the United States enforcing residential segregation on racial grounds; towns in Texas, North Carolina, Kentucky, Virginia and Missouri follow suit; the Baltimore ordinance is ruled unconstitutional by the Supreme Court in 1917.

1913 Following a discussion by the Cabinet on race relations, President
Apr. Woodrow Wilson introduces racial segregation in government workplaces.

1915 The Supreme Court decision in *Guinn* v *The United States* outlaws the
June 'grandfather clauses' used in the Southern states to disenfranchise black citizens. However, because of the increasing age of those affected, the practice is already losing its impact.

Nov. The NAACP leads protests against the film *Birth of a Nation* for its racism and obvious sympathies for white extremist organisations; the film encourages a resurgence of Ku Klux Klan activities.

1917 The United States enters World War One; 300,000 black Americans
Apr. will serve in the segregated armed forces.

July Whites attack black workers in East St Louis, Illinois, in protests against their employment in a factory, killing 40; the NAACP responds with 10,000-strong silent march along Fifth Avenue in New York City to protest against racism.

Aug. Seventeen whites are killed in clashes with black soldiers in Houston, Texas; 18 black soldiers are executed.

Nov. Black administrator Emmett J. Scott is appointed special assistant to the Secretary of War to advise on the part black Americans can play in the country's war effort. The Supreme Court rules in *Buchanan* v *Warley* that a Kentucky law banning blacks and whites from living in the same block is unconstitutional.

1918
July
The National Liberty Congress of Colored Americans appeals to Congress to make lynching a Federal rather than a state crime to increase the chances of successful prosecutions but the appeal is rejected. A 'Red Summer' of race riots erupts in over 25 American cities, including Chicago, Philadelphia and Washington DC; the disturbances last into October and over 100 black people are killed and another 1,000 injured.

1919
The Commission on Inter-racial Co-operation (later the Southern Regional Council) is formed by black and white civil leaders to work for improved race relations in the Southern states.

1920
Aug.
Black nationalist Marcus Garvey (1887–1940) advocates a 'back to Africa' policy at a 25,000-strong rally of his Universal Negro Improvement Association in New York City.

1920
Nov.
After a prolonged Ku Klux Klan campaign of intimidation, black people attempting to vote in Florida are attacked by white mobs.

1922
A Bill for firmer action to be taken against lynching is passed in the House of Representatives by 230 votes to 119 but falls in the Senate.

1923
The Supreme Court rules in *Moore* v *Dempsey* that excluding blacks from juries is inconsistent with the right to a fair trial; the decision follows a trial in which a black man is convicted of murder by an all-white jury.

1925
May
Black activist A. Philip Randolph (1885–1979) forms the Brotherhood of Sleeping Car Porters, a union in a predominantly black industry; attempts to affiliate to the largely white American Federation of Labour are rejected in 1928 and 1934 but succeed in 1936.

1927
Mar.
The Supreme Court rules in *Nixon* v *Herndon* that a Texas law excluding black voters from state Democratic primaries is unconstitutional; other methods of racial exclusion are soon developed.

1928
Nov.
Oscar De Priest is elected to the House of Representatives as a Republican from Illinois, the first black politician to be elected from a Northern state.

1929
Dec.
A 'Don't buy where you can't work' campaign is organised in Chicago to protest against white-owned businesses with predominantly black customers refusing to employ black workers; the campaign rapidly spreads to other black areas.

1930
The NAACP mounts a successful campaign against the appointment of a prominent racist judge to the Supreme Court.

1931
Apr.

The trial begins of the Scottsboro boys, nine black youths accused of raping a white woman, a controversial case which will raise questions about racism in the American justice system.

1933
Mar.

The NAACP opens a legal campaign against segregation in education by suing the University of North Carolina for its refusal to admit black students; the case is lost.

1934
Nov.

Arthur L. Mitchell is elected the first black Democratic member of the House of Representatives. A NAACP speaker protests at the AFL convention at the continuation of racial discrimination and the exclusion of black workers from affiliated unions.

1935

The Congress of Industrial Organisations (CIO) secedes from the AFL, opening up opportunities for increasing black unionisation.

1936
Dec.

The Supreme Court rules in *Gibbs* v *Board of Education of Montgomery County, Maryland*, that unequal pay for black and white teachers is unconstitutional. President Franklin D. Roosevelt appoints Mary McLeod Bethune (1875–1955) to his unofficial 'Black Cabinet' as director of the Division of Negro Affairs in the National Youth Administration.

1938
Dec.

The Supreme Court rules in *Missouri ex rel Gaines* that separate educational facilities provided by states for black students must be equal to those provided for whites.

1941
Apr.

The Supreme Court rules that separate facilities in railway carriages provided for black passengers must be equal to those provided for whites.

June

President Roosevelt issues Executive Order 8802 outlawing racial and religious discrimination in the defence industries and on government training schemes following a threat by A. Philip Randolph and other black leaders to mount a 100,000-strong protest march on Washington DC. The AFL rejects a resolution from Randolph protesting against the exclusion of black workers from affiliated trade unions.

July

President Roosevelt establishes a Fair Employment Practices Committee to monitor and act against racial discrimination in the defence industry. This and Executive Order 8802 are seen as the most radical civil rights actions taken by the government since Reconstruction although, in practice, the results prove disappointing.

Dec.

The United States enters World War Two; almost a million black Americans will serve in the segregated armed forces.

1942
June

Blacks and whites form the Congress of Racial Equality (CORE) in Chicago to take non-violent direct action against segregation and discrimination and begin with a restaurant sit-in; CORE becomes a national movement in 1943.

Oct.

Sixty Southern black leaders issue the 'Durham Manifesto'

demanding policies to encourage improved race relations in the United States.

1943
Jan.   The black assistant to the Secretary of War resigns in protest against segregation in the armed forces.

May–
Aug.   There are serious race riots in which 40 people die; troops are deployed to restore order in Mobile and Detroit.

1944
Apr.   The Supreme Court rules in *Smith* v *Allwright* that the exclusion of black voters from primary elections throughout the Southern states is unconstitutional; the ruling promises to open the way for renewed black participation in political activity, although many obstacles remain.

1945
Mar.   New York establishes a Fair Employment Practices Commission to combat racial discrimination, the first state to take this action.

Sept.   White students boycott classes in Gary, Indiana, in protest against attempts to desegregate education.

1946
June   The Supreme Court rules in *Morgan* v *Virginia* that segregation in interstate transport is unconstitutional but the decision has little real impact in the Southern states.

Dec.   President Harry S. Truman appoints a bi-racial Committee on Civil Rights to investigate segregation and racial discrimination and to recommend action.

1947
Apr.   CORE despatches 'Freedom Riders' to the Southern states to test the effectiveness of the June 1946 Supreme Court decision outlawing segregation in interstate bus travel.

Oct.   The Commission on Civil Rights issues a report entitled *To Secure These Rights*, condemning racism in the United States and calling for a programme to remove segregation.

1948
Jan.   The Supreme Court rules in *Sipuel* v *Oklahoma State Board of Regents* that states must provide equivalent legal education to blacks and whites after the university had denied admission to a black student.

Mar.   Black activist A. Philip Randolph tells a Senate committee that unless segregation in the armed forces is abolished he will encourage young blacks to refuse military service; he goes on to establish the League for Non-Violent Civil Disobedience Against Military Segregation.

May   The Supreme Court rules in *Shelley* v *Kraemer* that a covenant preventing the sale of a house to a black purchaser is not legally enforceable.

July   Following the Democratic National Convention's adoption of a civil rights policy, delegates from Mississippi and South Carolina leave to form the 'Dixiecrats', Democrats from the Southern states who oppose desegregation. President Truman issues Executive Order 9981 outlawing racial discrimination in the armed forces and government employment, opening the way for desegregation in these areas; the army chief of staff declares that segregation will only end in the armed forces when it ends in the wider society.

Oct.   The California Supreme Court rules that a state law banning inter-racial marriage is unconstitutional.

1950   The Supreme Court rules in *Sweatt* v *Painter* that equality in education
June   involves more than the provision of equal facilities and orders the admission of a black student to the University of Texas Law School. The court also declares in *McLaurin* v *Oklahoma State Board of Regents* that no distinction could be made on racial grounds against any student attending an educational institution.

1951   As racial segregation begins to be abandoned by leading colleges, the
Apr.   University of North Carolina becomes one of the first in the Southern states to attempt integration; Tennessee follows in 1952.

July   There are the worst racial disturbances in the North since 1919 as 3,000 whites attempt to prevent a black family moving into a white area of Cicero, Illinois; the National Guard is deployed.

Dec.   A backlash begins against increasing moves to combat segregation when the Florida NAACP organiser is killed in a bombing; within a year there will be at least 40 such bombings.

1952   The Tuskegee Institute reports for the first time since records have
Dec.   been kept that there have been no lynchings of black people over the past year.

1953   Black passengers begin a bus boycott in Baton Rouge, Louisiana to
June   secure desegregation of the transport system; the ten day action results in a compromise.

1954   President Dwight D. Eisenhower appoints J. Ernest Wilkins Assistant
Mar.   Secretary of Labor, the highest government post yet attained by a black American.

May   The Supreme Court rules in *Brown* v *Board of Education of Topeka, Kansas,* that racial segregation in public schools is unconstitutional. Chief Justice Earl Warren declares, 'We conclude that in the field of public education the doctrine of "separate but equal" has no place. Separate educational facilities are inherently unequal.' The result is the most significant victory for the NAACP in the civil rights cases it has mounted and opens a period of agitation and legislation that will be described as the 'Second Reconstruction'.

3.5 Chronology of black civil rights in the United States, 1954–90

1954
May
The Supreme Court decision in *Brown* v *Board of Education of Topeka, Kansas*, declares racial segregation in public education to be unconstitutional; the court's reversal of the 'separate but equal' ruling made in the 1896 decision *Plessy* v *Ferguson* opens up a wider struggle for civil rights. Over the next decade, despite initial disappointments, there will be an unprecedented wave of agitation and legislation.

Sept.
Public schools in Washington DC and Baltimore, Maryland, begin desegregation.

Oct.
The Defense Department announces that integration of the armed forces has been completely implemented.

Nov.
Three black Americans – Augustus Hawkins, Adam Clayton Powell and William L. Dawson – are elected to the House of Representatives, the largest number since the period of Reconstruction following the civil war.

1955
May
The Supreme Court announces that its ruling on the illegality of educational segregation is to be implemented 'with all deliberate speed', effectively undermining the radicalism of the ruling and providing an opportunity for states to delay implementation.

Nov.
The Interstate Commerce Commission bans segregation in interstate public transportation and connected facilities. The Supreme Court declares the segregation of recreational facilities in Baltimore, Maryland, unconstitutional.

Dec.
The refusal of NAACP activist Rose Parks to give up her seat to a white passenger on a bus in Montgomery, Atlanta, and her subsequent arrest, provokes a boycott of the city's buses by black passengers; the boycott continues until December 1956, when a Supreme Court ruling forces the integration of the city's transport. The boycott organisers form a Montgomery Improvement Association (MIA) to campaign for civil rights; a local minister, Martin Luther King Jr (1929–68), is appointed president and begins his rise to prominence as the voice of the black rights movement.

1956
Jan.
King's home in Montgomery is bombed as the campaign for black civil rights in the city intensifies.

Feb.
A black student is admitted to the University of Alabama by court order but she is expelled following a riot by white students.

Aug.- Sept	There are violent white protests as the authorities attempt to desegregate schools in Kentucky, Tennessee and Texas.
Nov.	The Supreme Court rules that segregation on public buses in Montgomery is illegal and the boycott ends in December. The boycotters' victory acts as a signal to black people of the efficacy of protest to secure civil rights.
Dec.	A six month bus boycott in Tallahassee, Florida, ends segregation.
1957 Feb.	The Southern Christian Leadership Conference (SCLC) is established with its headquarters in Atlanta, Georgia, to provide organisation for civil rights activity throughout the Southern states; the SCLC counterposes non-violent civil disobedience as a means of achieving change against the NAACP's non-confrontational campaign in the courts; King is elected president, a post he holds until his death in 1968.
May	Over 15,000 demonstrators, the majority black, gather at the Lincoln Memorial, Washington DC, to support a Voting Rights Bill introduced in Congress.
June	A black boycott of white businesses begins in Tuskegee, Alabama, in protest against gerrymandering of voting districts to weaken black political influence.
Aug.	The Civil Rights Act, the first major civil rights legislation since 1875, passes in Congress; the Act establishes a Commission on Civil Rights to investigate attempts to deny black citizens the right to vote and sets up a civil rights division in the Justice Department.
Sept.	There are violent white protests against attempts to desegregate schools in Alabama and Tennessee. President Eisenhower despatches Federal troops to Little Rock, Arkansas, to enforce school desegregation against the opposition of state governor Orval Faubus; the troops escort nine black children into the Central High School.
Dec.	New York City introduces Fair Housing Practice regulations to end racial discrimination in housing.
1958 May	A conference of senior black figures calls for the intensification of the campaign for black civil rights.
Aug.	The NAACP Youth Council begins a campaign of sit-ins to end segregation of lunch counters in Oklahoma City.
Oct.	Ten thousand students mount a Youth March for Integrated Schools in Washington DC.
1960 Feb.	Black students organise a sit-in to end lunch counter segregation in Greensboro, North Carolina; in two weeks the campaign has spread to 15 cities in five Southern states. Although the demonstrators are met with violence and legal harassment, restaurants desegregate voluntarily or following a court order. The campaign encourages a further development of non-violent direct action.
Mar.	President Eisenhower declares he is 'deeply sympathetic' to the black claim for civil rights and calls for the establishment of

bi-racial committees throughout the Southern states to negotiate change.

Apr. The Student Non-Violent Co-ordinating Committee (SNCC) is established at a conference in Raleigh, North Carolina, to provide central organisation for student civil rights activities.

May President Eisenhower signs a Civil Rights Act, strengthening the provisions of the 1957 legislation; Federal courts are empowered to appoint referees to combat racial discrimination in voting where a 'pattern or practice' of discrimination can be shown to exist and to register qualified black voters where obstacles have been placed in their way.

July Elijah Muhammad – leader of the 100,000 strong Nation of Islam – calls for the establishment of a black state in America, re-opening the division in the civil rights movement between those seeking integration into American society and those arguing for black separatism.

Nov. President John F. Kennedy is elected, winning an estimated two thirds of the black American vote. New Orleans is forced to end segregation in schooling by court order after attempting to prevent integration by closing the schools.

1961
May Black students and white supporters organised by CORE begin a campaign of 'Freedom Rides' in the Southern states to force implementation of new regulations prohibiting segregation in facilities connected with interstate buses. They meet with success in Virginia and North Carolina but are attacked in South Carolina. CORE claims within a year that the Freedom Riders have achieved their objectives. King, who acts as chairman of the riders' co-ordinating committee, calls the campaign a psychological turning point in the civil rights movement.

Dec. King leads a badly organised and unsuccessful campaign to end segregation in Albany, Georgia.

1962
Sept. The National Guard is deployed to end violent white protests against the admission by court order of George Meredith to the University of Mississippi.

Oct. King appeals to President Kennedy to announce a second 'Emancipation Proclamation' ending all racial segregation as the centenary approaches of Lincoln's proclamation freeing the slaves.

Nov. President Kennedy issues an Executive Order banning racial discrimination in federally funded housing projects.

Dec. King and other black leaders ask President Kennedy to provide economic aid to newly independent African states and to impose sanctions against the apartheid regime in South Africa; the rapid European decolonisation in Africa has a dramatic impact on the civil rights movement in the United States.

1963
Apr. King leads a campaign against segregation in Birmingham, Alabama, which meets with police violence; King is arrested and writes his

'Letter from Birmingham Jail', a denunciation of racism and a classic statement of non-violent civil disobedience. Following a violent attack on a 'Children's Crusade' agreement is reached in May on the gradual desegregation of public facilities. President Kennedy, who uses the event to win support for planned civil rights legislation, tells King that the Birmingham police chief has contributed as much for black rights as Lincoln by showing the violent face of racism.

June- Civil rights demonstrations are mounted throughout the United
Aug.   States to culminate in a March for Jobs and Freedom to Washington DC.

Aug.   A quarter of a million people (a third of them white) gather at the Lincoln Memorial in Washington DC in the largest ever civil rights demonstration; King makes his celebrated 'I have a dream' speech. President Kennedy meets the leaders and promises civil rights legislation.

Sept. Four girls are killed in the bombing of a black Sunday school at the 16th Street Baptist Church in Birmingham, Alabama, a building also used for civil rights meetings; two black youths are killed in the riots that follow.

Oct.   Over 200,000 black students boycott schools in Chicago in protests against *de facto* segregation.

Dec.   King meets President Lyndon B. Johnson (who has succeeded the assassinated Kennedy); Johnson, who will launch a 'Great Society' programme to combat poverty, promises to push civil rights legislation through Congress.

1964 The Twenty-fourth Amendment to the Constitution prohibits the use
Jan.   of poll taxes to deny black citizens the right to vote; this practice has been prevalent throughout the Southern states; in Selma, Alabama, blacks constituted a majority of the 29,000 population but only 350 were registered voters.

July   President Johnson signs the most far-reaching Civil Rights Act since 1875 in the presence of black leaders; the legislation prohibits racial discrimination in voting, employment and in public facilities, with a wide interpretation of what constitutes 'public', and establishes an Equal Employment Opportunity Commission. The signing is almost immediately followed by serious disturbances in Northern urban centres, including Harlem, Brooklyn, Jersey City, Philadelphia and Chicago; over 100 people are injured. As the riots continue into August, the National Guard is deployed to restore order.

Aug.   Three civil rights workers (one black and two white) are murdered by white extremists in Mississippi while attempting to register black voters; the killings bring home to many whites the intensity of the civil rights struggle.

Dec.   King is awarded the Nobel Peace Prize for his attempts to ensure the civil rights campaign is conducted on a policy of non-violence;

however, as the campaign spreads into the Northern states, pacifism is increasingly questioned. Congress passes the Economic Opportunity Act to improve black access to education and training.

1965
Jan. The civil rights movement begins a voter registration drive in Selma, Alabama, which continues into March. There are mass arrests of demonstrators, culminating in an attack by police in March which is dubbed 'Bloody Sunday' and criticised by President Johnson.

Mar. King leads a march from Selma to Montgomery to protest against interference in registering black voters; a white civil rights worker is murdered following a rally.

June The Council of Federated Organisations, a network of civil rights organisations including CORE and the SNCC, launches a 'Freedom Summer' voter registration drive in the Southern states.

Aug. President Johnson signs a Voting Rights Act banning the poll tax, literacy tests and other conditions imposed to restrict the registration of black voters. The United States experiences the worst racial disturbances in its history as the Watts district of Los Angeles erupts into violence following a clash between black youths and the police; 34 are killed, 900 injured and over 3,000 arrested. There are similar disturbances in Chicago.

1966
Jan. Robert C. Weaver becomes the first black American to serve in the Cabinet when he is appointed Secretary of Housing and Urban Development.

June King and the SNCC's Stokely Carmichael lead a 'March against Fear' from Memphis, Tennessee to Jackson, Mississippi following the shooting of James Meredith; during the march Carmichael uses the expression 'Black Power' in public for the first time and demands whites leave the march, opening divisions with King who favours integration and racial co-operation. The SNCC and CORE take up the slogan while the NAACP and King's SCLC reject its implications for the black civil rights movement.

July King launches a campaign to desegregate housing in Chicago; after he has reached agreement with the city authorities there is serious rioting following a dispute between black children and police.

Oct. The Black Panther Party is launched in Oakland, California, with a ten-point programme which includes armed resistance to police racism.

1967
Apr. King expresses opposition to the Vietnam War for its effect on President Johnson's 'War on Poverty' and the disproportionate casualties suffered by black soldiers.

May–
Oct. The United States experiences a summer of violence, with over 40 riots in urban centres; 26 people are killed in Newark in July and 40 in Detroit. President Johnson appoints a National Advisory Commission on Civil disorders under Illinois governor Otto Kerner; his report in March 1968 blames white racism for being at the root of

the 1967 disturbances and warns that the United States is becoming two communities, 'one white, one black, separate and unequal'.

1968
Apr. King is assassinated in Memphis, Tennessee; there is rioting in 125 urban centres across the United States. President Johnson signs a Fair Housing Act outlawing racial discrimination in the sale and renting of housing.

May The 'Poor People's Campaign', a coalition of blacks, poor whites, Native and Hispanic Americans led by Rev Ralph Abernathy (King's successor as leader of the SCLC) erect Resurrection City in Washington DC to press for civil rights; the campaign ends in failure in June.

Nov. Republican Richard Nixon wins the presidential election; Shirley Chisholm becomes the first black woman elected to the House of Representatives.

1969
Oct. The Supreme Court rules in *Alexander* v *Holmes County Board of Education* that segregation in public schooling must end 'at once', ending the delay encouraged by the 'with all deliberate speed' decision of 1955.

1970
Feb. It is revealed that President Nixon's domestic adviser, Daniel P. Moynihan, has suggested that 'the time may have come when the issue of race could benefit from a period of benign neglect'; black civil rights leaders issue a statement denouncing Moynihan's proposal as part of systematic attempt to 'wipe out nearly two decades of civil rights progress'.

June The NAACP accuses President Nixon of implementing a 'calculated policy to work against the needs and aspirations of the largest minority of its citizens'. The Commission on Civil Rights echoes this criticism in October when it calls for 'courageous moral leadership' from President Nixon following what it called a 'breakdown' in enforcing legislation against racial discrimination.

1971
Jan. Twelve black Congressmen boycott President Nixon's 'State of the Union' speech in protest against his policies on black civil rights. The Supreme Court declares that Southern states must obtain Federal approval for legislative changes that might affect black voting rights.

Mar. The Supreme Court declares in a case brought by the Equal Employment Opportunities Commission that employment tests that have the effect of discriminating against black applicants are unconstitutional.

Apr. The Supreme Court rules that using bussing – the moving of students from one area to another – as a means of desegregating education is not unconstitutional.

June The Supreme Court rules by five votes to four that it is not unconstitutional to avoid desegregating public facilities by closing them; the action was not considered discriminatory because it affected blacks and whites equally.

1972
May   The National Education Association reports that over 30,000 black teachers have been made redundant since 1954 because of educational desegregation.

June   The extension of the policy of bussing to achieve school integration is postponed until all court appeals have been exhausted or until January 1974; while the NAACP supports the practice, CORE opposes it and calls for an educational system that is 'separate but really equal'.

1973
Dec.   The district court in San Francisco, California, orders the city authorities to introduce employment quotas for minorities in the fire and police departments.

1976
June   The Supreme Court rules that it is unconstitutional for private schools to exclude black students on racial grounds.

1978
June   The Supreme Court rules in *Regents of the University of California* v *Bakke* that affirmative action procedures should not be over-rigid; Bakke, a white student, complained that he had been refused admission to the university's medical school because of racial quotas.

July   The Supreme Court upholds the constitutionality of the Bell Telephone System using a quota system to combat race and sex discrimination in employment.

1979
Feb.   The Civil Rights Commission reports that 46% of black school children are still attending racially segregated schools.

1988
Mar.   Congress rejects President Reagan's veto of the Civil Rights Restoration Act; the Act reverses a 1984 Supreme Court decision which placed limits on enforcement of previous civil rights legislation.

1990
Oct.   President George Bush vetoes the 1990 Civil Rights Act on the grounds that it seeks to introduce the 'destructive force of quotas' into employment; a Senate attempt to reverse the veto fails.

3.5.1 Effect of the 1965 Voting Rights Act on black voter registration in Southern states

	Registered black votes	
	1960	1966
Alabama	66,000	250,000
Arkansas	73,000	115,000
Georgia	183,000	303,000
Louisiana	180,000	300,000
Mississippi	159,000	243,000
North Carolina	22,000	175,000
South Carolina	210,000	282,000
Tennessee	58,000	191,000
Texas	227,000	400,000
Virginia	100,000	205,000

Source: Based on table in André Kaspi (ed.), *Great Dates in United States History* (New York, 1994), p. 192.

3.6 Chronology of serious racial disturbances and riots in the United States, 1863–1972

1863
July

There are four days of rioting in New York against the introduction of conscription into the Union Army to fight in the Civil War; there are attacks on blacks who are ineligible for conscription and whom whites fear will take their jobs; over a thousand people, mostly black, are killed or injured; there are similar disturbances over the issue in Boston, where 20 black people are killed.

1866
May

In three days of race rioting in Memphis, Tennessee, in which army veterans are particularly targeted, 46 blacks and two whites are killed; black women are raped and 12 black schools and four churches are destroyed by fire.

July

At least 35 people are killed and over a hundred injured in New Orleans when police attack a multi-racial Republican Party meeting.

1867
Apr.

The Ku Klux Klan, a white racist organisation formed to prevent freed slaves exercising their rights, holds its first national convention in Nashville, Tennessee.

1868
Sept.

There are race riots throughout Louisiana, the most serious of which takes place in New Orleans; over 200 black people are killed.

1875
Sept.

Over 20 black people are killed in a massacre in Clinton, Mississippi.

1876
July

Three months of serious racial disturbances begin in South Carolina, following the killing of five black people in Hamburg. President Ulysses S. Grant deploys Federal troops to restore order.

1883
Nov.

Whites kill four black people in a coup which ousts the racially integrated local government in Danville, Virginia.

1886
Mar.

Twenty black people are killed in racial violence in Mississippi.

1895
Mar.

Six black workers are killed when they are attacked by white rioters in New Orleans.

1898
Nov.

A white mob attacks the black section of Wilmington, North Carolina, killing at least 30 people and driving many from the town; the attack follows a press campaign to disenfranchise black voters.

1900
July

Black homes and schools are destroyed in four days of racial disturbances in New Orleans.

Aug.   White mobs attack the New York black ghetto of Harlem following the death of a police officer; the police refuse to move against the white rioters.

1906
Apr.   Three whites are killed in Brownsville, Texas, by black soldiers retaliating against continued racist abuse; the soldiers are dishonourably discharged by President Theodore Roosevelt but are exonerated following a court of enquiry in 1909.

Sept.   Eighteen blacks and three whites are killed in three days of race rioting in Atlanta, Georgia; the disturbances followed a press campaign to disenfranchise black citizens which included allegations of rape; a multi-racial Atlanta Civic League is formed after the disturbances to improve race relations.

1908
Aug.   There is a week of racial clashes in Springfield, Illinois, the birthplace of Abraham Lincoln, in which troops are deployed; in the aftermath a conference is called which establishes the National Association for the Advancement of Colored People in 1909.

1917
July   Over 40 black people are killed and 6,000 driven from their homes in riots in East St Louis, Illinois, triggered by the employment of black workers in a factory with Federal contracts; martial law is declared; the NAACP organises a silent march through New York City to protest against racism.

Aug.   Black soldiers and white civilians clash in Houston, Texas; two blacks and 17 whites are killed; 18 black soldiers are later executed for their part in the incident.

1919
July   A 'Red Summer' of race riots throughout the United States begins; between July and October over 100 people are killed and over 1,000 seriously injured in disturbances in 25 cities, including Washington DC, Chicago and Philadelphia; Federal troops are deployed to restore order. The National Liberty Congress of Colored Americans unsuccessfully asks Congress to make lynching a Federal rather than a state crime to increase the possibility of punishing perpetrators; 83 lynchings take place in 1918.

1920
Nov.   Black people attempting to vote in Florida are attacked by white mobs led by the Ku Klux Klan; the attacks follow a long campaign of intimidation conducted by the Klan.

1921
June   Over 60 blacks and 20 whites are killed in racial disturbances in Tulsa, Oklahoma, which follow black fears that a man accused of rape is about to be lynched.

1935
Mar.   There is serious rioting and looting in the New York Harlem ghetto following the killing of a black youth accused of stealing from a shop; a commission of enquiry says the roots of the disturbances were in 'resentments against racial discrimination and poverty in the midst of plenty'.

1941
Aug.
There are clashes between black and white civilians and soldiers in North Carolina.

1943
May
Four months of racial disturbances begin across the United States; over 40 people are killed and Federal troops are deployed in Illinois, Texas and New York.

1946
Aug.
Over a hundred black people are injured in racial clashes in Alabama and Pennsylvania.

1951
July
There are serious racial clashes in Cicero, Illinois, as whites protest against the attempt to house a black family in a white area; the National Guard is deployed to restore order.

Dec.
The murder by bombing of an NAACP organiser in Florida opens a period of racially motivated assassinations.

1952
Dec.
The multi-racial civil rights body, the Southern Regional Council, reports that over 40 racist bombings have taken place in the previous two years; the Tuskegee Institute reports that for the first time since records were kept in 1881, no lynchings of black people have taken place during the previous year.

1953
June
There is a race riot in Chicago as black families attempt to move into a previously all-white area.

1956
Jan.
The home of civil rights leader Martin Luther King Jr is bombed during the campaign against segregation in Montgomery, Atlanta; King continues to insist that civil rights campaigners maintain a policy of non-violent civil disobedience despite provocation.

Feb.
Whites riot in protest against the admission of a black student to the University of Alabama; she is expelled from the university.

Sept.
There are violent white protests against attempts by the authorities to end racial segregation of schools in Kentucky, Tennessee and Texas.

1957
Sept.
Violent white protests continue against attempts at educational integration in Alabama and Tennessee.

1958
June
A bomb explodes at the home of a black Baptist minister active in the civil rights campaign in Birmingham, Alabama.

1960
Feb.
There are white attacks on black and white civil rights demonstrators using the tactic of the 'sit-in' in an attempt to desegregate lunch counters in the Southern states; following racial attacks in Montgomery, Alabama, Martin Luther King Jr declares that passive resistance to segregation remains essential.

1962
Sept.
There is rioting by whites as United States marshals escort a black student into the University of Mississippi; the National Guard is deployed to maintain order. Six black churches are burnt down in Georgia.

1963
Apr.
Aggressive police action against civil rights protestors in Birmingham, Alabama, is met with international outrage; white bombings and attacks continue after agreement on desegregation is reached in May.

June   Mississippi NAACP organiser Medgar Evers (1925–63) is murdered by a white racist who is acquitted when he comes to trial.

Sept.   Four black girls are killed in the bombing of a church in Birmingham, Alabama; the bombing comes shortly after the Washington DC March for Jobs and Freedom.

1964
July   A month of serious disturbances which spread across the United States begins in Harlem following the shooting of a black youth by white police; as the rioting spreads to Brooklyn, Jersey City, Philadelphia and Chicago, over 100 people are seriously injured, there are millions of dollars worth of damage to property and the National Guard is mobilised; the rioting erupts two weeks after the Congress passes a sweeping Civil Rights Act.

Aug.   Three civil rights activists (two black and one white) are murdered in Mississippi.

1965
Mar.   A violent police attack on civil rights marchers in Selma, Alabama, is criticised by President Lyndon Johnson.

Aug.   There are serious racial disturbances in the Watts section of Los Angeles following a clash between black youths and white police; an estimated 30,000 people (almost a third of the black population) participate in riots in which 34 people are killed, over 1,000 seriously injured and almost 4,000 arrested; the rioters are protesting over police racism, unemployment and the disproportionate effect of the Vietnam War on black youth; President Johnson declares that 'legitimate grievances' do not excuse rioting and Martin Luther King Jr says the rioters will damage the civil rights movement.

1966
July   Two black people are killed and over 350 arrested in clashes with police in Chicago following a dispute between police and children over the use of a fire hydrant; Martin Luther King Jr and the city mayor respond by establishing a committee on police–community relations. Four people are killed in racial disturbances in Cleveland, Ohio.

Sept.   There is rioting in Dayton, Ohio, and in Atlanta, Georgia.

1967
May   The United States experiences the worst period of racial disturbances in the country's history as there are riots in over 40 cities, spreading into October; the most serious clashes are in Newark (where 26 are killed), Detroit (where 40 are killed), Boston, New York City, Washington DC and Atlanta; President Johnson appoints a National Advisory Commission on Civil Disorders under Illinois governor Otto Kerner; Kerner reports in March 1968 that 'white racism' is responsible for the disturbances and that the United States is in danger of becoming two nations, 'one white, one black, separate and unequal'.

1968
Feb.   Three black students are killed by police in a demonstration against segregation at a college in South Carolina.

Apr.	There is rioting throughout black areas of the United States following the assassination of Martin Luther King Jr; in disturbances in 125 cities, 46 people are killed, over 2,500 seriously injured and there are over 20,000 arrests.
July	A gun fight between black nationalists and police in Cleveland, Ohio, sets off riots in which eight black people and three white police officers are killed.
Aug.	Three people are killed and hundreds seriously injured during riots in Miami.
1969 June	A wave of race riots begins in Connecticut and spreads through the summer to Louisiana, Florida and Massachusetts.
1970 Jan.	Federal Bureau of Investigation director J. Edgar Hoover claims that seven police officers had been killed and over 100 injured in attacks by black militants in the past year.
May	Six black people are killed by police in riots in Augusta, Georgia. Two black students are killed in a demonstration in Mississippi. There are further clashes into the summer in Florida, Connecticut and North Carolina.
1971 Feb.	Two people are killed during clashes in a black school boycott in Wilmington, North Carolina.
May	There are riots in New York City during protests against reductions in education and welfare spending.
June	Clashes take place between black and white servicemen in Texas; there are riots in Tennessee, Florida and Georgia.
1972 Jan.	Two black youths and two white deputy sheriffs are killed in racial clashes in Baton Rouge, Louisiana.

3.6.1 Lynching of black people in the United States, 1882–1968

State	Number of lynchings	State	Number of lynchings
Alabama	299	Nebraska	5
Alaska	0	Nevada	0
Arizona	0	New Jersey	1
Arkansas	226	New Mexico	3
California	2	New York	1
Colorado	3	North Carolina	86
Delaware	1	North Dakota	3
Florida	257	Ohio	16
Georgia	492	Oklahoma	40
Idaho	0	Oregon	1
Illinois	19	Pennsylvania	6
Indiana	14	South Carolina	156
Iowa	2	South Dakota	0
Kansas	19	Tennessee	204
Kentucky	142	Texas	352
Louisiana	335	Utah	2
Maine	0	Vermont	0
Maryland	27	Virginia	83
Michigan	1	Washington	1
Minnesota	4	West Virginia	28
Mississippi	539	Wisconsin	0
Missouri	69	Wyoming	5
Montana	2	Total	3,446

Source: Derived from statistics compiled by the Tuskegee Institute, Alabama, and cited in W. Augustus Low and Virgil A. Clift (eds), *Encyclopaedia of Black America* (New York, 1984), p. 542.

3.7 Chronology of the rise and fall of apartheid in South Africa, 1948–1994

1948
May
A National Party–Afrikaner Party alliance takes office on an apartheid programme; the policy is described by the government as 'separate but equal'.

1949
June
The Prohibition of Mixed Marriages Act bans marriages between blacks and whites.

1950
May
The Immorality Amendment Act outlaws sexual relations between blacks and whites. The Population Registration Act empowers the government to classify the South African population according to racial origin.

June
The Suppression of Communism Act outlaws the Communist Party and defines Communism as 'any doctrine or scheme which aims at bringing about any political, economic, social or industrial changes in South Africa by the promotion of disorder or disturbances or which aims at encouraging feelings of hostility between the White community and non-White community'.

July
The Group Area Act – the cornerstone of apartheid – sets a framework for the division of South Africa into separate areas on a racial basis.

1951
June
The Bantu Representation Act places black interests in the hands of government-appointed chiefs. The Separate Representation of Voters Act removes Cape Coloureds from the electoral roll.

Dec.
Leaders of the African National Congress (ANC) write to Prime Minister Malan seeking the repeal of apartheid legislation and direct black parliamentary representation.

1952
Apr.
The ANC and the South African Indian National Congress hold nationwide meetings as a preliminary to a 'defiance campaign' against apartheid laws.

June
The Native Laws Amendment Act restricts the movements of black workers. The Natives (Abolition of Passes and Co-ordination of Documents) Act – the 'pass law' – requires all black South Africans over 16 to carry a reference book and to show it to the police on demand. The 'defiance campaign' opens; 1,500 protesters are arrested on the first day and 8,000 in the course of the year.

1953
Mar.
The South African appeal court declares racial segregation unlawful unless equal facilities are provided; Prime Minister Malan

says his government would write racial discrimination into legislation.

Sept.   The Native Labour (Settlement of Disputes) Act outlaws strikes by black workers.

Oct.   The Reservation of Separate Amenities Act strengthens racial segregation in public facilities and transport.

1954
Jan.   The Bantu Education Act restricts educational opportunities for black children.

May   The Native Resettlement Act provides for forced removal of the black population from areas designated as white.

1955
Feb.   Black people are moved into segregated townships in Cape Western province, following the announcement by Native Affairs minister Verwoerd that the opening stages of implementation of apartheid policy are beginning.

June   A Congress of the People – convened by the ANC, the Indian and Coloured communities, liberal whites and the black trade unions –adopts a Freedom Charter for a multi-racial South Africa; the meeting is broken up by police.

1956
Mar.   The Tomlinson Commission (appointed in 1951) rejects the possibility of racial integration, recommends the resettlement of the majority of South Africa's black population in 'Bantustans' with increased spending on their development; black people will be allowed in white areas only as temporary migratory workers.

Apr.   The ANC, Coloured, Indian and liberal white organisations call for a boycott of transport in Cape Town as segregation is introduced.

May   The Industrial Coalition Act restricts skilled jobs to white workers and bans mixed-race trade unions. The Bantu Education Amendment Act extends segregation to private schools.

Dec.   One hundred and fifty-six participants in the 1955 Congress of the People are charged with treason.

1957
Jan.   The 'Treason trial' of anti-apartheid activists opens; hearings continue until May and are then adjourned until January 1958; during the recess charges against 61 people are withdrawn.

1958
Mar.   The ANC demands an end to apartheid, a black minimum wage and black participation in government.

Oct.   Nine hundred black women are arrested in demonstrations against an extension of the pass laws.

Nov.   Thirty of the 91 defendants in the 'Treason trial' are charged with treasonable conspiracy.

1959
Jan.   Prime Minister Verwoerd announces plans to establish eight black states as a 'positive' aspect of apartheid.

May   The first all-black local authority, the Transkei Territorial Authority, is established.

June   The ANC organises a 'Freedom Day' boycott of businesses supporting apartheid policies and calls for an international boycott of South African goods.

1960
Feb.

British Prime Minister Macmillan delivers his 'wind of change' speech to the South African Parliament and warns that Britain cannot support apartheid.

Mar.

Sixty-seven people are killed and 178 wounded by police in the Sharpeville Massacre during demonstrations against the pass laws. Against the background of international condemnation, the government proclaims a state of emergency and bans the ANC and other black political organisations.

Apr.

The UN Security Council unanimously calls for the South African government to abandon its apartheid policies.

Dec.

Prime Minister Verwoerd announces the extension of apartheid to the 1.5 million coloured population.

1961
Mar.

A special court acquits 28 anti-apartheid activists of plotting to overthrow the government.

Dec.

The ANC begins armed resistance to apartheid with bombings in Johannesburg and Port Elizabeth.

1962
Jan.

Prime Minister Verwoerd announces two million Xhosa will be given self rule in Transkei as part of what he describes as 'separate development'.

June

The General Law Amendment (Sabotage) Act give the government extensive new powers against anti-apartheid activity.

Nov.

The UN General Assembly calls for economic and diplomatic sanctions against South Africa.

1963
May

The Transkei Self-Government Act sets out conditions under which Transkei will be granted limited home rule.

July

Seventeen anti-apartheid activists, including Nelson Mandela and Walter Sisulu, are arrested in Rivonia and charged with plotting to overthrow the government; they are acquitted in December but immediately re-arrested.

1964
Jan.

The Odendaal Commission (appointed in September 1962) recommends continuing apartheid policy on the grounds that groups living in South Africa differ 'physically and spiritually and harbour strong feelings against each other' and proposes establishing ten non-white homelands.

May

Transkei's all-black legislative assembly opens.

June

The 'Rivonia trial' concludes with life sentences for eight ANC leaders; ANC Deputy President Mandela declares that violence was the only course open to them.

1965
Jan.

The Bantu Laws Amendment Act gives the government wider powers to remove rights of black people living in white areas.

1966
Oct.

The UN General Assembly withdraws South Africa's mandate to administer South West Africa (Namibia) but the government declares it will continue to control the territory.

1967
June

The General Laws Amendment Act (the 'Terrorism Act') provides the government with greater powers to combat what it defines as treason.

1968
Feb.

The Prohibition of Mixed Marriages Amendment Act nullifies mixed-race marriages entered into by male South Africans abroad.

May

The Prohibition of Political Interference Act bans multi-racial political parties.

Oct.

The opening of the Ovamboland legislative council marks a further step in South Africa's policy of separate development.

1969
Mar.

The South West Africa Affairs Act empowers the government to apply South African laws, including apartheid legislation, in South West Africa (Namibia).

Sept.

The UN Special Committee on Apartheid reports the failure of economic sanctions and criticises the United States, Britain, Japan and West Germany for ignoring the boycott.

1970
Feb.

The Bantu Homelands Citizenship Act declares black South Africans citizens of the appropriate homeland (whether or not they live in one).

1971
Mar.

Prime Minister John Botha announces his willingness to discuss the apartheid policy with leaders of African states.

June

The International Court of Justice declares South Africa's administration of Namibia illegal.

1972
June

Bophuthatswana joins Transkei as a self-governing black homeland; Ciskei follows in August and North Sotho in October.

1973
Feb.

Venda and Gazankulu become self-governing black homelands.

May

The Bantu Labour Relations Regulation Amendment allows black workers the right to strike following a wave of industrial action.

1974
Jan.

The opposition United Party-controlled Johannesburg announces an end to segregation in parks and libraries and other aspects of 'petty apartheid'; other local authorities, including one controlled by the National Party, follow suit.

Nov.

A majority of the black homelands refuse to accept proposals for full independence if they are denied a share in the country's wealth.

1975
June

Britain, France and the United States veto a UN Security Council vote to impose an arms embargo on South Africa. The independence of neighbouring Mozambique from Portugal provides a base for ANC guerrillas.

1976
June

There is a rising in Soweto, a township near Johannesburg, as thousands of school children demonstrate against the imposition of Afrikaans in education; by the end of the year over 500 are killed as anti-apartheid protests intensify.

| Oct. | Transkei becomes the first black homeland to be granted full independence; three million Xhosa lose their South African citizenship. |

1977
Aug.   Prime Minister Vorster offers increased political power to South Africa's Indian and Coloured communities but confines future black political activity to the homelands.

Sept.   The death in police custody of Black Consciousness Movement leader Stephen Biko provokes international protests and renewed violence in black townships.

Oct.   The government bans 18 anti-apartheid organisations and arrests leaders.

Dec.   Bophuthatswana becomes the second black homeland to receive independence.

1978
Sept.   P. W. Botha succeeds Vorster as Prime Minister and declares that he intends to improve race relations while retaining apartheid.

1979
Aug.   Prime Minister Botha declares his acceptance of a multi-racial society, proposes the end of petty apartheid and the establishment of a 'constellation' of South African states.

Sept.   Venda becomes the third black homeland to receive full independence. The South African Labour Minister announces that black workers can join the trade union of their choice, although multi-racial unions remain illegal.

1980
Apr.   Demonstrations by Coloured school children against unequal spending on education open weeks of class boycotts.

June   The ANC claims responsibility for four bombings at South African oil refineries as part of a wave of attacks on economic targets.

1981
Jan.   South African forces destroy three ANC guerrilla bases in Mozambique.

Feb.   The government establishes a multi-racial President's Council to consult with Indian, Coloured and white government-appointed representatives, the first mixed-race body since 1948; black South Africans remain excluded on the grounds that their political arena is in the homelands.

Aug.   Black squatters on the outskirts of Cape Town (mainly migrant workers' families) are deported to the Transkei homeland.

Nov.   As black trade union activity becomes increasingly politicised, 14 union leaders are arrested under the Suppression of Communism Act.

1982
Mar.   Prime Minister Botha expels 16 conservative members of the ruling National Party for opposing his reform policies.

July   Large-scale black strikes and disturbances begin in the Johannesburg gold mines.

Dec.   South African forces attack alleged ANC headquarters in Lesotho. ANC bombings delay the opening of South Africa's first nuclear power facility.

1983
May   ANC guerrillas explode car bomb outside the South African Air Force headquarters in Pretoria. Government responds by raiding the ANC base in Mozambique.

Aug.   A United Democratic Front (UDF) is formed by 550 trade unions, community and religious bodies as a multi-racial umbrella anti-apartheid organisation; government declares the million-strong body a front for the banned ANC.

Nov.   Prime Minister Botha wins overwhelming support in an all-white referendum on proposals to grant limited legislative power to the Indian and Coloured communities; the communities themselves are divided over the plans. There is a widespread black boycott of elections to townships councils with limited authority.

1984
Feb.   South Africa and Angola agree on withdrawal of South African troops from Angola and an end to Angolan support of SWAPO guerrillas; the agreement falters by the end of the year.

Mar.   South Africa and Mozambique negotiate the Nkomati Accord under which Mozambique agrees to close ANC guerrilla bases in the country; there is a decline in ANC armed action in South Africa.

Aug.   There are widespread boycotts in elections to the coloured chamber of a new tri-cameral parliament.

Sept.   Botha is elected South Africa's first executive President; he appoints the first Cabinet ever to include non-white members, with Indian and coloured ministers without portfolio.

Nov.   The UDF and black trade unions launch a major strike against government policies; the white business community criticises the detention without trial of strike leaders.

1985
June   South African forces raid ANC bases in Botswana. The ANC announces it will intensify guerrilla attacks in South Africa.

July   President Botha introduces an indefinite state of emergency giving police sweeping powers as communal violence grows in black townships.

Aug.   Black and Asian members of the UDF are charged with treason. President Botha announces there is no question of ending apartheid.

Sept.   President Botha announces proposals for change, including restoration of citizenship (but not political rights) to blacks deprived of it under the homelands scheme, but he refuses to negotiate with the ANC.

Nov.   Black unions establish the Congress of South African Trade Unions (COSATU) and call for Botha's resignation and abolition of the pass laws.

1986
Jan.   President Botha says that South Africa has 'outgrown' apartheid, proposes the release of ANC leader Nelson Mandela and offers black participation in a national advisory council.

Mar.   President Botha lifts the state of emergency; over this period more than 750 people have been killed and 8,000 arrested.

Apr.   President Botha announces that the pass laws will be repealed.

May   As tension grows in the ruling National Party over Botha's reform policy, South African forces attack alleged ANC bases in Botswana, Zambia and Zimbabwe.

June   President Botha reimposes the state of emergency; a thousand anti-apartheid activists are arrested. Over 65% of black workers join a one-day general strike called to commemorate the 10th anniversary of the Soweto rising.

Oct.   The United States imposes economic sanctions on South Africa.

Dec.   President Botha declares that South Africa is threatened by 'revolutionary onslaught' and strengthens the state of emergency.

1987
July   Afrikaner liberals hold discussions with ANC leaders in Senegal and issue the Dakar Declaration calling for an end to apartheid.

1988
Sept.   The government withdraws a planned extension of the Group Areas Act, the cornerstone of apartheid.

Dec.   Nelson Mandela is moved to a half-way house rather than being returned to prison after medical treatment.

1989
Feb.   Frederick de Klerk succeeds Botha as National Party leader.

May   Reform is promised by de Klerk but he denies the possibility of black majority rule in South Africa.

Sept.   Elections see a fall in National Party support; newly elected President de Klerk promises reform and meets leading opposition figures.

Oct.   Former ANC leader Walter Sisulu and seven other prominent black nationalists are released from prison; ANC holds its first rally in South Africa since being banned in 1962.

Nov.   President de Klerk desegregates South African beaches and promises to repeal the Separate Amenities Act.

Dec.   President de Klerk meets Nelson Mandela to discuss government–ANC negotiations.

1990
Jan.   Mandela appeals for the government to enter into negotiations to prevent 'civil strife and ruin'.

Feb.   President de Klerk announces an end to the ANC ban, the legalisation of the Communist Party, Pan-Africanist Congress and other opposition organisations and calls for 'reconstruction and reconciliation'; Mandela is released after 27 years in prison.

1991
June   The dismantling of apartheid legislation begins with the repeal of the Group Areas Act.

1992
Oct.   The Constitutional Amendment Act opens the way for black membership of the Cabinet.

1993
Feb.   President de Klerk appoints the first black Cabinet members.

1994
Apr.

South Africa holds its first multi-racial elections; the ANC takes 62% of the vote.

May

Mandela is inaugurated as President with de Klerk as deputy.

BIOGRAPHIES

Abbott Robert Sengstacke (1879–1940) United States civil rights activist and journalist. Born in Georgia, Abbott practised law until founding a black newspaper, the *Chicago Defender* in 1905. The *Defender* became a potent weapon in the campaign against racial discrimination and segregation and encouraged black Americans to migrate to the Northern states. A member of the State Race Relations Commission following the Chicago race riots of 1919, Abbott was also prominent in the National Urban League.

Abernathy Ralph (1926–90) United States clergyman and civil rights leader. Ordained as a Baptist minister in 1948, Abernathy became pastor of the First Baptist Church in Montgomery, Alabama, in 1951. He acted with Martin Luther King Jr (1929–68) as a leader of the successful 1955–56 Montgomery bus boycott, going on to become founding secretary-treasurer of the SCLC in 1957. A close aide to King, Abernathy became SCLC vice president in 1961. Appointed SCLC president following King's assassination in 1968, Abernathy organised the Poor People's Campaign and Resurrection City in Washington DC. He resigned the SCLC presidency in 1977, ran unsuccessfully for Congress in 1978 and supported the Republican presidential candidate Ronald Reagan in 1980. His autobiography *And the Walls Came Tumbling Down* (1989) aroused controversy over his criticisms of King.

Afonso I (?–c1545) Ruler of the Kongo kingdom (present day Angola and Congo) from 1506. The son of a Christian convert, Afonso protested to King Manuel of Portugal over the activities of Portuguese traders in copper, ivory and slaves in the Kongo. Beginning in 1526 he issued a number of decrees in which he unsuccessfully attempted to place limits on the slave trade. In 1540 a group of traders attempted to assassinate Afonso in church but his authority was not strong enough to secure the expulsion of the Portuguese.

Allen Richard (1760–1831) United States clergyman and black rights leader. Born a slave, Allen became a Methodist preacher and, with his owner's encouragement, worked to buy his freedom, taking the name Allen. In response to increasing racism among white Methodists in Philadelphia, Allen, with fellow preacher Absalom Jones (1746–1818), established the first independent black organisation in the United States, the Free African Society, as a mutual aid group in 1787. The Society developed into the African Church of Philadelphia and in 1794 Allen founded what would become the first independent black denomination, the Africa Methodist Episcopal Church, and was appointed its first bishop in 1799. With Jones, Allen organised black relief activities during a yellow fever epidemic in 1793 and raised a black militia unit in the 1812 war with Britain. Allen, with Jones and the abolitionist James Forten (1766–1842), opposed the American Colonisation Society's attempts to encourage black emigration. He also served as president of the first Negro Convention.

Anthony Susan Brownell (1820–1906) United States abolitionist and female suffrage activist. Active in the Massachusetts temperance movement from 1848 to 1863, Anthony worked for the American Anti-Slavery Society from

1856 to 1861 and in 1863 founded the Women's Loyal League to campaign for abolition. Following the abolition of slavery in 1865, Anthony concentrated on the suffrage campaign, forming the National Woman Suffrage Association with Elizabeth Cady Stanton in 1869.

Attucks Crispus (1723–70) American independence activist. The son of a slave and a native American, Attucks escaped from slavery in 1759 and became a sailor. After attending meetings condemning British taxation of the American colonies, Attucks wrote a protest letter to the provincial governor. He was killed with four other demonstrators by British soldiers in a clash in Boston on 5 March 1770 and became one of the first casualties in the developing rebellion against Britain.

Bailey Gamaliel (1807–59) United States abolitionist journalist. Bailey edited the first anti-slavery newspaper in the western United States, the *Cincinnati Philanthropist* (later the *Daily Herald and Philanthropist*) from 1836–43, continuing publication despite attacks by pro-slavery demonstrators. In 1847, Bailey was appointed editor of the *National Era*, the American and Foreign Anti-Slavery Society's weekly paper. He retained this position until his death and was responsible for the serialisation of *Uncle Tom's Cabin* in the early 1850s.

Baker Ella (1903–86) United States civil rights activist. Granddaughter of slaves, Baker joined the Young Negroes Co-operative League in 1930, becoming its national director in 1931. After becoming active in the NAACP in 1940, Baker was director of branches from 1943 to 1946 and led a campaign to desegregate New York City schools. A co-founder of the civil rights fundraising group In Struggle in 1956, Baker moved to Atlanta to become organiser of the SCLC in 1957, leading a voter registration drive. An opponent of over-centralised leadership, Baker left the SCLC in 1959, was prominent in the organisation of the SNCC in 1960 and played an important part in desegregation of the Democratic Party in Mississippi. Returning to New York in 1964, she continued to campaign for civil rights and in support of African independence struggles.

Benezet Anthony (1713–84) United States abolitionist. A Quaker, Benezet taught free and slave blacks in Philadelphia before encouraging the Quakers to establish a school for free blacks in 1773. He persuaded the local Quakers to oppose slavery and was prominent in the campaign to establish the Pennsylvania Society for the Abolition of Slavery in 1775. Benezet rejected white supremacist views, wrote numerous anti-slavery pamphlets and conducted an extensive correspondence on the subject with, among others, Benjamin Franklin, Granville Sharpe and John Wesley. Four hundred black mourners attended his funeral.

Bethune Mary McLeod (1875–1955) United States educationalist, civil rights and feminist activist. In 1904, Bethune founded the Daytona Normal and Industrial Institute for Negro Girls (later the Bethune–Cookman College). A member of the National Urban League executive board and an active opponent of the Ku Klux Klan, Bethune was founder and president of the National Association of Colored Women's Clubs from 1924 to 1928, she established the National Association of Colored Women in 1926 and was president of the National Council of Negro Women from 1935 to 1949. President Franklin Roosevelt (1882–1945) appointed her a special advisor on Minority Affairs in 1935 and from 1936 to 1944 she was Director of the Division of Negro Affairs of the National Youth Administration.

Bibb Henry (1815–54) United States abolitionist and Pan-Africanist activist. The son of a slave and her owner, Bibb escaped from slavery in 1842 and lectured against the institution while campaigning for the abolitionist Liberty Party in Michigan. Bibb escaped with his wife to Canada when the 1850 Fugitive Slave Act came into force and established the first black Canadian newspaper, the *Voice of the Fugitive.* With other abolitionists, he formed the Refugee Home Society Plan to provide 25 acre plots of land to emancipated slaves. Bibb also founded the North American Convention of Colored People and its offshoot, the American Continental and West India League, a movement for Pan-Africanist unity.

Birney James Gillespie (1792–1857) United States abolitionist and politician. A lawyer, Birney worked as an agent for the American Colonisation Society from 1832 to 1834 before becoming an abolitionist. In 1834 he freed slaves he had inherited and was prominent in organising the Kentucky Anti-Slavery Society in 1835. Appointed executive secretary of the American Anti-Slavery Society in 1837, Birney sided with the gradualists in the argument which split the Society in 1839, arguing that emancipation could be achieved legally through political and religious pressure. He was vice-president of the World Anti-Slavery Convention in London in 1840. A member of the abolitionist Liberty Party, he was nominated as the party's presidential candidate in 1840 and 1844.

Blyden Edward Wilmot (1832–1912) United States emigrationist and Liberian politician. Born in St Thomas in the Caribbean, Blyden moved to the United States and then emigrated to the black African republic of Liberia in 1850. He worked as an academic and was active in encouraging black American emigration to Liberia. Blyden was Liberia's Secretary of State from 1864 to 1866, Minister of the Interior from 1880 to 1882, ambassador to Britain in 1877–78 and 1892, and Director of Education from 1901 to 1906. Among his many works on the black experience is *Christianity, Islam and the Negro Race.*

Bogle Paul (c1825–65) Jamaican cleric and civil rights activist. Born a slave, Bogle was appointed deacon of the Baptist church in Stony Gut in the early 1860s, and worked with George Gordon (c1820–65) to improve the conditions of the local poor. In October 1865 Bogle and Gordon led two protest marches into Morant Bay, the second of which developed into a riot in which several whites were killed. Following a declaration of martial law,

Bogle was arrested and executed after a summary trial. After Jamaican independence, Bogle was named a national hero.

Boukman (dates unknown) Haitian slave revolt leader. Boukman led a black slave rising in 1791, joining forces with mulattos fighting against discriminatory legislation which limited political rights to whites and free blacks. During the rebellion a large number of plantations were destroyed and 10,000 slaves and mulattos were killed.

Brougham Henry (1778–1868) British politician and abolitionist. A radical lawyer, Brougham became MP for Camelford in 1810, making abolitionism a prime campaigning issue. He stood unsuccessfully for a seat in the slave trading port of Liverpool but was returned for Winchelsea in 1816. Becoming a peer and appointed Lord Chancellor in 1830, Brougham played a leading part in ensuring the progress of the legislation which abolished slavery.

Brown John (1800–59) United States abolitionist. Born into an anti-slavery family, Brown helped finance the publication of David Walker's 1829 *An Appeal to the Coloured Citizens of the World*, gave land to fugitive slaves and worked with the Underground Railroad. In 1855 he killed five people in a pro-slavery town in Kansas in retaliation for an attack on an anti-slavery town. To further his plan for a slave uprising, Brown led a 22–strong raid on the federal arsenal at Harper's Ferry in October 1859. Brown was captured, convicted of treason and executed in December. After his death, he was seen as an abolitionist martyr by many Northerners.

Brown William Wells (c1814–84) United States writer and abolitionist. The son of slave mother and slave-owner father, Brown escaped from slavery in 1834, adopting the name of a Quaker who helped him in educating himself. Brown lectured for the Massachusetts and New York Anti-Slavery Societies and worked with the Underground Railroad. Following the success of his autobiography, *Narrative of William W. Brown, a Fugitive Slave* (1847), Brown lectured on abolitionism in the United States and Europe, publishing *The American Fugitive in Europe* in 1855. Brown went on to produce a number of novels and historical works with slavery and emancipation as a theme. A novel on the relationship between President Thomas Jefferson and his slave Sally Hemmings was banned in the United States until 1969.

Bruce Blanche Kelso (1841–98) United States politician. Born a slave in Virginia, Bruce established a black school in 1861 and, following emancipation in 1865, became a planter, revenue collector and school superintendent. A member of the United States Senate from 1875 to 1881, Bruce was the first black American to serve a full term. He went on to serve as a Treasury registrar from 1871 to 1889 and District of Columbia recorder of deeds from 1889 to 1893.

Butler Tubal Uriah ('Buzz') (1891–1977) Trinidadian civil rights activist and politician. Born in Grenada, Butler served in the British Army in World War One and moved to Trinidad in 1921. Successively a pipe fitter and a pastor,

Butler joined the Trinidad Workingman's Association and led a hunger march in 1935. The British colonial authority's attempt to arrest him led to riots throughout the Caribbean in 1936. Butler was imprisoned for sedition from 1937 to 1939 and detained without trial from 1939 to 1945. Butler was denied power by the British governor in 1950, despite his British Empire Workers', Peasants' and Ratepayers' Union having won a majority of seats. He moved to England, where he lived until 1956.

Buxton Thomas Fowell (1786–1845) British MP and abolitionist. A Quaker and social reform activist, Buxton was elected MP for Weymouth in 1818. One of the founders in 1823 of the Society for the Mitigation and Gradual Abolition of Slavery Throughout the British Dominions, Buxton became the body's parliamentary spokesman on the retirement in 1825 of William Wilberforce (1759–1833). With the passing of abolition legislation in 1833, Buxton wrote *The African Slave Trade and Its Remedy* (1839), encouraging the British government to negotiate anti-slavery treaties with African rulers. An expedition sent to the Niger delta in 1841 met with disaster and disappointment and its failure was said to have contributed to Buxton's death.

Carmichael Stokely (1941–98) United States civil rights activist. Born in Trinidad, Carmichael moved with his family to Harlem and participated in voter registration drives and civil rights demonstrations before graduating from Howard University in 1964. Becoming a full-time worker with the Student Nonviolent Coordinating Committee (SNCC) in 1964, he was appointed chairman in 1966. On a march in Mississippi, Carmichael used the expression 'Black Power', which was soon taken up by radical activists. Carmichael left the SNCC in 1968, becoming Black Panther Party prime minister, resigning in 1969. He co-wrote *Black Power: The Political Liberation of America* in 1970 and in 1973 moved to Uganda, where he became a citizen and changed his name to Kwame Touré. He later returned to the United States.

Casas Bartolomé de las (1474–1566) Spanish cleric and advocate of African slavery. Born in Seville, de las Casas accompanied Columbus on his third voyage to the Americas in 1498. Settling in Hispaniola in 1502, de las Casas soon expressed concern at the Spanish treatment of the indigenous population. In 1511 he recommended the importation of Africans on the grounds that they were more suited to hard labour. It was from this point that the growth of African slavery in the New World began. He later protested that he had intended Africans to work as free labourers rather than slaves and criticised their treatment. Ordained in 1510, he joined the Dominicans in 1522 and was appointed Bishop of Chiapas in 1543. Unpopular among the colonists of New Spain (Mexico), de las Casas returned to Spain in 1547. Continuing his concern with the indigenous population, de las Casas wrote a treatise on their slavery in 1552.

Céspedes Carlos Manuel de (1819–74) Cuban revolutionary and abolitionist. Born into a plantation family settled in Cuba since 1517, Céspedes completed his law studies in Spain, where he was involved in the 1843 revolution and exiled to France. On his return to Cuba, Céspedes became a lawyer and writer and joined an underground movement seeking independence from Spain. As leader of the independence forces in Oriente province, he declared Cuban independence in October 1868 and said that, 'A free Cuba cannot be a slave Cuba.' Céspedes freed his own slaves but as a supporter of overall gradual abolition came under criticism from both supporters and opponents of slavery. He accepted slave recruits into his rebel army with their owners' permission (who, in turn, would then be compensated). General slave emancipation was proclaimed on his election as president of the revolutionary government in April 1869. Deposed in 1873, Céspedes was executed by Spanish soldiers.

Chisholm Shirley Anita St Hill (born 1924) United States politician. The first black woman to be elected to Congress, Chisholm served in the New York State Assembly as a Democrat from 1964 to 1968 and in the House of Representatives from 1969 to 1983. A nursery teacher, Chisholm worked in child welfare from 1959 to 1964 and her autobiography, *Unbought and Unbossed*, was published in 1970. In 1972 she unsuccessfully sought nomination as Democratic presidential candidate. Returning to teaching, she was co-founder of the National Political Congress of Black Women.

Christophe Henri (1767–1820) Haitian revolutionary leader. Born in Grenada, Christophe moved to Saint Domingue (now Haiti) after working as a sailor. Joining the revolt against France led by Toussaint L'Ouverture (1746–1803), Christophe became a general in the rebel forces. After independence, he divided the island with Alexandre Pétion (1770–1818) and became President of Haiti in 1807. He proclaimed himself King Henri I in 1811 but committed suicide following an army mutiny against him.

Cinquez Joseph (Cinque) (c1811–1879) African slave rebellion leader. A member of the West African Mendi people, Cinque was taken captive by the Ley people and sold to a Spanish slave trader. In 1839 Cinque led the seizure of the slave ship *Amistad*, sailing from Cuba, and attempted to force the crew to return the vessel to Africa. However, the *Amistad* was taken in custody by the USS *Washington*. Cinque and others were charged with piracy. Cinque learnt some English and the rudiments of Christianity before being granted his liberty in 1841. He returned to Africa to find his village destroyed and his family missing and lived with missionaries. Shortly before his death he requested a Christian burial.

Clark Septima Poinsette (1898–1987) United States civil rights activist. Born in South Carolina, Clark was dismissed from her post as a teacher for refusing to resign from the NAACP in 1956. A member of the SCLC, Clark organised Freedom Schools in the Southern states to assist black Americans through literacy tests imposed as a condition for voting.

Clarkson Thomas (1760–1846) British abolitionist. After winning a Cambridge University prize for an essay on slavery in 1785 (published in 1786 as *An Essay on the Slavery and Commerce of the Human Species, Particularly the African)*, Clarkson met anti-slavery activist Granville Sharp (1735–1813). In 1787 they formed the Society for Effecting the Abolition of the Slave Trade, with Clarkson taking responsibility for research. He was also instrumental in persuading William Wilberforce (1759–1833) to press the campaign in the House of Commons. Clarkson's pamphlet, *A Summary View of the Slave Trade and of the Probable Consequences of its Abolition* (1787), gave a graphic account of the horrors of the trade. Clarkson visited France following the 1789 Revolution in an unsuccessful attempt to persuade the National Assembly to promote legislation against slavery. Following the abolition of British participation in the slave trade in 1807, Clarkson co-operated with Thomas Fowell Buxton (1786–1845) to establish the Society for the Mitigation and Gradual Abolition of Slavery Throughout the British Dominions, of which he was a vice president.

Clay Cassius Marcellus (1810–1903) United States abolitionist. Clay advocated gradual emancipation of slaves while serving three terms in the Kentucky legislature from 1835 to 1840. He established an anti-slavery weekly, the *True American*, in 1845, but the press was destroyed by pro-slavery demonstrators. Clay renewed publication in Ohio and then returned to Louisville, Kentucky, where he renamed the paper the *Examiner.*

Clay Henry (1777–1852) United States politician. A lawyer, Clay was elected to the Kentucky state legislature in 1803 and to the United States Senate in 1806. A founding member of the American Colonisation Society in 1816, and president from 1836, he favoured the gradual abolition of slavery. Clay was closely involved in formulating the 1820 Missouri Compromise and the Compromise of 1850, both of which attempted to resolve the problem of a nation divided between slavery and anti-slavery. He was unsuccessful in his attempts to become President in 1824, 1832 and 1844.

Cleaver (Leroy) Eldridge (1935–98) United States activist and writer. Imprisoned for attempted murder in 1958, Cleaver read widely in politics and history, including writing by Malcolm X (1925–65). On his release in 1966 Cleaver joined the Black Panther Party, succeeding Huey Newton (1942–89) as Minister of Information in 1967. His collection of political essays, *Soul on Ice*, was a best-seller in 1968. In the same year, Cleaver stood as the Peace and Freedom Party's presidential candidate. Urging black Americans to mount an armed rising, but facing parole violation charges, Cleaver fled to Algeria where he remained in exile for seven years, criticising the Panthers' turn to community politics. Cleaver returned to the United States in 1975, proclaiming himself a born-again Christian and a conservative in *Soul on Fire* (1978).

Coffin Levi (1798–1877) United States abolitionist. A Quaker businessman, Coffin became involved in the Underground Railroad when he moved to Indiana in 1826. He also published an abolitionist newspaper from his store. During his 20 years of activity, he provided a haven for thousands of fleeing slaves, becoming known as 'President of the Underground Railroad' and his home as 'Grand Central Station'. Coffin's store also sold goods produced by free blacks. Following emancipation in 1865, Coffin played a prominent part in the Western Freedmen's Aid Society, raising $100,000 in Europe for its activities. He was a delegate to the International Anti-Slavery Conference in Paris in 1867.

Coffy (died 1763) African slave rebellion leader. Born in West Africa, Coffy led a rising of slaves in the colony of Berbice (now part of Guyana). As divisions grew between Berbice-born and African-born slaves, Coffy relinquished leadership of the rebellion and committed suicide. Following Guyana's independence, Coffy became the country's first national hero.

Colbert Jean-Baptiste (1619–83) French administrator. Born into a merchant family, Colbert rose rapidly in the service of King Louis XIV, and was Controller General of Finance from 1685 and Secretary of State for the Navy from 1688. In these positions he administered a programme that carried France into a position of dominance in Europe. As Navy Secretary he built the Atlantic fleet by forcing African slaves into the crews, along with criminals. Colbert promoted the Code Noir, the ordinance on the treatment of slaves in French colonies issued in 1685.

Craft Ellen (1826–97) United States slave escapee. Born in Georgia, Craft escaped from slavery with her husband William through the Underground Railroad. The couple moved to England where William produced a description of their experiences in *Running a Thousand Miles for Freedom* in 1868. They later returned to Georgia and became farmers.

Crummell Alexander (1819–98) United States clergyman, writer and emigrationist. Denied admission to the Episcopal Church seminary because of his colour, Crummell was eventually ordained in 1844 and graduated from Cambridge University in 1853. A missionary and academic in Liberia from 1853–73, Crummell became convinced there was no future for black people in the United States and worked with the American Colonisation Society to encourage black emigration to Liberia. Following his return to the United States, Crummell participated in the 1893 Pan-African Congress in Chicago and was involved in the establishment of the American Negro Academy in 1897. In his inaugural address to the Academy, Crummell first used the expression 'the talented tenth'.

Cudjoe Colonel (dates unknown) Jamaican slave leader. Taken from West Africa to Jamaica as a slave, Cudjoe escaped to the island's Central Mountains in 1690 and became a Maroon leader. The First Maroon War with the English colonial authorities followed attacks on plantations led by Cudjoe and his brothers. After a treaty agreed in 1738, Cudjoe and his followers were granted their freedom. Cudjoe Day is celebrated in Jamaica on the first Monday in January.

Cuffe Paul (1759–1817) United States businessman and emigrationist. Born free, Cuffe worked on whaling and cargo vessels before establishing a trading business with his brother which prospered through blockade running in the War of Independence. Cuffe developed a fleet and a shipyard. An activist for black rights, in 1780 he led protests over the taxation without representation of blacks denied the right to vote in Massachusetts. He opened a school for black children in 1797. Pessimistic about the future of free black Americans, Cuffe advocated black emigration to Africa and in 1814 unsuccessfully petitioned the government for funds. In 1815 he led an expedition of 40 black Americans to Sierra Leone at his own expense. The settlement succeeded despite local white opposition.

Delany Martin Robison (1812–85) United States abolitionist and emigrationist. Born free, Robison began practising medicine in 1843, published a newspaper, the *Mystery*, from 1843 to 1847, and acted as co-editor with Frederick Douglass (1818–95) of the *North Star* from 1847 to 1849. Delany initially opposed the emigrationist American Colonisation Society, but changed his position following the passage of the Fugitive Slave Act in 1850, convening three emigration conventions from 1854 to 1858. His book *The Condition, Elevation, Emigration, and Destiny of the Colored People of the United States, Politically Considered*, published in 1852, advocated black separatism and aroused abolitionist criticism. In 1859 he visited Liberia and what is now Nigeria to begin development of a black American settlement. On his return to the United States, Delany became a major in the Union army, worked for the Freedmen's Bureau and stood unsuccessfully for the post of South Carolina lieutenant-governor in 1874. He continued writing and practising medicine until his death.

Dessalines Jean-Jacques (c1758–1806) Haitian revolutionary leader. Taken as a slave to Haiti from Guinea, Dessalines joined the revolt against the French led by Toussaint L'Ouverture (1746–1803) in 1791, becoming one of the leading figures. In 1803 he led the defeat of an attempted French invasion. Appointed governor, Dessalines proclaimed himself Emperor Jacques I in 1804 but was assassinated by army officers two years later.

Douglass Frederick (born Frederick Bailey) (1818–95) United States abolitionist and civil rights leader. Following an unsuccessful attempt in 1836, Bailey escaped from slavery to New York in 1838, changed his name to Douglass and married. After addressing the American Anti-Slavery Society, Douglass went on a lecture tour, published the *Narrative of the Life of Frederick Douglass* in 1845 and conducted abolitionist propaganda in England. On his return to the United States in 1847, he continued abolitionist activity, working with the Underground Railroad, and became involved in the campaign for women's rights. Arguing against dependence on white abolitionists and increasingly favouring slave rebellion, Douglass broke with William Lloyd Garrison (1805–79) and in 1847 set up the *North Star* (*Frederick Douglass' Paper* from 1851 to 1860). During the 1861–65 Civil War, Douglass met President Lincoln (1809–65) a number of times to discuss black issues and worked for the recruitment of black soldiers. In 1867 he rejected an offer by President Andrew Johnson to head the Freedman's Bureau and in 1870 became editor of the *New National Era*. Appointed president of the Freedman's Savings and Trust company in 1874, Douglass was appointed a United States Marshal in 1877 and recorder of deeds for Washington DC in 1880. From 1889 to 1891, Douglass was American consul-general to Haiti but resigned in protest against American business methods.

Du Bois William Edward Burghardt (1868–1963) United States academic, writer, civil rights and Pan-African activist. The first black American to be awarded a Ph.D. from Harvard in 1895, Du Bois taught at Atlanta University from 1897 to 1914. An organiser of the 1900 London Pan-African Conference, Du Bois published the influential *The Souls of Black Folk* in 1902, and played a leading part in forming the Niagara Movement in 1905 and the NAACP in 1909. Du Bois edited the NAACP journal *Crisis*. He became a member of the Socialist Party in 1911 and received the NAACP's Springarn Award in 1920. A supporter of the concept of the 'talented tenth', Du Bois rejected the conciliatory policies of Booker T. Washington (1856–1915) and actively confronted racism. By the 1930s Du Bois was taking an increasingly Pan-Africanist position and in 1934 he severed his connection with the NAACP, disagreeing with the movement's integrationism. After World War Two, Du Bois was involved in organising Pan-African conferences, was accused and acquitted of being a communist in 1951, joined the Communist Party in 1959 and moved to Ghana, where he died. Among his many works are *The Suppression of the Slave Trade in the United States of America 1638–1870* (1896), *Black Reconstruction* (1935) and *Dusk of Dawn* (1940).

Equiano Olaudah Benin (1745–?) Anti-slavery activist and writer. Born in Benin (now Nigeria), Equiano was kidnapped with his sister (from whom he was separated), and taken as a slave to Virginia in 1756. Moved to England in 1757, he was sold and taken to Montserrat, where he bought his freedom and returned to England. Appointed as commissary for stores in the abortive Sierra Leone settlement scheme in 1786, Equiano became increasingly active in the campaign against the slave trade and slavery. In 1792 he became a member of the radical London Corresponding Society. He is best known for his two volume autobiography, *The Interesting Narrative of the Life of Olaudah Equiano, or Gustavas Vassa, the African: by Himself*, originally published in 1790.

Evers Medgar Wiley (1925–63) United States civil rights activist. After army service in World War Two, Evers graduated from Alcorn State University and became the NAACP Mississippi field secretary. Active in black voter registration and leading boycotts of racially discriminating white-owned businesses, Evers was shot outside his home in 1963. A white supremacist charged with the killing was tried twice in 1964 but all-white juries failed to reach a verdict. He was finally convicted by a mixed jury in 1994.

Farmer, James (1920–99) United States civil rights leader. Farmer declared on graduating from Howard University in 1941 that his ambition was to 'destroy segregation'. Farmer worked for trade unions and civil rights groups before becoming founding director of the Congress of Racial Equality (CORE) in 1942 and leading sit-ins in segregated Chicago restaurants. In 1961 Farmer organised the Freedom Rides to integrate interstate transport and to expose the depths of segregation in the Southern states. He missed the opportunity to address the 1963 March on Washington by refusing to accept bail following his arrest at a demonstration. Farmer left CORE in 1966 and in 1969 accepted the offer of a government post from President Nixon. He severed all connection with CORE in 1976 and unsuccessfully attempted to form a new civil rights organisation in 1980.

Farrakhan Louis Haleem Abdul (born 1933) United States religious and black separatist leader. Born Louis Eugene Walcott, Farrakhan was recruited to the black Muslim Nation of Islam by Malcolm X (1925–65) in 1955. He opposed Malcolm X when he left the movement in 1965, succeeding him as leader of the Harlem Mosque. Farrakhan (as he became in 1965), resigned when the movement abandoned black nationalist separatism in 1975, establishing a rival Nation of Islam. Farrakhan's body – with its advocacy of racial separatism, black nationalism and economic self-sufficiency – soon eclipsed its rival. Farrakhan – despite offending liberal opinion because of his alleged anti-semitism – emerged as a leading black figure with his organisation of the 1995 Million Man March on Washington. In 1996 he reportedly asked President Nelson Mandela for land in South Africa for resettlement of a million black Americans.

Fauset Jessie (1882–1961) United States writer and black activist. A teacher, Fauset was literary editor of the NAACP journal *The Crisis* from 1920 to 1923 and was then appointed managing editor. A prominent figure in the Harlem Renaissance, Fauset's novels have useful material on the 'Talented Tenth' and issues affecting the black middle class in the 1920s and 1930s.

Forten Charlotte (1837–1915) United States abolitionist activist. The descendant of abolitionists, Forten joined the Massachusetts Anti-Slavery Society before she was 18 and in 1856 became the first black teacher of white students in the United States. Forced to give up education through ill-health, she became a correspondent for the *National Anti-Slavery Standard* and the *Atlantic Monthly*. At the end of the American Civil War she worked assisting emancipated slaves.

Forten James (1766–1842) United States businessman and abolitionist activist. A seaman during the American War of Independence, Forten became owner of a sailmaking company. In 1800 a petition against slavery he organised with Richard Allen (1760–1831) was rejected by Congress and in 1812 he organised, again with Allen, a 2,500-strong black force to defend Philadelphia during the war with Britain. Forten encouraged William Lloyd Garrison (1805–79) to take up abolitionist activity and organised the American Anti-Slavery Society in 1833. He was also active in temperance and peace movements.

Fortune Timothy Thomas (1856–1928) United States Pan-African activist and journalist. Born a slave, he became a printer and attended Howard University after emancipation. He established two newspapers, the *New York Age* in 1879 and the *New York Freeman* in 1884, and was co-organiser of the Afro-American Press Association. Fortune formed the National Afro-American League (a precursor of the NAACP) to agitate for black nationalism in 1890. Among his many works are *Black and White: Land, Labor and Politics in the United States* (1884) and *The Negro in Politics* (1886).

Garnet Henry Highland (1815–82) United States clergyman, abolitionist and emigrationist. Born a slave, he escaped in 1824. Originally an advocate of emancipation through peaceful political action, Garnet divided the 1843 National Negro Convention with a 'Call to Rebellion' in which – inspired by David Walker (c1796–1830) – he urged a slave revolt and general strike. In 1849 he became a supporter of emigrationism, establishing an African Civilisation Society, though he remained an abolitionist propagandist and lectured on the subject in England and Scotland. In 1852 he moved to Jamaica as a missionary but on his return to the United States had lost much of his influence. In 1873 Garnet called for an invasion of the Spanish Caribbean colony of Cuba to emancipate the slaves. In 1881 he was appointed United States minister to Liberia but died within two months of his arrival.

Garrison William Lloyd (1805–79) United States journalist and abolitionist. Editor of a temperance newspaper, and initially a supporter of the American Colonisation Society, Garrison became an advocate of immediate emancipation after meeting the abolitionist Benjamin Lundy in 1829. Garrison was imprisoned for attacking slave owners in Lundy's *The Genius of Universal Emancipation* and from 1831 to 1865 he published *The Liberator*, an abolitionist paper with a small circulation but a wide influence. He formed the New England Anti-Slavery Society in 1832, attracting support from Wendell Phillips (1811–84) and the writer Henry Thoreau (1817–62). Garrison divided the American Anti-Slavery Society (established in 1833) with his demand for equal rights for women and for a more active campaign against slavery. His radical position dominated the Society and he was the organisation's president from 1843 to 1865. He refused to vote for a government that permitted slavery to continue, causing a split with Frederick Douglass (1818–95) over the efficacy of using the Constitution to combat the institution, and advocated the separation of the free North from the slave South. Lincoln's 1863 Emancipation Proclamation won Garrison's support.

Garvey Marcus Mosiah (1887–1940) Jamaican Pan-Africanist leader. A printer at 14, Garvey worked in Central and Latin America before settling in London in 1912 where he worked for the Pan-Africanist *Africa Times and Orient Review*. Returning to Jamaica in 1914, Garvey established the Universal Negro Improvement Association (UNIA), moving its headquarters to Harlem in 1917. Building on black migration to the North and disappointment with the results of participating in World War One, Garvey's UNIA emphasised black economic self-reliance and political self-determination and aimed at a spiritual (and physical) return to an independent and unified Africa. Garvey was elected UNIA president-general at its first convention in 1920. The UNIA set up a number of businesses, including the Black Star Steamship Line, and a journal, *The Negro World*. Opposed by the NAACP and the government, Garvey was convicted on mail fraud charges in 1922 following the shipping line's collapse. Released in 1925, Garvey returned to Jamaica, where he presided over two UNIA conventions and became a Kingston municipal councillor. Moving to London in 1935, Garvey continued publishing his journal *Black Man* and held annual UNIA conventions in Canada but died in poverty. Garvey was proclaimed Jamaica's first national hero and influenced both Rastafarianism and the Nation of Islam.

Hall Prince (c1735–1807) United States Masonic and emigrationist leader. Born in Barbados, Hall fought in the American War of Independence. In 1777 he was an organiser of a petition to abolish slavery in Massachusetts. Unable to find a Freemason's lodge that would accept black members, he established the first black lodge in 1784 which was granted official recognition in 1787. Among the lodge members was the activist cleric Richard Allen (1760–1831). Hall called on fellow masons to work to abolish slavery and to 'bear up under the daily insults you meet within the streets of Boston'. In 1787, Hall petitioned the Massachusetts legislature to provide funds for the voluntary return of poor black Americans to Africa and later sued unsuccessfully for equal education for black children.

Henson Josiah (1789–1883) United States abolitionist activist. Born a slave in Maryland, Henson became a Methodist Episcopal preacher in 1828, escaping from slavery in 1830. Active in the Underground Railroad, Henson met Harriet Beecher Stowe (1811–96), who reputedly based her influential *Uncle Tom's Cabin* on his experiences. He travelled to England to be given an award by British abolitionist campaigners.

Heyrick Elizabeth (née Coltman) (1769–1831) British abolitionist activist. A Quaker influenced by the ideas of the radical Thomas Paine (1737–1809), Heyrick organised a sugar boycott in Leicester before taking a prominent part in the founding of the Birmingham Ladies Society for the Relief of Negro Slaves (later the Female Society for Birmingham), of which she was treasurer. Heyrick led the Leicester Ladies Anti-Slavery Society and helped establish a coalition of women's abolitionist groups. Her pamphlet *Immediate not Gradual Abolition* (1824) criticised the official position of the Society for the Mitigation and Gradual Abolition of Slavery Throughout the British Dominions and its male leaders. After attempts by, among others, William Wilberforce (1759–1833) to suppress this view, the Society adopted her position in 1830.

Honeychurch Mary (1795–1865) British abolitionist activist. A travelling minister for the Society of Friends (the Quakers), and the mother of ten children, Honeychurch devoted much of her attention to the abolitionist movement. She was secretary of the Birmingham Ladies Society for the Relief of Negro Slaves (later the Female Society for Birmingham) from 1825 to 1836 and treasurer from 1845 to 1861. She was also active in the temperance movement.

Jackson Jesse Louis (born 1941) United States civil rights activist and politician. Jackson became an activist while studying at the Chicago Theological Seminary, joining the SCLC in 1965 and became an associate of Martin Luther King Jr (1929–68). In 1967 was appointed national chairman of Operation Breadbasket, the black community organisation. An organiser of Resurrection City in 1968 (when he was also ordained), Jackson left the SCLC in 1971 to head Operation PUSH (People United to Save (later Serve) Humanity) and in 1984 unsuccessfully sought nomination as the Democratic presidential candidate, hampered by accusations of anti-semitism through his association with Nation of Islam leader Louis Farrakhan (born 1933). Jackson established the National Rainbow Coalition in 1986, made a second attempt at the nomination in 1988 and left Operation PUSH in 1989. Following a period as an unofficial diplomat (he secured the release of Iraqi hostages in 1991), Jackson returned to Operation PUSH in 1996.

Jacobs Harriet Ann (1813–97) United States abolitionist activist. Born a slave, and sexually abused, Jacobs escaped in 1835, living in hiding in North Carolina until she reached New York in 1842. Here she became an abolitionist activist and, after gaining her freedom through purchase, wrote *Incidents in the Life of a Slave girl: Written by Herself* (1861), making hitherto unexpressed points about the sexual abuse of female slaves. During the 1861–65 Civil War, Jacobs raised money for black refugees, going on to raise funds in England to build a black orphanage in Georgia and to work in education. In 1896 she was involved in the establishment of the National Association of Colored Women.

Johnson Lyndon Baines (1908–73) United States politician. A Democratic Congressman from 1937 to 1949 (serving in the Navy from 1941 to 1942) and Senator from 1949, Johnson was elected Vice-President in 1960 and succeeded President Kennedy (1917–63) on his assassination. He won the 1964 election by a landslide. A staunch advocate of civil rights, Johnson found a success in pushing through legislation that had eluded his predecessor, including the 1964 Civil Rights Act, the 1965 Voting Rights Act and the 1968 Fair Housing Act. However, Johnson's escalation of the war in Vietnam undermined his hopes of building a 'Great Society' and, as rioting intensified in black ghettos and protests against the effects of the war grew, he withdrew as presidential candidate in 1968.

Jordan Edward (1800–69) Jamaican civil rights activist and journalist. Born free in Jamaica, Jordan became prominent as a campaigner for civil rights for free blacks and established the newspaper, *The Watchman*, in 1829. He used the newspaper to attack the British authorities and agitate against slavery. In 1832 he was imprisoned for six months for sedition. Following emancipation,

Jordan became a member of the House of Assembly, where he agitated for a franchise reform and served as Speaker from 1861 to 1864.

Kennedy, John Fitzgerald (1917–63) United States politician. Following World War Two service in the Navy, Kennedy was a Democratic Congressman from 1947 to 1952 and a Senator from 1953 to 1960, when he was elected President. In office, Kennedy appeared unwilling to alienate his Southern 'Dixiecrat' supporters by pushing promised civil rights legislation forcefully. The measures he did propose were successfully taken up by his successor Lyndon Johnson (1908–73) following Kennedy's assassination in 1963.

King Martin (Michael) Luther Jr (1929–68) United States civil rights leader. Appointed a pastor in Montgomery, Alabama, in 1954, King came into prominence during the 1955–56 bus boycott, when he was elected president of the Montgomery Improvement Association. In 1957, he became founding president of the Southern Christian Leadership Conference (SCLC), taking major responsibility for fund-raising and propaganda. Committed to non-violent civil disobedience, King's attempts to build alliances with liberal whites provoked accusations of Communist sympathies. In the early 1960s, King was involved in a number of campaigns – notably in Albany, Georgia and Birmingham, Alabama, and on the Selma-Montgomery march – and made his celebrated 'I have a dream' speech at the 1963 march on Washington. From 1966 King was increasingly challenged by younger black activists advocating black self-defence while riots in the Northern ghettos undermined his pacifist teaching. King turned to economic issues and to criticism of the war in Vietnam and was murdered while supporting a garbage workers' strike in Memphis. King's birthday was designated a national holiday in the United States in 1983.

Knight Anne (1781–1862) British abolitionist, feminist and radical activist. A Quaker from an abolitionist family, Knight formed a branch of the Women's Anti-Slavery Society in Chelmsford, Essex, in 1830, and worked with Thomas Clarkson (1760–1846). An advocate of immediate emancipation without compensation, Knight lectured on abolitionism in France in 1834. A feminist, she criticised the attitude of the predominantly male leadership of the Society for the Mitigation and Gradual Abolition of Slavery Throughout the British Dominions and their attempts to prevent women participating in the 1840 World Anti-Slavery Convention. Following the success of the abolition campaign, Knight was active in Chartism and the campaign for women's rights, establishing the first society for women's suffrage in 1851. The free slave village of Knightsville in Jamaica was named after her.

Lincoln Abraham (1809–65) United States politician. Largely self-educated, Lincoln worked as a storekeeper, postmaster and lawyer before being elected to the Illinois legislature and then to the House of Representatives in 1847. An unsuccessful candidate for the Senate in 1855 and 1858 (when a series of debates with his opponent Stephen Douglas secured him a national political reputation), Lincoln was elected as President in 1860 with less than 40% of the vote. The election of this prominent abolitionist precipitated the Confederacy's secession and the ensuing civil war. Wary of alienating the border states, Lincoln reversed the emancipation of slaves in Missouri proclaimed by General John Fremont in 1861. Lincoln issued a preliminary emancipation announcement in September 1862 after a Union victory at Antietam, following this with the Emancipation Proclamation of 1 January 1863 freeing the slaves in the Confederacy. Though largely symbolic – the Union had no means of enforcing abolition in the South – the proclamation paved the way for the 1865 Thirteenth Amendment. Lincoln believed, however, that freed blacks should remove themselves from the United States. Re-elected in 1864, Lincoln's second inaugural speech declared the war was being fought to end slavery. He was assassinated a week after the Union victory in April 1865 by John Wilkes Booth, a Confederate sympathiser.

Lovejoy Elijah Parish (1802–37) United States abolitionist journalist. Founding editor of a Presbyterian gradualist abolitionist newspaper, the *St Louis Observer*, in 1833; pro-slavery demonstrators forced Lovejoy to move to Illinois in 1836. Here he set up a newspaper advocating immediate emancipation of the slaves, the *Alton Observer*, and helped form the Illinois Anti-Slavery Society. His presses were destroyed three times by pro-slavery mobs and Lovejoy was killed attempting to protect a new press. His killing in 1837 provided a source of effective abolitionist propaganda in the Northern states.

Lundy Benjamin (1789–1839) United States abolitionist activist. A Quaker saddler, Lundy founded the anti-slavery Union Humane Society in Ohio in 1815 and, after taking up abolitionist activity full time, established a magazine, the *Philanthropist*, in 1819. This was succeeded in 1821 by the *Genius of Universal Emancipation*. William Lloyd Garrison (1805–79) became associate editor in 1829 but left following disagreement with Lundy's support for establishing colonies for freed slaves outside the United States. In 1836 – following the demise of the *Genius* – Lundy began publishing the *National Enquirer*, which was edited (as the *Pennsylvania Freeman*) from 1838 by John Greenleaf Whittier (1807–92).

Malcolm X (born Malcolm Little) (1925–65) United States black nationalist activist. Serving a ten year sentence for burglary, Little joined the Nation of Islam and after parole in 1952 he was ordained, taking the name Malcolm X and becoming the movement's leading orator. Malcolm X initially denounced whites and advocated a separate black state. In 1964 he broke with the Nation after being suspended for declaring the assassination of President Kennedy (1917–63) an example of 'chickens come home to roost' and travelled to Mecca. On his return to the United States, he adopted the name El-Hajj Malik El-Shabbazz, established the Organisation of Afro-American Unity, and softened his view that all whites were devils. Though still an advocate of violence in self-defence, Malcolm X increasingly sought co-operation with other civil rights activists. He was assassinated by three members of the Nation of Islam after he had denounced their leader as a 'racist' and a 'faker'.

Mandela Nelson Rolihlahla (born 1918) South African politician and anti-apartheid activist. Educated at Fort Hare University from 1938 to 1940, Mandela was expelled for political activism. Active in the ANC, Mandela formed the ANC Youth League with Walter Sisulu (born 1912) in 1942 and became ANC deputy president in 1952. He was given a suspended prison sentence for organising the Defiance Campaign and was acquitted on a charge of treason in 1961 when he formed the underground ANC armed wing, Umkhonto we Sizwe. Sentenced to life imprisonment in 1964 following the Rivonia Trial, Mandela remained incarcerated until 1990. He was awarded the Nobel Peace Prize in 1993 and was elected as South Africa's first post-apartheid President in 1994, serving until his retirement in 1999. Among his writings are *No Easy Walk to Freedom* (1965) and *Long Walk to Freedom* (1995).

Mansfield William Murray (1st Earl of Mansfield) (1705–93) British lawyer. Called to the Bar in 1730, Mansfield was elected to the House of Commons and was appointed solicitor general in 1742. In 1754 he became attorney general, serving at the same time as leader of the Commons. He was appointed chief justice of the King's Bench in 1756 and it was in this post that he issued the Somerset judgment in 1772, ruling that a runaway slave could not forcibly be removed from England with the words, 'I cannot say this case is allowed or approved by the law of England; and therefore the black must be discharged.' Later appointed Speaker of the House of Lords, Mansfield resigned as chief justice in 1788.

Marryshow Theophilus Albert (1887–1958) Grenadian anti-colonialist activist. An advocate of independence for Britain's Caribbean colonies and the establishment of a West Indies Federation, Marryshow founded a newspaper, *The West Indian*, in 1915, and conducted anti-colonialist activity through the Caribbean and in Britain. He was elected first president of the Caribbean Labour Congress in 1945 and became a member of the Federation of the West Indies Parliament Upper House in 1958.

Marshall Thurgood (1908–93) United States lawyer and civil rights activist. Marshall began practising law in 1933 and was chief counsel for the NAACP from 1938 to 1950. Marshall was director and chief counsel for the NAACP Legal and Defense Educational Fund from 1940 to 1961, winning the first of 29 Supreme Court victories in 1940. Marshall presented the argument that resulted in the landmark 1954 Supreme Court ruling that educational discrimination was unconstitutional. He was appointed to the Appeal Court (against Southern opposition) in 1961 and solicitor general in 1965. In 1967 he was appointed the first black Supreme Court justice, a position he retained until his retirement in 1991. In the Supreme Court, Marshall took a generally liberal position.

Mott Lucretia (1793–1880) United States abolitionist, feminist and temperance activist. A Quaker, Mott became active in the abolitionist movement in the 1830s and was a delegate (denied admission as a woman) to the 1840 World Anti-Slavery Convention in London. In 1860 she delivered a celebrated 'I am no advocate of passivity' speech to the Pennsylvania Anti-Slavery Society. Mott harboured fugitive slaves and, following emancipation in 1865, agitated for black suffrage.

Muhammad Elijah (born Robert Poole) (1886–1975) United States religious and black nationalist leader. Born in Georgia, Muhammad joined the Moorish Science Temple while working as an automobile worker. In 1930 he formed a rival Nation of Islam, a movement advocating black self-reliance and economic self-sufficiency. By 1960 the Nation, which had spread from Detroit to Chicago, had 80 temples and claimed over 15,000 members. Muhammad expelled the prominent member Malcolm X in 1965 for advocating a move to radical political activity.

Nabuco de Arajo Joaquím Aurelio Barreto (1849–1910) Brazilian politician and abolitionist activist. Born into an aristocratic family in the north east of the country, Nabuco was elected to the Chamber of Deputies in 1878. Two years later he established the Brazilian Anti-Slavery Society with André Rebouças. The campaign to end slavery succeeded in 1888. Nabuco retired from public life in 1890 but served as Brazil's ambassador to the United States from 1905 to 1910.

Nanny (dates unknown) Jamaican Maroon leader. Nanny was a prominent Maroon activist in Jamaica in the early 18th century and established Nannytown, a stronghold in the Blue Mountains during the First Maroon War. Nannytown was destroyed by British troops in 1734 and Nanny's fate is unknown. She was declared a National Hero of Jamaica in the 1970s.

Newton John (1725–1807) British slave trader and abolitionist activist. Newton entered the slave trade in 1745 but himself became the slave of a black owner. He escaped, became a Christian, but remained in the slave trade, commanding a slave ship for four years before retiring because of ill-health. As a clergyman, he was an anti-slave trade activist, declaring in 1797 that 'the blood of many thousands of our helpless, much injured fellow creatures is crying against us'. In *Thoughts upon the African Slave Trade*, published in 1808, Newton graphically described conditions on slave ships: 'The slaves lie in two rows, one above the other like books upon a shelf.' Newton died shortly after the trade was abolished in British possessions.

Parks Rosa Louise McCauley (born 1913) United States civil rights activist. A long-standing NAACP activist, Parks triggered the 1955–56 Montgomery bus boycott and the Supreme Court anti-discrimination decision that followed by refusing to give up her seat to a white passenger. Following the boycott, Parks was harassed by racists and lost her job as a seamstress. She moved to Detroit where she and her husband lived in relative poverty. She worked as administrative assistant to a Congressman from 1965 to 1987 and remained active in the civil rights and anti-apartheid movement. In 1987 she was co-founder of a project to encourage black education and employment.

Payne Clement Osbourne (1904–47) Caribbean civil rights activist. Born in Trinidad, Payne was prominent in the National Unemployed Movement from 1934 to 1935 and the Negro Welfare, Cultural and Social Association from 1935 to 1937. In 1937 he became founding president of the Federated Workers' Trade Union and secretary of the Workers' United Front Committee in 1938. His deportation from Barbados by the British colonial authorities in 1938 provoked widespread rioting.

Pease Elizabeth (1807–97) British abolitionist, feminist and radical activist. Member of a prominent Quaker family, Pease led the Darlington Women's Anti-Slavery Society in the mid 1820s. In 1828 she published the *Address to the Women of Great Britain* with Jane Smeal. A Chartist, Pease worked to encourage working class women to become active in the anti-slavery campaign. Following the success of abolitionism, Pease was involved in peace, temperance and anti-vivisection campaigns.

Pennington James (1809–79) United States abolitionist and civil rights activist. Born a slave, Pennington escaped in 1830 and was aided by Quakers. Following his ordination as a Presbyterian minister, Pennington was elected to the General Convention for the Improvement of the Free Colored People and in 1843 was elected as Connecticut delegate to the World Anti-Slavery Convention in London. Fearing a return to slavery under the 1850 Fugitive Slavery Act, Pennington's supporters purchased his freedom in 1851. As organiser of the New York Legal Rights Association, Pennington sued a railroad company for its racial segregation policies and, although the case failed, achieved changes in the company's discriminatory practices.

Phillips Wendell (1811–84) United States abolitionist activist. Phillips came to prominence with a speech denouncing the murder of anti-slavery activist Elijah Lovejoy (1802–37). He gave up his law practice in 1837 to join abolitionists grouped around William Lloyd Garrison (1805–79) and advocated an end to slavery even at the cost of preserving the Union. A delegate to the 1840 World Anti-Slavery Convention in London, Phillips attacked what he saw as the moderate approach adopted by President Lincoln (1809–65) to emancipation during the 1861–65 Civil War. He refused to allow the dissolution of the American Anti-Slavery Society (succeeding Garrison as president in 1865) until the passage of the Fifteenth Amendment enfranchised the freed slaves. Phillips remained an activist, supporting women's suffrage, workers' rights, prohibition and currency reform.

Powell Colin Luther (born 1937) United States soldier. The son of Caribbean immigrants, Powell was educated at the City College of New York, George Washington University and the National War College, was commissioned into the army in 1958 and served in Vietnam. After holding a number of staff and command appointments, Powell served as assistant for national security to President Ronald Reagan from 1987 to 1989 and was then appointed chairman of the Joint Chiefs of Staff, a post he held until his retirement in 1993. A prominent figure in the 1990–91 war against Iraq, Powell resisted urgings to stand as a presidential candidate in 1996. In 2001 he was appointed Secretary of State in the Republican administration.

Prosser Gabriel (c1775–1800) United States slave leader. A devout Christian, Prosser planned the first major slave insurrection in the United States, intending to establish an independent black state in Virginia. Prosser's force was to capture the arsenal in Richmond and kill all whites except Methodists and Quakers. An estimated 1,000 slaves assembled outside the city but were dispersed by a violent storm and then attacked by the state militia. Prosser and 34 supporters were captured, tried and hanged.

Randolph Asa Philip (1889–1979) United States trade union and civil rights leader. Co-founder in 1912 of a black employment agency, Randolph set up a magazine in 1917, *The Messenger* (renamed *The Black Worker* in 1929). An unsuccessful Socialist Party candidate, Randolph was founding president of the black union, the Brotherhood of Sleeping Car Porters, in 1925, a post he retained until 1968. In 1941, Randolph threatened President Franklin Roosevelt (1882–1945) with a black mass march on Washington DC to protest against lack of employment opportunities, forcing Roosevelt to issue Executive Order 8802 barring discrimination in the defence industry. Randolph's League for Nonviolent Civil Disobedience against Military Segregation, formed in 1947, encouraged President Harry Truman (1884–1972) to outlaw segregation in the armed forces in 1948. He was founding president from 1960 to 1966 of the Negro American Labor Council, formed to combat discrimination in the union movement. Randolph was director of the 1963 March on Washington for Jobs and Freedom and in 1965 formed an institute to examine the causes of poverty.

Revels Hiram Rhoades (1822–1901) United States civil rights activist and politician. Born free in North Carolina, Revels became a Methodist Episcopal preacher, serving in the 1861–5 Civil War as a chaplain and recruiter of black troops to the Union Army. In 1870, Revels became the first black American to be elected to the Senate and served one year. In 1876 he became editor of the *South Western Christian Advocate* and was later president of Alcorn State University, Mississippi.

Russwurm John Brown (1799–1851) United States black activist and journalist. Born in Jamaica, Russwurm moved to the United States and became the country's first black graduate in 1826. In 1827 he co-founded the first black newspaper in the United States, *Freedom's Journal*, with Samuel Cornish (c1795–1859). In 1830 Russwurm left to settle in Liberia where he became superintendent of schools and published the *Liberia Herald* until 1850.

Schoelcher Victor (1804–93) French politician and abolitionist activist.

During a campaign against slavery in the French colonies, Schoelcher visited the Caribbean in 1829–30. He was a leading member of the French Society for the Abolition of Slavery, founded in France in 1834. Initially a supporter of gradualist emancipation, his experiences led him to support immediate freedom for the slaves. As Under-Secretary to the Navy with responsibility for the colonies in 1848, he supervised the drafting of legislation which abolished slavery throughout the French colonies. Exiled in 1850, Schoelcher returned to France in 1870 and was subsequently elected to the National Assembly.

Scott Dred (c1795–1858) United States slave. Born in Virginia, Scott was taken by his owner to Missouri in 1827 and subsequently, by a new owner, to the Illinois and Wisconsin territories from 1833 to 1838. In 1846, the son of a former owner claimed in the Missouri state court that Scott was a free man because he had lived in a free territory. The court ruled against Scott in 1852 and the Supreme Court declared in 1857 that as a slave Scott was ineligible to take action in a Federal court. However, Scott was freed by his owner in the same year and worked briefly as a hotel porter before dying of tuberculosis.

Sharp Granville (1735–1813) British abolitionist activist and social reformer. A draper and then a civil servant, Sharp became prominent as an abolitionist through his involvement in legal attempts to secure the liberty of slaves who had landed in Britain, notably in the Somerset case of 1772. His support for the 1776 American Declaration of Independence forced his resignation from the civil service. In 1787, Sharp supported the establishment of a colony in Sierra Leone for freed slaves and in the same year became chairman of the newly formed Society for Effecting the Abolition of the Slave Trade (Sharp's proposal for the inclusion of the word Slavery was rejected). Sharp's main role was propaganda against the slave trade. With the success of the campaign in 1807, Sharp joined Thomas Clarkson (1760–1846) and Thomas Fowell Buxton (1786–1845) in forming the Society for the Mitigation and Gradual Abolition of Slavery Throughout the British Dominions. In the same year, he was appointed chairman of the British and Foreign Bible Society.

Sharpe Samuel (1801–32) Jamaican slave leader. An educated slave who served as a Baptist deacon, Sharpe spent 1831 planning and organising a rising which opened at the end of December in St James, amidst rumours that emancipation had been granted but was being withheld by the island's white assembly. The rebellion, which lasted over a week and became known as the 'Baptist War', spread across Jamaica until the rebels held a third of the island. two hundred slaves were killed and over 200 properties destroyed. Sharpe was captured and hanged in Montego Bay early in 1832. The rising encouraged rapid moves towards emancipation by Britain.

Singleton Benjamin ('Pap') (?–1892) American migration leader. A freed slave in Tennessee, Singleton concluded that it was impossible for emancipated slaves and their former owners to co-exist and advocated separation. He first formed a Tennessee Real Estate and Homestead Association but then encouraged black migration from the Southern states to

Kansas, leading what became known as the 'Exodusters'. As the migrants met with continuing racial hostility, Singleton advocated a return to Africa.

Smalls Robert (1839–1915) United States politician. Born a slave, Smalls became a shipping pilot and seized a Confederate blockade-runner, the Planter, and its slave crew in 1862, sailing it into Union waters. Appointed the Planter's captain, Smalls served the Union during the Civil War, becoming a notable figure and meeting President Lincoln (1809–65). After the war, he served two years in the South Carolina House of Representatives and three years in the state Senate. After a conviction for bribery, for which he was pardoned, Smalls served five terms in the House of Representatives from 1875 until his retirement in 1887.

Smeal Jane (dates unknown) British abolitionist and radical activist. A Quaker, Smeal formed and led the Glasgow Ladies' Emancipation Society in the mid 1820s. In 1828 she published *Address to the Women of Great Britain* with Elizabeth Pease, encouraging women to participate in abolitionist activity. An active Chartist, Smeal praised the part played by working and middle-class women co-operating in the abolition campaign.

Smith Gerrit (1797–1874) United States abolitionist activist. A supporter of the American Colonisation Society, Smith left to join the American Anti-Slavery Society, becoming a close associate of William Lloyd Garrison (1805–79) and Frederick Douglass (1818–95). Initially committed to a peaceful campaign – his home in New York was a station on the Underground Railroad and he provided funds for land for black settlement – Smith supported the armed struggle against slavery in Kansas in the mid 1850s and was involved in discussions on the 1859 Harper's Ferry raid. Smith was an unsuccessful and avowedly abolitionist candidate for President in 1848, 1856 and 1860.

Stanton Elizabeth Cady (1815–1902) United States abolitionist and feminist activist. Cady became associated with abolitionism through her cousin Gerrit Smith (1797–1874) and was closely associated with Lucretia Mott (1793–1880). She was denied a seat, with other women delegates, at the 1840 World Anti-Slavery Convention in London. Although she remained an anti-slavery activist, she split with Smith and Frederick Douglass (1818–95) over the issue of black male suffrage coming before women's rights.

Still William Lloyd (1821–1902) United States abolitionist activist. Originally a farm worker, Still moved from New Jersey to Philadelphia in 1844 and learned to read and write. Taking a job as a clerk with the Pennsylvania Anti-Slavery Society, Still went on to become chairman of the local Vigilance Committee formed to oppose operation of the Fugitive Slave Act. As an 'Underground Railroad' conductor, Still was involved in the escape of 649 slaves and published a book on the subject in 1872. He was active in anti-segregation campaigning, established an association to collect information on black lives in 1861 and served on the Freedman's Aid Commission formed at the end of the American Civil War to assist freed slaves.

Stowe Harriet Beecher (1811–96) United States writer, abolitionist and suffrage activist. Her novel *Uncle Tom's Cabin*, serialised from 1851 to 1852 in the Washington anti-slavery newspaper, the *National Era*, and published in book form in 1852, played an important part in encouraging abolitionist sentiment in the Northern states as the Civil War approached. Stowe's knowledge of slavery, abolitionism and the Underground Railroad, derived from her observation of life in Kentucky. Following publication, she lectured on slavery in the United States and Europe. Her next work, *A Key to Uncle Tom's Cabin*, provided documentary evidence on slavery. A further book on slavery, *Dred: A Tale of the Great Dismal Swamp* followed in 1856.

Tappan Arthur (1786–1865) United States abolitionist activist. A businessman, Tappen and his brother, Lewis, were initially financial supporters of abolitionism and other reforming activities. Arthur Tappan was elected first president of the American Anti-Slavery Society in 1833. In the split in the Society between gradualists and radicals which took place in 1839, Arthur Tappan sided with the gradualists and in 1840 was founding president of the American and Foreign Anti-Slavery Society.

Tappan Lewis (1788–1873) United States abolitionist activist. A businessman in partnership with his brother, Arthur, Lewis Tappen was prominent in anti-slavery societies. With Arthur, Lewis went with the gradualists in the argument which split the American Anti-Slavery Society in 1839. He was a delegate at the World Anti-Slavery Convention in London in 1843. On his retirement in 1849 he devoted the bulk of his time to the campaign against slavery.

Terrell Mary Church (1863–1954) United States civil rights activist and educationalist. A teacher at the first black American college, Wilberforce University, from 1884, Terrell lived in Europe before being elected first president of the National Association of Colored Women, 1896–1901. A lecturer against lynching and on black women's rights and suffrage, Terrell was a delegate to the International Congress of Women in Zurich and organised the black vote for the Republican Party. From 1950 to 1953 she led a successful campaign against racial discrimination in Washington DC.

Toussaint L'Ouverture (born Pierre Dominique Toussaint Breda) (1745–1803) Haitian slave revolt leader. Born a slave, Toussaint became a plantation overseer. Freed in 1777, Toussaint joined the slave rebellion in 1791, was soon appointed commander and organised an effective guerrilla force. He became known as 'L'Ouverture' because of his ability to find an 'opening' in battle. He expelled the French in 1797, repelled a British invasion the following year and crushed a mulatto rising in 1799. Toussaint introduced a constitution and appointed himself governor in 1801. After negotiating a treaty with France in 1802 following an invasion, Toussaint was captured and died in a dungeon at Fort-du-Joux in the Jura. His life was celebrated in poems by Wordsworth and Lamartine.

Trotter William Monroe (1872–1934) United States civil rights activist. Trotter founded the militant *Boston Guardian* in 1901, opposing the accomodationist policies of Booker T. Washington (1856–1915) and demanding full equality. He was arrested for heckling Washington in 1903. A founding member of the Niagara Movement in 1905, Trotter refused to join the NAACP because of suspicion of the motives of white supporters. Trotter continued his civil rights activities, including picketing the showing of the film Birth of a Nation in 1915. Denied a visa by the government to attend the 1919 Paris Peace Conference as a representative of the National Equal Rights League, Trotter crossed the Atlantic as a ship's cook. He supported a Japanese motion to condemn racial discrimination in the League of Nations Covenant, a motion opposed by the United States and Britain.

Truth Sojourner (born Isabella Baumfree) (1797–1883) United States abolitionist and women's rights activist. Freed by the New York State Emancipation Act in 1827, she changed her name to Sojourner Truth after a religious revelation in 1843 and joined an abolitionist community called the Northampton Association of Education and Industry. Following the publication of her biography in 1850, Truth became an abolitionist lecturer and attended women's rights conventions. At a convention in 1851 she made her celebrated defence of women's and black rights in a speech in which she apocryphally declared, 'Ain't I a Woman?'. She worked with the National Freedmen's Relief Association and the Freedmen's Bureau from 1864 to 1868, with the American Woman Suffrage Association in the 1870s and was an active supporter of the Exodusters.

Tubman Harriet (c1821–1913) United States abolitionist activist. A 'conductor' on the Underground Railroad known as 'Moses', Tubman was born a slave but escaped to Philadelphia in 1849. Becoming involved in the abolitionist movement, she returned south to lead over 200 people to freedom from 1850 to 1860, including her brother and sister. Her activities led to slave owners offering rewards totalling $40,000 for her capture. During the 1861–5 Civil War, Tubman acted as a scout and spy for the Union forces. She set up a home in New York for elderly freed slaves unable to work and was active in the women's suffrage movement.

Turner Nat (1800–31) United States slave leader. Following a short-lived escape in 1821, Turner become a popular Christian preacher among slaves from 1825 to 1830. During this period he used the opportunity to plan a slave insurrection. In 1831 Turner and six supporters opened the rising by killing 60 whites as a preliminary to raising more recruits and capturing the arsenal at Jerusalem, Virginia. But only another 60 joined the rebels, who were finally dispersed by the militia. Briefly at liberty, Turner was tried and hanged. The rebellion terrorised white Southerners and undermined the myth of slave contentment.

Vesey Denmark (c1767–1822) United States slave leader. Born in the Danish West Indies, Vesey settled with his new owner in Charleston, Virginia, in 1783. In 1800 Vesey won $600 in a lottery and purchased his freedom, working as a carpenter. An admirer of the 1791–1804 Haiti slave revolt and dissatisfied with the treatment of free blacks, Vesey began organising a rising of urban and plantation slaves in which they would seize arms, kill as many whites as possible and destroy Charleston. A black servant warned the authorities on the eve of the rising in June 1822. Vesey was captured, found guilty of attempted insurrection and hanged with 34 others.

Walker David (c1796–1830) United States abolitionist activist. Son of a slave father and free mother, Walker set up a used clothing store in Boston in the 1820s and became a member of black societies opposing slavery and discrimination. A regular contributor of articles to *Freedom's Journal*, the first black American newspaper, Walker became prominent in anti-slavery campaigning in Boston. In 1829 he published *An Appeal to the Coloured Citizens of the World*, a response to growing racism and the apparent indifference of whites to slavery. Walker called for the violent overthrow of slavery in America and the Caribbean. Despite threats from supporters of slavery, Walker refused to seek safety in Canada, publishing a third edition of the *Appeal* in 1830. His sudden death, long viewed with suspicion, may have been due to tuberculosis.

Washington Booker Taliaferro (1856–1915) United States educationalist and activist. Born a slave, Washington worked in coal mines and as a houseboy, paying his way to graduation. A teacher, he established the Tuskegee Normal and Industrial Institute in Alabama in 1891. He was later prominent in establishing the National Negro Business League. Washington delivered the Atlanta Compromise speech at the Cotton States Exposition in 1895, a plea for racial co-operation and an argument for black economic and educational advance rather than agitation for political and civil rights. His urging of moderation when racial segregation was intensifying and lynching increasing was criticised by other black leaders, including W. E. B. Du Bois (1868–1963) and William Monroe Trotter (1872–1934), who went on to form the Niagara Movement in 1909. Washington appeared before he died to have recognised the limitations of his programme of compromise, notably in an article he wrote in 1912 entitled 'Is the Negro Having a Fair Chance?'.

Weaver Robert Clifton (born 1907) United States politician. Weaver held a number of administrative posts before World War Two, including social assistant with the Housing Authority from 1937 to 1940 and assistant with the National Defense Advisory Committee in 1940. During the war he was involved with the mobilisation of black labour and then became an academic before serving as New York state rent commissioner from 1955 to 1959. In 1961 President John F. Kennedy appointed Weaver as administrator of the Housing and Home Finance Agency. In 1966, President Lyndon B. Johnson appointed him the first black cabinet member as head of the Department of Housing and Urban Development, a post he held until 1968, when he returned to academic life.

Wedgwood Josiah (1730–95) British abolitionist activist. A member of the prominent pottery family and a Unitarian, Wedgwood took an early interest in social and political reform. He was active with Thomas Clarkson (1760–1846) and Granville Sharp (1735–1813) in forming the Society for Effecting the Abolition of the Slave Trade in 1787, joined the organisation's committee and produced its seal. Wedgwood wrote in 1788 that ending the slave trade was 'the only probable means of withholding the heavy hand of cruelty and oppression from those who now groan under it'.

Wells-Barnett Ida Bell (1862–1931) United States journalist, civil rights and feminist activist. Born a slave, Wells-Barnett became a teacher but was dismissed in 1891 for criticising inadequate facilities in segregated black schools. In 1894 she unsuccessfully sued a railway company which ejected her from a train for refusing to travel in a designated black coach. The Memphis offices of *Free Speech* were wrecked by whites angered by articles she wrote on lynching and inter-racial relationships in 1892. Wells-Barnett continued her anti-lynching campaign, lecturing in Britain in 1893–94 and leading a deputation to President McKinley in 1898. She was a founder member of the National Association of Colored Women in 1896, the NAACP in 1910 and the Alpha Suffrage Club in 1913, and an early supporter of Garvey's UNIA. She continued to promote civil rights in her journalism.

Wheatley Phyllis (c1753–1784) North American slave and poet. Born in Senegal, Wheatley was taken as a slave to Boston at the age of seven. Educated by her owners, Wheatley wrote her first poem, *On being brought from Africa to America*, at 13. She was sent to England when she was 20 and her collection, *Poems on various subjects, religious and moral*, which appeared in 1773, was the first book published in Britain by a black woman. She came to prominence as a writer in the late 1760s. Although her only reference in the collection to her experiences appears in the line, 'Some view our sable race with scornful eye', Wheatley was seen as an example by the abolitionists of the early 19th century. Wheatley received her freedom in 1778 and married but died in poverty.

White Walter Francis (1893–1955) United States civil rights activist and journalist. Born in Georgia, White became an NAACP activist and as a journalist reported on lynchings and racial clashes. He was appointed NAACP national secretary in 1930 and was influential as an advisor to President Franklin D. Roosevelt in the establishment of the Fair Employment Practice Committee. After World War Two White was an advisor to the United States delegations to the United Nations. Among his many writings are *Rope and Faggot: A Biography of Judge Lynch* (1929), *A Rising Wind: A Report of the Negro Soldier in the European Theater of War* (1945) and *How Far the Promised Land?* (1955).

Whittier John Greenleaf (1807–92) United States abolitionist activist and poet. Whittier put forward his abolitionist views in a pamphlet, *Justice and Expediency*, in 1833, and attended the national anti-slavery convention. A member of the Massachusetts legislature in 1834–35, Whittier stood unsuccessfully for Congress as a candidate for the anti-slavery Liberty Party in 1842, going on to be a founder member of the Republican Party. Corresponding editor from 1847 to 1859 of the abolitionist weekly, the *National Era*, Whittier continued to write against slavery until emancipation in 1865.

Wilberforce William (1759–1833) British politician and abolitionist activist. Elected as a Tory Member of Parliament in 1780, Wilberforce turned to social reform after joining the evangelical Clapham Sect in 1784. Following a speech on the subject in 1789, Wilberforce was identified with Thomas Clarkson (1760–1846) and Granville Sharp (1735–1813) as a leading figure in the anti-slave trade movement. As the parliamentary voice of the Society for Effecting the Abolition of the Slave Trade, Wilberforce presented the first bill to end the trade in 1791. It was defeated by 163 votes to 66. Wilberforce continued the parliamentary campaign, raising the issue annually, and legislation was finally passed in 1807. He initially opposed emancipation but was persuaded by Thomas Fowell Buxton (1786–1845) to become vice president of the Society for the Mitigation and Gradual Abolition of Slavery Throughout the British Dominions. Wilberforce retired from the Commons in 1825 and played little direct part in the passage of emancipation legislation. An Act abolishing slavery was passed a few days before Wilberforce's death. He was once asked by King George III, 'How go on your black clients, Mr Wilberforce?' Wilberforce's other activities included prison reform, opposition to pornography, and overseas missionary work. He was, however, less liberal towards working-class interests and was a member of a secret government committee appointed in 1817 to repress popular discontent.

Wilkins Roy (1901–81) United States civil rights activist. After working his way through college, Wilkins became a journalist on a black American newspaper and became active in the National Association for the Advancement of Colored People (NAACP) in Kansas. In 1931 he was appointed the NAACP assistant executive secretary and in 1934 replaced W. E. B. Du Bois (1868–1963) as editor of the NAACP journal, the Crisis. An adviser to the government on black participation in the armed services during World War Two, Wilkins held a number of positions in the NAACP before becoming executive secretary in 1955, at a point when the civil rights movement was entering its most active period. Wilkins retired in 1977.

Williams Eric Eustace (1911–81) Trinidad and Tobago writer and politician. Awarded an Oxford D.Phil. in 1938 for his thesis, 'The Economic Aspect of the West Indian Slave Trade and Slavery', Williams taught at Howard University in the United States from 1939. In 1948 he was appointed head of the Caribbean Commission research branch but resigned in 1955 in protest at its tendency towards colonialism. Returning to Trinidad, Williams formed the People's National Movement in 1956 and was chief minister from 1956 to 1959, premier from 1959 to 1962 and prime minister on independence in 1962, an office he held on his death. Among his many books are *Capitalism and Slavery* and *From Columbus to Castro: The History of the Caribbean 1492–1969*.

GLOSSARY OF TERMS, EVENTS AND MOVEMENTS

Abolitionism The movement in Britain, Western Europe and the Americas which organised opposition to the slave trade and slavery. As early as the 16th century, the French political philosopher Jean Bodin (1530–96) declared slavery to be both immoral and counterproductive, while in 1639 Pope Urban VIII condemned the slave trade for depriving its victims of their liberty. In the 18th century, slavery came under increasing criticism from rationalists, who believed it to contravene the concept of the rights of man, and Quakers, who denounced the institution as anathema to Christianity. The Somerset case of 1772, mounted by Granville Sharp (1735–1813), provided an encouragement to abolitionism and between 1777 and 1804 slavery was abandoned in the Northern part of the United States following its independence from Britain. Although both Britain and the United States ended their involvement in the slave trade in 1807–08, slavery continued in the Southern states, South America and the Caribbean (where it was abolished by Britain in its territories in 1834 and by France in 1848). In the United States, where slavery was seen by Southern planters as an economic necessity, abolitionism (against a background of slave resistance and Southern repression) took a more militant line. Leading abolitionists included William Lloyd Garrison (1805–79) and Frederick Douglass (1818–95). *Uncle Tom's Cabin*, published by Harriet Beecher Stowe (1811–96) in 1852, roused Northern opinion. Abolitionism culminated in the United States with the Emancipation Proclamation of 1863 and the Thirteenth Amendment to the Constitution in 1865. Pressure then turned to the Spanish Caribbean and South America, where slavery was gradually abolished through the latter half of the 19th century.

ACMHR See Alabama Christian Movement for Human Rights.

Affirmative action Policies in the United States intended to increase the numbers of people from groups believed to have suffered discrimination in, for example, employment and education. Affirmative action can take the form of allowing people to compete equally by removing obstacles or by setting quotas to ensure members of the group are proportionally represented. The expression was first used in an order on Federal contracts issued by President John F. Kennedy (1917–63) in 1961. Initially, Federal orders required businesses carrying out contracts for the government to do so without regard to race. This developed into taking the racial – and, later, gender – balance of employees in the businesses into account when awarding contracts. By the 1970s, however, there was growing disagreement over the effectiveness and equity of affirmative action. In 1989, the Supreme Court ruled that state and local action based on race was unconstitutional unless it was intended to redress a specific (rather than general) instance of discrimination. The court extended this to Federal action in 1995, effectively barring affirmative action intended to counteract racial discrimination by society generally.

African Civilisation Committee An organisation established in Britain in 1839 by the abolitionist Thomas Fowell Buxton (1786–1845), with the support of other groups, to attempt to undermine the international slave trade by encouraging the development of settlements in Africa. Buxton was able to win the support of the Whig government for the Committee's objectives but the organisation collapsed in 1843 following a disastrous Niger expedition in 1840–42.

African Emigration Association An organisation founded in the United States in 1881 which advocated the return of black Americans to Africa. The Association was the first to put forward – in a declaration presented to Congress in 1886 – what would become the Pan-Africanist call for a 'United States of Africa'.

African Institution The successor organisation to the Society for Effecting the Abolition of the Slave Trade, formed following the ending of the slave trade by Britain in 1807. The Institution worked, largely unsuccessfully, to persuade other European powers to follow Britain's lead in abolishing the trade and to encourage Africans involved in the sale of slaves to take up other activities. The Institution was succeeded by the Society for the Mitigation and Gradual Abolition of Slavery Throughout the British Dominions in 1823.

African Methodist Episcopal Church The oldest autonomous black organisation in the United States, established with the former slave Richard Allen (1760–1831) as its founding bishop in Philadelphia, Pennsylvania. Allen had formed the Baltimore African Church in 1787 when white Methodists refused to allow fellow black worshippers to sit in pews or take Holy Communion. This amalgamated with a number of smaller Methodist bodies to form the African Methodist Episcopal church, which was formally recognised in 1816.

African Union Society A body formed by free black Americans in 1780 in Newport, Rhode Island, to provide support for widows and orphans, to retain records of manumission (the certificates of liberty granted to individual slaves), and to formulate plans for a return to Africa. An agreement was reached with the British authorities to move 12 black families to Sierra Leone but was abandoned.

Agency Committee A body led by Thomas Clarkson (1760–1846) from 1831 to 1834 as a breakaway from the Society for the Mitigation and Gradual Abolition of Slavery Throughout the British Dominions. The Committee was largely financed by Quakers. It employed three full-time agents to establish local societies, of which there were soon 1,200 organising petitions demanding an immediate and unconditional end to slavery and seeking to persuade voters to demand pledges to support anti-slavery legislation from Parliamentary candidates. Despite the Committee's opposition to compensation to slave owners and a transitional period of apprenticeship for emancipated slaves, the Committee and the Society worked closely together. The Committee presented the free trade economic arguments for abolition but stressed the moral and humanitarian aspects.

Alabama Christian Movement for Human Rights (ACMHR) A movement active in the campaign for black civil rights in the United States from 1956 to 1962. Formed by the Baptist ministers, the Rev. Fred Shuttlesworth and the Rev. Vernon Johns, when the activities of the National Association for the Advancement of Colored People were banned in Alabama, the movement organised demonstrations and filed law suits against racial discrimination.

Alexander v Holmes County Board of Education In this 1969 case – which concerned the attempt by some Southern states to continue racial segregation in education by using public funds to support private white schools – the United States Supreme Court declared that educational segregation ordered under 1954 *Brown* v *Board of Education of Topeka* decision should be undertaken 'at once' rather than 'with all deliberate speed'.

American Anti-Slavery Society The organisation was established as a loose confederation of abolitionists in Philadelphia in December 1833 by William Lloyd Garrison (1805–79), Theodore Dwight Weld (1803–95), Arthur Tappen (1786–1865), Lewis Tappen (1788–1863), Lucretia Mott (1793–1880), Levi Coffin (1798–1877) and James Birney (1792–1857) to oppose slavery in the United States. Prominent black founders included Frederick Douglass (1818–95), Henry Highland Garnet (1815–82), David Walker (c1796–1830), Harriet Tubman (c1821–1913) and Martin R. Delany (1812–85). The Society's Constitution declared its objective to be 'the entire abolition of Slavery in the United States' and to 'elevate the character and condition of the people of color, by encouraging their intellectual, moral, and religious improvement, and by removing public prejudice'. The Society organised propaganda meetings and publicity (including an annual almanac and *The Slave's Friend*, a monthly for children) and sponsored anti-slavery petitions to be sent to Congress. Within five years there were over 1,350 societies with almost 250,000 members. In 1839 the Society divided over differences in strategy, with a moderate wing led by the Tappan brothers leaving to form the American and Foreign Anti-Slavery Society. Garrison, whose followers favoured a more agitational policy (and, unlike the Tappen supporters, women played a greater part in organisation) retained influence over the Anti-Slavery Society. The Society remained in existence until the adoption of the Fifteenth Amendment to the Constitution in 1870 guaranteeing citizenship rights to freed slaves.

American and Foreign Anti-Slavery Society Established in 1839 by Arthur Tappen (1786–1865) and Lewis Tappen (1788–1863) as a moderate breakaway from the American Anti-Slavery Society, the organisation favoured a policy of moral persuasion and political action rather than agitation and was instrumental in the establishment of the Liberal Party in 1840.

American Colonisation Society The American Society for Colonising the Free People of Color was established in 1817 by Congressmen Henry Clay (1777–1853) – with former President James Madison at its head – to encourage the emigration of free blacks (who numbered approximately

250,000) from the United States to Africa. The Society was an uneasy alliance between moderate abolitionists and slaveholders intent on preserving the institution. By attempting to heighten black fears of white attitudes, the Society effectively intensified racial tensions. The Society transported 86 free blacks in 1820. A prominent member, Jehudi Ashmun (1794–1828), proposed the establishment of an American empire in Africa and purchased land for $300 in what became the black republic of Liberia in 1847. The Society – which assisted in the emigration of 13,000 free blacks in the first 50 years of its existence at a cost of $2 million – came under increasing criticism as the anti-slavery campaign intensified from the 1830s. William Lloyd Garrison (1805–79) denounced the Society as a ploy to perpetuate slavery. Although the Society failed to persuade the United States Congress to allocate funds to assist its activities, state legislatures in Maryland, Missouri, New Jersey, Pennsylvania and Virginia provided financial support in the 1850s. In the later 19th century, the Society concentrated on missionary and education work and was finally dissolved in 1964.

American Negro Academy Established in Washington DC in March 1897 by the clergyman and writer Alexander Crummell (1819–97), the Academy was intended to promote academic achievement among black Americans to act as a counter to white racism. In his opening address Crummell referred to a 'talented tenth' which would become an intellectual elite to provide leadership to black Americans.

Amistad **incident** A mutiny in May 1836 in which 49 slaves led by Joseph Cinque (c1811–78) seized the *Amistad*, which was transporting them from Havana, Cuba, where they had been sold. The slaves ordered the crew to sail to Africa but the ship went north and was intercepted by an American naval vessel which took it to Montauk Point, Log Island. Abolitionists and black American societies raised funds to secure former President John Quincy Adams to defend the slaves on mutiny and piracy charges. Judge A. T. Judson, ruling the slaves had been illegally smuggled into Cuba, set them free but the slave traders appealed. Judson's ruling was finally upheld by the Supreme Court in January 1841. The captives returned to Africa, the majority of them to Sierra Leone.

Amis des Noirs (Fr. 'friends of the blacks') An anti-slavery association established in France in 1788. In common with other European organisations, this was an elite movement which attempted to achieve its ends by working through official channels rather than organising a mass movement to agitate for the abolition of slavery. France finally abolished slavery in 1848.

An Appeal to the Coloured Citizens of the World A pamphlet produced by David Walker (c1796–1830) in 1829 calling on slaves in the United States and the Caribbean to rebel against their owners. The *Appeal* was a response to increasing racism and the apparent indifference of whites to slavery. Walker – a free black who was the son of a slave – declared, 'We must and shall be free, I say, in spite of you. You may do your best to keep us in wretchedness and misery, to enrich you and your children; but God will deliver us from under you.' The pamphlet was smuggled into Southern states, where it was banned, and a slave owner offered a $3,000 reward for Walker's death. Walker, refusing an opportunity to escape to safety in Canada, died suddenly (possibly from tuberculosis despite allegations of poisoning) after producing a third edition of the *Appeal*.

Anti-Slavery Society (Britain) See Society for Effecting the Abolition of the Slave Trade, and Society for the Mitigation and Gradual Abolition of Slavery Throughout the British Dominions.

Apartheid (Afrikaans 'apartness') The system of institutionalised racial discrimination practised in South Africa from 1948, when it was introduced by the National Party, until 1991, when President Frederick de Klerk announced its final abandonment. The party had declared in its 1948 manifesto, 'The choice before us is one of two divergent courses: either that of integration, which would in the long run amount to national suicide on the part of the whites; or that of apartheid.' The main apartheid legislation included the Prohibition of Mixed Marriages Act 1949 and the Immorality Act 1957 (which banned inter-racial sexual relations), the Population Registration Act (which categorised South Africa's population on a racial basis), the Group Areas Act 1950 (which segregated housing), the Natives Act 1952 (which extended pre-existing requirements for black South Africans to carry passes), the Separate Amenities Act 1953 (which segregated transport and other public facilities) and the Bantu Education Act 1953 (which segregated education). The politicians introducing apartheid pointed to the 'separate but equal' segregation practised in the United States.

Apostolic letters Popes wrote a number of letters on the subject of the slave trade and slavery which were intended to influence the behaviour of members of the church. Nicholas V's letter of January 1455 – written in the crisis that followed the Ottoman capture of Constantinople – was taken as an approval of slavery. Nicholas authorised the Portuguese king to 'subdue all Saracens and pagans whatsoever, and all other enemies of Christ wheresoever placed... and to reduce their persons to perpetual slavery'. Pius II wrote to a bishop leaving for Africa in October 1462, at a time when Portugal was extending its influence, that Christian converts should not be enslaved. Paul III wrote to the Archbishop of Toledo criticising the slave trade in May 1537, as did Urban VIII in April 1622 to the Apostolic Chamber of Portugal. Urban condemned those who 'reduce to slavery the Indians of the Eastern and Southern Indies'. Criticisms continued in a letter written by Benedict XIV to the Bishop of Brazil in December 1743. In December 1839, Pope Gregory XVI wrote of his pain that Christians in the past 'did not hesitate to reduce to slavery, Indians, negroes and other wretched peoples, or else, by instituting or developing the trade of those who had been made slaves by others, to favour their unworthy practice'. He called for an end to both the trade and slavery. The letter forbade 'any Ecclesiastic or lay person from presuming to defend as permissible this traffic in Blacks under no matter what protest or excuse, or from publishing or teaching in any manner whatsoever, in public or privately, opinions contrary to what we have set forth in this Apostolic letter'.

Apprenticeship A system which the British authorities attempted to impose in its Caribbean colonies following the abolition of slavery in 1834, primarily to protect the interests of estate owners (who were also awarded £20 million compensation). Of the 750,000 slaves in the region, only those under six years of age were to be granted immediate liberty. The remainder were to work for their former owners for 63 hours a week, 40 of which were unpaid. This 'apprenticeship' was intended to continue for six years for field workers and four years for domestic workers and was to be supervised by salaried magistrates posted from Britain. Only Antigua refused to introduce the system and slaves on the island were granted full emancipation on 1 August 1834. In Jamaica and British Guiana (now Guyana), free slaves attempted to avoid apprenticeship by leaving the estates and establishing 'free villages'. More widely, the system proved difficult to enforce and was abandoned on 1 August 1838.

Asiento de negros (Sp. 'negroes' contract') An agreement negotiated from the 16th to the mid 18th century by the Spanish Crown with an individual or a government granting a monopoly on the import of slaves into Spanish American and Caribbean colonies. From 1600 to 1750 an estimated 450,000 slaves were imported under these agreements. The first *asiento* was negotiated by Spain with a Genoese company in 1517 for the import of 1,000 slaves a year over an eight year period. A second agreement – for 4,000 slaves a year – was signed with a German company in 1528 and later agreements were entered into with Portugal, France and Britain. The most important *asiento* was entered into with the British South Sea Company as part of the 1713 Treaty of Utrecht, under which the Company (with George I as a governor from 1718) was to transport 4,800 slaves a year for 30 years. The agreement proved unprofitable to the Company and, although renegotiated in 1748, was abandoned in 1750 in return for a payment from Spain of £100,000.

Atlanta Compromise The central message of a speech made by the black American activist and educationalist Booker T. Washington (1856–1915) at the Cotton States International Exposition in Atlanta in 1895. Washington advocated a moderate path for black advance through education, economic activity, the acquisition of property and the development of what he described as 'high character'. In this way, Washington argued, equality would follow. He condemned political agitation for equality and migration from the Southern to the Northern states. Washington was criticised by other black activists – and accused of having been selected by whites as a black leader – and opposition to his views played some part in the establishment of the National Association for the Advancement of Colored People (NAACP) in 1909.

Atlanta Riots Following a white campaign to exclude black citizens from the electoral roll, and reports of attacks on white women by black men, white mobs attacked black areas in Atlanta, Georgia, in September 1906. Blacks attempting to defend themselves were arrested and 12 people – the majority of them white – were killed in clashes. Black activists and white liberals established the Atlanta Civic League in an effort to prevent further clashes. Following the riots, legislation was introduced to deny black people the vote.

Bantustans Areas of land (later known as Homelands) allocated to black South Africans under Land Acts passed in 1913 and 1936. The black population – 81% of the country's total – was granted 13% of the land, dispersed throughout the country and largely agriculturally inferior. Under the Bantu Homelands Consolidation Act of 1971, the white apartheid regime granted the areas a spurious independence which was not recognised by any government outside South Africa. Transkei became 'independent' in 1976, Bophutatswana in 1977, Venda in 1979 and Ciskei in 1981. With the end of apartheid, the areas were reabsorbed into South Africa.

Baptist War A rising of 60,000 slaves in the British Caribbean colony of Jamaica led by Samuel Sharpe (1801–32), a Baptist deacon, from December 1831 to January 1832 following rumours that freedom granted by the British government was being withheld by the island's white-controlled assembly. A third of the island remained under control of the rebels for a week in which 200 were killed by local militia and troops. The authorities offered an amnesty to all who returned to their estate within ten days but over 340 slaves were executed in the aftermath. The alarm generated by the rising – in which over 200 properties were destroyed and damage was estimated at over £1 million – speeded progress towards emancipation.

Barbados Riots (1876 and 1937) The riots which broke out on the British Caribbean island of Barbados in April 1876 followed long-standing grievances over the conditions of the population since the abolition of slavery, particularly unemployment. Black rioters fought the police and destroyed warehouses and plantations before troops were mobilised at the end of the month. Eight rioters were killed and eight police injured. There were riots in 1937 against the deportation of the radical Clement Payne in which police opened fire, killing 14 demonstrators and wounding over 40.

Barracão (Port. 'shed') A shelter or barracks constructed to hold slaves on the coasts of Portuguese African colonies before their transportation. For two centuries, Portugal dominated the Atlantic slave trade.

Bens do evento (Port. 'goods from an event') Expression used in Brazil to describe blacks who were assumed to be slaves and were returned to their owners and, if none could be found, publicly auctioned. The term had originally denoted recaptured escaped animals.

Berbice Rising Slave rebellion in the Dutch South American colony of Berbice which took place on two plantations in February 1763, following a smaller rising the previous year. Slaves led by Coffy, Atar and Akkara killed whites and established a base to make further attacks. In March, a rebel proposal to divide the island into a white area and a territory for freed slaves was rejected by the colony's governor. In the attack that followed with troops from across the Caribbean, Coffy committed suicide and 3,000 slaves surrendered with little resistance. A third of the white population (350 at the outset) fled or were killed in the rising. The Dutch authorities declared a general amnesty in late 1763.

Birmingham bombing The murder in a white racist bombing of four girls attending Sunday school at 16th Street Baptist Church, in Birmingham, Alabama, on 15 September 1963. The incident occurred at the height of the civil rights struggle in the United States and three weeks after the 250,000 strong march on Washington DC.

Black Codes Legislation in the southern United States following the Confederate defeat in the 1861–65 Civil War which attempted to keep the freed slaves under subjection and were modelled on the former slave codes. The Codes, which varied in severity in different states, restricted civil rights and free speech, imposed curfews and forbade the ownership of land or weapons. The military governors who controlled the South until 1877 suspended the operation of the codes, the terms of which were also ostensibly outlawed by the 1866 Civil Rights Act and Fourteenth Amendment to the United States Constitution in 1868, which guaranteed the rights of citizenship to black Americans. The colonial powers France and Spain also issued black codes in the 17th and 18th centuries governing the treatment of slaves.

Black Manifesto A declaration at the National Black Economic Development conference in 1969 calling for black Americans to be paid reparations of $500 million by white Christian churches and Jewish synagogues as compensation for the part allegedly played by those institutions in slavery. There are organisations in Britain and the United States campaigning for reparations to be paid to the descendants of slaves and to Africa by the states that benefited economically from slavery.

Black Moses Name used to describe the black abolitionist Harriet Tubman (1823–1913) for her role in the Underground Railroad. Tubman, an escaped slave herself, helped over 250 slaves to liberty, including members of her family.

Black Muslims See Nation of Islam.

Black Panther Party Black American radical organisation (known as the Black Panther Party for Self-Defense) founded in Oakland, California, by Huey P. Newton (1942–89) and Bobby Seale (born 1936) in October 1966, initially to protect the black community against police violence. They were joined in the leadership by Eldridge Cleaver (born 1935) in 1967. The Panthers, who openly carried weapons and were involved in armed clashes with the police, called for community control of education and the police. In 1968–69, the Panthers reported that 28 members had been shot by police. By the late 1960s, the Panthers developed a revolutionary Marxist–Leninist ideology and developed alliances with white radical groups, arousing criticism from other black organisations which stressed racial contradictions in society. In the early 1970s the Panthers shifted towards more traditional political tactics (Seale won a third of the votes when he ran as candidate for mayor of Oakland in 1973) and community politics, establishing free health clinics, breakfast programmes for ghetto youth and classes. However, within a few years the Panthers had effectively ceased to exist, weakened by the arrests of Newton and Seale and Eldridge's self-exile in Algeria.

Black Power A term that emerged during the 1960s campaign for black civil rights in the United States, partly out of disappointment with the results of the non-violent integrationist policies of Martin Luther King Jr (1929–68). The expression – which argued the need for the destruction of the economic and political system to guarantee black liberation and implied armed revolution – was first used by Stokely Carmichael (1941–98) in 1966 on a march in Mississippi. The Black Panther Party was a notable advocate of black power but its abandonment of a call for black armed struggle in 1972 marked the final waning of any significant support for the concept.

Black Seminoles Fugitive North American slaves who joined the native American Seminoles in Florida from the early 18th century onwards. The purchase of Florida from Spain by the United States in 1819 was encouraged by slave owners in the neighbouring state of Georgia to cut off this means of escaping slavery. United States troops attacked the Seminole settlements, forcing many to flee to Mexico.

Boston Anti-emigration Declaration An angry response by black American leaders in 1862 to a suggestion by President Abraham Lincoln (shortly before he issued the Emancipation Proclamation) that the black population should emigrate to Africa or Latin America with Federal assistance. The declaration – made public at a meeting in Boston, Massachusetts – said that if black people wished to leave they would do so in their own time and at their own expense and warned, 'we don't want to go now... if anybody else wants us to go, they must compel us'.

Brazilian Anti-slavery Society Established in 1880 by black abolitionist Luis Gonzaga Pinto da Gama and André Rebouças with Joaquim Nabuco as president and with the support of the Emperor of Brazil. The Society established campaigning newspapers in Rio de Janeiro and other cities. Among other leading members was Antonio Bento, editor of the journal *Redemption* and an organiser of an 'underground railroad' which assisted the escape of slaves into the interior of the country.

Brazilian Black Front (*Frente Negra Brasileria*) Established in São Paulo in 1931 by Arlindo and Isaltino Veiga Santos, Jose Correira Leite, Gevasio Morais and Alberto Orland as a political movement to unite black and mulatto Brazilians to secure equal economic and social treatment. The Front gathered significant support and registered as a political party. The Front was repressed with all other parties under the Vargas dictatorship. When it re-emerged, the movement concentrated on cultural rather than political activities.

Brigands' Wars A series of confrontations in the British Caribbean colonies of Grenada, St Lucia and St Vincent in 1795. British troops put down a rising of Black Caribs in St Vincent. The Caribs were deported from the colony. On Grenada and St Lucia, both of which were under French influence, the slave population rose in response to the proclamation of emancipation made in the French Revolution, but the rising was crushed by British forces.

British and Foreign Anti-Slavery Society A predominantly Quaker body established by Joseph Sturge in 1839 (with Thomas Clarkson as president) which worked to internationalise the success of the abolition campaign in Britain by exhorting other countries to follow Britain's lead. The Society's attempt to prevent the import of foreign sugar produced by slaves placed it out of step with contemporary free trade sentiment while its moralising aroused antagonism abroad. The Society provided financial assistance to the newly founded French Society to Abolish Slavery in 1840.

Brown v Board of Education of Topeka, Kansas A landmark civil rights case in the United States in which the Supreme Court unanimously ruled in 1954 that it was unconstitutional to establish separate educational institutions on the basis of race. In 1954 educational segregation was required in 17 Southern states and in the District of Columbia. Although the Supreme Court decision *Plessy* v *Fergusson* in 1896 upheld segregation generally, provided separate facilities were 'equal', expenditure was often biased towards white schools despite legal action by the NAACP on the issue. Oliver Brown – represented by an NAACP legal team – demanded that his daughter be given equal educational conditions to her white friends in Topeka, Kansas. In the Supreme Court, Chief Justice Earl Warren asked whether segregation deprived 'the children of the minority group of equal educational opportunity?' and answered that the court believed it did. Implementation of desegregation was passed to district courts, which were ordered to act with 'all deliberate speed'. The vagueness of the phrase allowed a long drawn out delay of integration.

Bussa's Rebellion Slaves in the British Caribbean colony of Barbados rose under the leadership of an African-born slave driver named Bussa in April 1816. Supported by free blacks, the revolt spread over the island and took four days to be suppressed by the militia. One white was killed. Over 200 participants were executed and others were transported to Sierra Leone.

Bussing A policy adopted in some areas of the United States in an attempt to achieve a racial balance in schools by transporting students. The policy, though partially successful, met with many objections and in some areas encouraged white parents to remove their children from the public sector. While the NAACP supported the policy, other black organisations – notably CORE in 1972 – called instead for 'separate but really equal' schools.

Carter v Texas An important civil rights case in 1900 in which the United States

Supreme Court ruled that it was unconstitutional to systematically exclude black Americans from juries on racial grounds. The difficulty remained, however, of proving that systematic exclusion was taking place where there were no black members of the pool from which jurors were chosen. The Supreme Court reinforced the decision in *Norris* v *Alabama* in 1935 in which it pointed to a failure to allow qualified black citizens to become members of the jury pool.

Caudrillas (Sp. 'led ones') Term used to describe the work gangs of slaves in Spanish America operating in groups of 10–15 under the direction of a *capitan*. Slaves in the gangs were allowed to work a day a week for themselves on small plots of land allocated to them to produce food. The useful life expectancy of a slave in a work gang was under ten years.

Chicago Defender Black American newspaper founded in May 1905 by Robert S. Abbott (1870–1940) which campaigned against racial discrimination and advocated black migration from the Southern states to the North. By 1919 the paper was selling 130,000 copies and angered white Southerners with reports of lynchings and crimes committed against black people and regular comparison of black wages in different areas of the country. The *Defender* encouraged the 'Great Migration' of the 1920s with the slogans 'The Flight out of Egypt' and 'Bound for the Promised Land'. The paper became a daily in 1956.

Chicago Riot The most serious of the race riots in the United States during the 'Red Summer' of 1918. Clashes began after a black youth was killed for swimming in an area of Lake Michigan restricted to whites and police refused to arrest the white responsible. In almost two weeks of rioting, 38 people (23 blacks and 15 whites) were killed, over 500 injured and a thousand black families driven from their homes. In the aftermath, President Woodrow Wilson accused whites of being responsible.

Címmarones (Sp. 'runaways') Fugitive slaves in Latin America and Caribbean. The expression was originally used to describe rebellious slaves from the indigenous population but was soon extended to African slaves who had escaped, either as individuals or in mass revolts. They often attempted to build communities away from the European presence and were particularly concentrated in the northern and coastal provinces of Colombia and Venezuela, along the coasts of Peru, Ecuador and Central America, in the interior of Brazil. In both South America and the Caribbean they mixed with the indigenous population.

Citizens' Commission on Civil Rights A body established in the United States in 1982 by Democrats and Republicans who had been active in the 1960s civil rights movement. Commission members feared that President Ronald Reagan was undermining the gains of the 1960s and that the official Commission on Civil Rights was failing in its role of monitoring enforcement of the law. The Citizens' Commission set itself the role of

191

monitoring enforcement, publishing reports and acting as a pressure group.

Civil Rights Act, 1875 The 1875 Civil Rights Act was the last such legislation passed in the United States until 1957. Section 1 of the Act declared, 'that all persons within the jurisdiction of the United States shall be entitled to the full and equal enjoyment of the accommodations, advantages, facilities, and privileges of inns, public conveyances, on land or water, theaters, and any other places of public amusement; subject only to the conditions and limitations established by law, and applicable alike to citizens of every race and color, regardless of any previous condition of servitude'.

Civil Rights Act, 1957 The 1957 Civil Rights Act was the first such legislation passed in the United States since 1875. The Act created a Commission on Civil Rights, appointed an assistant attorney general to oversee civil rights matters, and attempted to prevent infringement of the right to vote.

Civil Rights Act, 1960 The 1960 Civil Rights Act attempted to strengthen the provisions of previous legislation on preventing the infringement of the rights of black Americans to vote. The legislation allowed the appointment of voting referees in areas in which a pattern of discrimination on racial grounds had been found.

Civil Rights Act, 1964 The 1964 Civil Rights Act, the most sweeping such legislation passed in the United States, attempted to strengthen all previous such legislation. Among the Act's provisions were the abolition of literacy tests for voting, the opening of 'any place of public accommodation... without discrimination or segregation on the ground of race, color, religion or national origin', the strengthening of the Civil Rights Commission, and an outlawing of discrimination in education and employment.

Civil Rights Act, 1968 Also known as the 'Fair Housing Act', the 1968 Civil Rights Act attempted to prevent racial discrimination in the United States in the provision of housing. Part of the Act declared it unlawful 'to refuse to sell or rent after the making of a bona fide offer, or to refuse to negotiate for the sale or rental of, or otherwise make unavailable or deny, a dwelling to any person because of race, color, religion, or national origin'.

Coartación (Sp. 'limitation') The procedure under which slaves in Spanish America could negotiate a price for which they could buy their own freedom, often by paying in instalments. The first formal agreements emerged in the early 18th century, becoming a central part of the slave code in Cuba in 1842. Urban slaves who worked in skilled trade were in the best position to benefit from this practice. There were examples of similar arrangements in all the slave-owning areas of the Americas.

Code Noir (Fr. 'Black Code') Detailed regulations on the treatment of slaves in the French Caribbean colonies of Guadeloupe, Martinique and Saint Domingue set out in an ordinance of Louis XIV in March 1685, based largely on the fear that ill-treatment of slaves by their owners would provoke revolt. The code – the 'Ordinance concerning the discipline of the Church, and the condition of Slaves in the West Indian Colonies' – included minimum standards of food, clothing and housing sufficient to ensure survival and slaves were allowed to complain about their conditions to the King's agent. A slave should be baptised as a Christian and not forced to work on Sundays or holy days. Slave families were not to be separated and slaves were allowed to marry with their owner's permission. Sexual relations between owners and slaves were forbidden and sexual attacks on slaves were an offence. The owner was to provide care for elderly and sick slaves and manumission was allowed after 20 years' work. Punishment for attempted escape ranged from mutilation to death and striking an owner was a capital offence. Free blacks were granted equivalent civil rights to whites. However, despite a liberal element in the code, many of the rights were gradually abrogated in the 18th century and by the end of the century the British abolitionist William Wilberforce (1759–1833) declared the code was largely ignored. There were similar codes on the treatment of slaves in the Spanish and Portuguese Caribbean and American colonies.

Código Filipino (Port. 'Philippines Code') A code of laws introduced in Portugal in 1603 which included provisions on slavery and slave trading. The code was fully effective in Brazil until the country's independence in 1822 and sections remained in force for much of the 19th century.

Código Negro (Sp. 'Black Code') Instructions issued by King Charles IV governing the treatment of slaves in Spanish America. Slave owners were ordered to ensure their slaves received religious instruction and were baptised, that they were given holidays on church feast days, were allowed to hire themselves out for wages on Sundays and that they were given permission to marry. Punishment floggings of over 25 lashes were banned and priests were given authority to ensure that the code's conditions were observed. The code was withdrawn in 1794 following protests from plantation owners, particularly in Cuba and Santo Domingo, but many of the religious provisions remained effective.

Colonisation The encouraging of free blacks to emigrate to Africa emerged in North America in the 18th century and was thought to have advantages among sections of both the black and white community. Among free blacks there was a consciousness that whites would never allow equality (though others felt it was essential to stay and struggle both against slavery and for full legal rights). The black trader Paul Cuffe (1759–1817) favoured colonisation, won the support of members of the US Congress and the British government, and shortly before his death organised a shipment of 38 free blacks to Sierra Leone and was planning annual voyages. Whites' motives were more complex – some felt the existence of free blacks in America threatened slavery, others believed white society would always discriminate, while others saw black colonists as a useful means of spreading Christianity in Africa. An American

Colonisation Society was founded in 1817 to encourage free Africans to emigrate as an alternative to emancipation and had a number of prominent slaveholders among its members. The concept of colonisation was increasingly criticised as the campaign for the abolition of slavery intensified from the 1830s but interest rose among black Americans in the 1850s as the pursuit of fugitives slaves intensified and following the collapse of Reconstruction in the South in 1877.

Colored Farmers' Alliance An organisation established in the United States in 1886 to work for an improvement in the condition of black farmers. By 1890 the Alliance was strongly organised in 12 states, with a large number of local branches in other areas of the country. The Alliance initially co-operated with the white National Farmers' Alliance but the two organisations severed links when whites accused the CFA of favouring black aspirations over those of whites when the CFA called for a black cotton pickers' strike.

Company of Royal Adventurers Trading to Africa Established in England in 1663 with a monopoly on the supply of slaves to the English colonies in the Caribbean and North America. The Company was backed by merchants in Bristol and London and had King Charles II, the Duke of York and Prince Rupert among its leading members. The Company issued a gold coin – the guinea – to commemorate its activities and the source of what was expected to be significant profits. However, the Company collapsed through mismanagement and was succeeded in 1672 by the more efficient Royal African Company.

Compromise of 1850 An attempt to resolve an outstanding dispute (following the failure of the Wilmot Proviso which had attempted to prohibit slavery in all lands acquired from Mexico) on the status of California and New Mexico following their seizure from Mexico in the 1846–48 war. Northern abolitionists hoped the institution of slavery would die out if expansion of the United States was limited in non-slave areas. The US Congress broadly accepted a proposal from Senator Henry Clay (1777–1852). California was to be admitted to the Union with a constitution prohibiting slavery, two territories of New Mexico and Utah were to be organised without any reference to slavery, the slave trade was abolished in Washington DC, and harsher legislation over the treatment of escaped slaves was introduced to replace the 1793 Fugitive Slave Act. However, hopes that the Compromise represented a solution of the slavery question in the new territories was disappointed.

Congress of Racial Equality (CORE) United States civil rights organisation founded by James Farmer (born 1920) in Chicago in 1942 as the Chicago Committee of Racial Equality. The organisation was initially multi-racial and favoured integration, organising picketing and sit-ins at segregated public facilities and it led the Freedom Rides of the early 1960s. In 1966 CORE adopted the slogan 'Black Power' and argued for the American blacks to control their own communities and provide goods and services for themselves. CORE's influence waned in the 1970s, particularly after a court case which questioned the organisation's fund raising methods.

CORE See Congress of Racial Equality.

The Crisis Magazine of the National Association for the Advancement of Colored People (NAACP), established under the editorship of W. E. B. Du Bois (1868–1963) in November 1910. By the 'Red Summer' of 1918 circulation reached 100,000 but slumped during the depression of the early 1930s. As well as maintaining a constant criticism of racism in the United States, *The Crisis* played a significant part in encouraging the flowering of black writing during the Harlem Renaissance of the 1920s.

Denmark Vesey Conspiracy Denmark Vesey (1767–1822), a slave who had bought his freedom after a lottery win, and an admirer of the Haitian Revolution, planned a rising with four slaves to take place in South Carolina in July 1822. As the conspiracy developed (and Vesey sought the support of the Haitian government), as many as 90,000 slave became involved. Despite betrayal by a domestic slave, Vesey continued the attempt but was thwarted by the state militia. Over a hundred slaves were arrested and 35, including Vesey, were executed.

Dred Scott case In the Dred Scott case, the Supreme Court ruled in 1857 that black Americans (whether slave or free) were not United States citizens and that the section of the 1820 Missouri Compromise barring slavery in the territories north and west of the state of Missouri was unconstitutional. The bench which made the ruling had a majority of Southern judges. Scott had been born a slave in Virginia but had eventually moved with his owner to a territory in which slavery was banned. In 1840 Scott and his wife returned with the slave owner to St Louis, where slavery was legal. When the owner died Scott sought freedom for himself, his wife and their two children. An all-white jury agreed in 1850 that two year's residence in a free territory made him free. This was reversed by the Missouri Supreme Court in 1852 and the case reached the US Supreme Court in 1856 where Scott's right to sue for his freedom was rejected. Northern abolitionist opinion was angered by Chief Justice Taney's declaration that blacks were 'so far inferior, that they had no rights which the white man was bound to respect'.

Dutch West India Company A trading company established in 1621 by the States-General of the Netherlands to compete with Spain and Portugal in their Caribbean and South American colonies and on the west coast of Africa. The Company – which was granted a trade monopoly, together with military and financial support by the States-General – had its most significant success against Portugal (occupying part of Brazil from 1630–54) and also acquired ports in West Africa from which to export slaves. It was, however, unable to acquire the dominance in the slave trade that it sought. The Company also administered the North American colony of New Netherlands (New York from 1644) but ceded the area to England in 1667. Ultimately less successful than its East Indies counterpart, the Company was placed under state control in 1791 before being dissolved in 1794.

Elemento servil (Port. 'servile element') A euphemism for slaves in Brazil in the period leading up to the abolition of the institution in 1888.

Elmina The first fortification built by the Portuguese on the West African coast in what is now Ghana in 1482, Elmina's full name was São Jorge da Mina. The Portuguese entered into trading agreements with inland African states and Elmina became a central focus of the trade in slaves, gold and ivory. Elmina was granted the status of a city in 1486. The city was captured by the Dutch in 1637, and this – combined with their seizure of northern Brazil from the Portuguese – provided them with the opportunity to dominate the Atlantic slave trade. The Dutch sold the fort to Britain in 1872.

Emancipados (Port. 'emancipated people') Free Africans in Brazil (also known as *Africanos livres*) whose rights were guaranteed by King João VI in 1818 and who were officially declared free by Brazilian courts or Anglo-Brazilian arbitration commissions. The *emancipados* were subject to an apprenticeship with government or private employers for 14 years which, in practice, differed little from actual slavery.

Emancipation Proclamation Issued by President Abraham Lincoln (1809–65) on 1 January 1863, the proclamation declared that all slaves 'within any State, or designated part of a State ... in rebellion ... shall be then and forever free'. In June 1862 Lincoln had signed a bill abolishing slavery in the Federal territories and in September had declared his intention to promulgate a proclamation in the Confederate states if they did not end their rebellion. In all, the proclamation granted freedom to 3,120,000 slaves. Despite the urging of abolitionists (and apparent support from Northern public opinion), slaves in parts of the South that had been captured by Union forces were not granted their freedom.

Emancipation War See Baptist War.

Emigrationism A policy developed in the British North America and then in the United States based on the view that black people would only find freedom by returning to Africa or by moving to their own territory. In 1773 a group of slaves in Massachusetts sought permission from the colonial authorities to be allowed to work to raise money to return to Africa. In 1787 members of the African Society in Boston asked for aid to buy land in Africa. Leading proponents of emigrationism included Paul Cuffe (1759–1817), Martin Delaney (1812–85), Alexander Crummell (1819–97) and Marcus Garvey (1887–1940). Negro Conventions met regularly in the United States from 1830 to 1864 to discuss emigration to Canada. In 1878, 207 black Americans from South Carolina sailed to Liberia and missions were sent to Ethiopia in 1903 and to the British Gold Coast colony (now Ghana) in 1915. Emigrationists opposed the white-controlled American Colonisation Society (the founder of the African republic of Liberia) which, they believed, intended to strengthen slavery in the United States by forcing free blacks to return to Africa.

Encomienda (Sp. from *encomendar*, 'to entrust') The system in the Spanish Americas by which colonists (*encomenderos*) were granted rights over a specified number of the indigenous population from whom they could extract tribute in gold or kind. In return the colonists maintained order and were to protect the indigenous population and instruct them in Christianity. The grant did not include land but in practice colonists also took over territory and turned the population into forced labourers. The Spanish Crown attempted to end abuses of the system under the Law of Burgos in 1512 and the New Law of the Indies in 1542 proved ineffective. However, as the indigenous population declined through ill-treatment and illness, the system lapsed, to be replaced with plantations using African slaves. The system ended officially in 1687.

Enforcement Act The Enforcement Act of 1870 attempted to guarantee voting rights to black Americans and to counter the intimidation by white racist groups such as the newly founded Ku Klux Klan. Section 1 of the Act declared, 'That all citizens of the United States who are or shall be qualified to vote by law at any election... shall be entitled to vote at all such elections, without distinction of race, color, or previous condition of servitude.'

Exodusters Freed slaves who moved from the Southern states – where their conditions worsened following the end of Reconstruction and the withdrawal of Federal troops in 1877 – to Kansas and the west. In 1879 there was a mass migration of 40,000 people and within a year the black population of Kansas had risen to 43,000. There was a similar migration to Oklahoma, where there were proposals that the area should become a solely black territory.

Fifteenth Amendment The 1870 amendment to the United States Constitution which attempted to prevent interference of the right to vote. Section 1 of the amendment declared, 'The right of citizens of the United States to vote shall not be denied or abridged by the United States or any State on account of race, color or previous condition of servitude.'

Fort Pillow Massacre The murder of 300 unarmed black Union soldiers captured by Confederate forces during the 1861–65 American Civil War. The troops carrying out the massacre at Fort Pillow, Tennessee, were commanded by General Nathan Bedford Forrest, who went on to establish the Ku Klux Klan in Tennessee in 1866.

Fourteenth Amendment The 1868 amendment to the United States Constitution which guaranteed rights of citizenship to black people. The first section of the amendment declared, 'All persons born or naturalised in the United States and subject to the jurisdiction thereof, are citizens of the United States and of the State wherein they reside. No State shall make or enforce any law which shall abridge the privileges or immunities of citizens of

197

the United States.' Section 2 guaranteed the right to vote of all male citizens over the age of 21.

Free Birth Law See Rio Branco Law.

Free by '63 The slogan of the National Association for the Advancement of Colored People and other groups as the civil rights campaign in the United States intensified in the 1960s, culminating in the August 1963 March on Washington for Jobs and Freedom. The year marked the one hundredth anniversary of President Lincoln's Emancipation Proclamation.

Freedmen's Bureau The Bureau of Refugees, Freedmen and Abandoned Lands – established as a Federal agency by the US government in March 1865, largely to provide aid to four million freed slaves. The Bureau was headed by Major General Oliver Howard and established over 2,000 black schools and colleges for almost 250,000 students, built hospitals, negotiated employment contracts and investigated claims of discriminatory treatment. Although 4,000 former slave families were settled on government-owned land in the Southern states, President Andrew Johnson thwarted the Bureau's wider ambitions by pardoning former slave owners, allowing them to retain their estates and forcing freed slaves to become sharecroppers. However, the Bureau – discredited with charges of corruption and inefficiency, denied sufficient federal funds and accused of being the political tool of the Radical Republicans – was wound up in 1872.

Freedom's Journal The first black American newspaper, established in March 1827 in New York City by the Jamaican-born journalist John Brown Russwurm (1799–1851) and the Presbyterian clergyman Samuel Cornish (c1795–1859) to campaign for the abolition of slavery and improvement in the treatment of free blacks. The Journal's first editorial declared, 'We wish to plead our own cause. Too long have others spoken for us.' The paper was re-established as the equally short-lived *Rights for All* in 1830.

Free Soil Party A political party formed in New York in 1848 by a number of anti-slavery groupings, including the Liberal Party and a dissident section of Democrats known as the 'Barnburners'. The Free Soilers were not abolitionists but opposed any extension of slavery into the territories and the admission of new slave states to the Union. Martin Van Buren ran as the party's presidential candidate in 1848 under the slogan 'Free soil, free speech, free labor and free men'. Van Buren was unsuccessful but the party won over 291,000 votes and 13 seats in the House of Representatives. Two members were elected to the Senate on a Free Soil Democratic ticket, Salmon P. Chase in 1848 and Charles Sumner in 1851. However, the secession of the 'Barnburners' in 1852 undermined the party's candidate in that year's presidential election, John P. Hale, although he polled 156,000 votes. The Free Soilers joined the emerging Republican Party in 1856.

French West Indies Company The *Compagnie des Indes Occidentales* was established by the French finance ministry in 1664 with a monopoly of slave trading to the French Caribbean. Although the Company had some success in promoting tobacco plantations in Saint Domingue, its activities were opposed by planters and traders – there was a planters' revolt in Martinique in 1666 – and its was dissolved after a decade of activity.

Fugitive Slave Acts Legislation in the United States which provided for the return of escaped slaves between states. Magistrates were empowered to rule on whether or not a person was a fugitive slave and to impose a $500 fine on anyone who assisted the slave. Enforcement was relaxed by Northern states as they abolished slavery, to the anger of the South. A second, and harsher, act was passed as part of the Compromise of 1850. A slaveholder simply had to produce the escaped slave and an affidavit of ownership to a judge for the slave to be returned. Law officers were forced to assist slaveholders seeking the return of their property. The 1850 Act threatened heavy penalties for ignoring its provisions and denied escaped slaves the right to testify or to trial by jury. However, a number of trials under the Act intensified the conflict between slavery and anti-slavery supporters. In 1860, South Carolina blamed Northern nullification of the acts as one cause of secession and the ensuing Civil War. Both Acts were repealed by the Union Congress in 1864.

'Gag rule' A procedure adopted by the United States House of Representatives in 1836 under which anti-slavery petitions received by the House were to be laid on the table without discussion or action. A campaign against the rule led by former President John Quincy Adams led to over 200,000 petitions being sent to the House from Northern states in one session. The rule was rescinded in 1844.

Gideon's Band United States abolitionist activists, predominantly women, who went to the South Carolina Sea Islands from March 1862, following their capture by Union forces, to educate freed slaves and to oversee their work as free labourers. Band members taught former slaves to read and sew and took responsibility for distributing clothing and supplies despatched by the Northern freedmen's aid associations established in November 1861.

'Grandfather clauses' A means in the southern United States of preventing black citizens from voting by restricting the ballot to descendants of people who had the vote on 1 January 1867, before Reconstruction attempted to assert black rights. The system began in Louisiana, where a clause was written into the state constitution. The practice was declared unconstitutional by the Supreme Court in the case of *Guinn* v *United States* in 1915.

Guadeloupe Rising A rebellion by slaves from Angola in the French Caribbean colony of Guadeloupe in 1656. The rebels appointed two African kings and planned to kill all whites on the island. The rebellion failed, partly due to the reluctance of slaves from other parts of Africa to join, and the majority of the participants were executed.

Harper's Ferry Raid An attack on the Federal armoury at Harper's Ferry on 16 October 1859, led by the white abolitionist John Brown (1800–59) who hoped

199

to provoke a local slave rising to enable him to establish a base from which to launch further raids on slave owners. Brown rejected appeals by the radical black abolitionists Frederick Douglass and Henry Highland Garnet (who himself had called for a slave rising in 1843) to abandon the plan. Of the 22 men involved in the assault, five were black. After capturing the armoury, Brown took 60 whites hostage in a rifle factory. Ten of the attackers were killed by the militia and soldiers led by Colonel Robert E. Lee (later Confederate commander in the Civil War). Brown and the survivors were tried and executed, although Brown's attacks on slavery during his trial won sympathy in the Northern states and heightened the bitterness leading to the outbreak of the Civil War in 1861.

Havana Company The Havana Company was established in the Spanish Caribbean colony of Cuba in 1740 at a time when a growing concentration on sugar cane production increased demand for slaves to work the plantations. The Company was formed to stimulate agricultural development by organising the importation of more slaves and to regulate the export trade. However, the Company proved itself to be inefficient and was responsible during its 21 year existence for importing fewer slaves than the 10,000 the British were able to during their ten month occupation of Havana in 1762.

Hispaniola Rising The first recorded slave rebellion in the Americas which began in December 1522 on an estate belonging to Don Diego, the son of Christopher Columbus, on Hispaniola (now Haiti). Twenty slaves from Diego's estate joined slaves from a neighbouring estate and fled into the mountains, where they conducted a guerrilla war against the Spanish authorities. Diego led a force against them and they were captured and hanged.

Indentured labour A form of servitude in North and South America and the Caribbean, initially confined to Europeans. Under the system, an individual was given passage in return for an agreement to work on cotton, rice, sugar or tobacco plantations for four to seven years or until he was 21, at which point he would be released and sometimes allowed a plot of land. The 20 Africans landed at Jamestown by a Dutch ship in 1619 arrived as indentured workers. The system was not as profitable as slavery, which replaced it.

'Jim Crow' laws Legislation in many American states from the 1880s to the 1960s which enforced segregation by ordering business owners and public institutions to keep blacks and whites separate and outlawed mixed race marriage. The derivation of the term 'Jim Crow' is obscure but is believed to refer to a black character (played by a white performer) in a minstrel show. The Supreme Court decision *Plessy* v *Fergusson* in 1896 upheld segregation, and by implication 'Jim Crow', with its ruling that the provision of 'separate but equal' facilities was constitutional. The Southern states were completely segregated by 1900. Examples of 'Jim Crow' were a Florida law forbidding marriage 'between a white person and a negro, or between a white person and a person of negro descent to the fourth generation' and segregation of mental hospitals, barbers and burial for blacks and whites in Georgia. In

Mississippi there was a fine of $500 and/or six months imprisonment for a person convicted of 'printing, publishing or circulating... matter urging or presenting for public acceptance or general information, arguments or suggestions in favor of social equality or intermarriage between whites and negroes'. While the NAACP led legal action against segregation in the 20th century (with the Supreme Court decision *Brown* v *Board of Education of Topeka* a landmark victory in 1954), direct action by, for example, the Freedom Riders and during the lunch counter sit-ins of the 1960s, pushed integration forward.

Kansas–Nebraska Act Legislation passed in the United States in 1854 which attempted to resolve differences between the North and the South over the organisation of the Kansas and Nebraska territories. The South opposed the provision of 1820 Missouri Compromise banning slavery in the territories. The Kansas–Nebraska Act made concessions to the South by repealing the anti-slavery clause and creating two territories in which popular (or 'squatter') sovereignty would decide the issue. The result was the conflict of 'bleeding Kansas' as both sides attempted to force the decision their way, intensifying the divisions leading to civil war in 1861.

'King Cotton' A reference to the importance of cotton as a crop in the Southern United States. The bulk of the labour force involved in the crop's production consisted of slaves. The invention by Eli Whitney of the cotton gin in 1793 simplified the production process and increased the demand for slaves in the 'New South': Alabama, Louisiana, Mississippi and Texas. By 1850 almost two thirds of plantation slaves were involved in cotton production, with slaves constituting 40% of the Southern population. Over 35% of slaves in the entire Americas were in the Southern United States.

Ku Klux Klan White racist organisation founded by former Confederate soldiers led by ex-general Nathan Forrest (responsible for a massacre of unarmed black soldiers during the Civil War) in Tennessee in 1866, initially to prevent freed slaves from exercising voting and other civil rights. Klan members – organised in an Invisible Empire led by a Grand Wizard – wore white robes to hide their identity. The Klan waned following legislation which authorised the use of Federal troops to counter its activities in 1871 but Southern blacks were already being terrorised out of political activity. The Klan revived in 1915 and by the mid 1920s was two million strong and politically influential not only in the Southern United States but also in parts of the North and West. Following collapse in the mid 1940s there were further revivals in the 1950s and 1960s (when Klan members murdered civil rights workers) and again in the 1980s, partly feeding on white grievances against affirmative action.

Ladina/ladino (Port. 'cunning') Term used in the Portuguese colony of Brazil to describe an African who was able to speak Portuguese and had absorbed elements of Portuguese culture and Christianity. The term was also used in Spanish to describe an African slave born in Spain.

Las Siete Partidas (Sp. 'the seven parts') A code of laws compiled between 1256 and 1265 by Alfonso the Learned based on Roman, Arab and Visigoth law. The code formed the basis of rules governing the treatment of slaves in Spanish territories. The code recognised slavery as an integral part of the Spanish economy and set out three categories of slaves: prisoners who had been engaged in war against the Catholic faith, the children of slaves, and free people who had voluntarily surrendered their liberty. Slaves had a number of rights, including the right to a smallholding of land, the right to marry and to manumission. Owners were forbidden to kill or ill treat their slaves. The code was said to have been responsible for a more favourable treatment of slaves by owners under the authority of Spain than in for example, British colonies or the United States.

'Law of the free womb' See Rio Branco Law.

Lei Áurea (Port. 'Golden Law') The legislation abolishing slavery which came into effect in Brazil on 13 May 1888.

Lei do ventre livre (Port. 'Law of the free womb') See Rio Branco Law.

'Letter from Birmingham Jail' A seminal statement on civil rights and non-violent disobedience written by Martin Luther King Jr (1929–68) when he was in prison during a campaign in Birmingham, Alabama in 1963. King had been criticised by white clergymen for leading 'unwise and untimely' demonstrations. King vividly described the black experience in the United States – 'harried by day and haunted by night by the fact that you are a Negro, living constantly on tiptoe stance never quite knowing what to expect next' – and declared, 'We know from experience that freedom is never voluntarily given by the oppressor; it must be demanded by the oppressed.'

Liberal Party The first political party in the United States to put forward the abolition of slavery as a central plank. James G. Birney ran as the party's presidential candidate in 1840, when he received little support, and in 1844, when he won 62,000 votes. The Liberals united with other groups in 1848 to form the Free Soil Party.

Louisiana Rising A slave rising in which 400 slaves led by Charles Deslondes (a free mulatto from Santo Domingo) destroyed plantations and killed two whites, forcing others to flee in panic to New Orleans. As the revolt spread, over 600 troops were deployed against them. In fighting outside New Orleans, which the rebels were attempting to capture, 66 slaves were killed and 17 captured. The leaders were executed and their heads displayed on poles in the city. There were further risings in the state in September and October 1840.

Manumission The freeing of a slave by an owner. The practice was initially more common among Spanish and Portuguese slave owners than, for example, British, Dutch or North Americans. However, from 1780 to 1810 there were increasing examples in the United States, with the free population rising from

4,000 to 94,000 over this period. Alarm generated by the success of the Haitian Revolution, and by increasing slave rebelliousness in the Southern states, prompted South Carolina and Mississippi to ban manumission in 1822, followed by Arkansas in 1858 and Maryland and Alabama in 1860.

'March against Fear' A civil rights demonstration in the United States in 1966 which followed the shooting of James Meredith in Tennessee. The march, which was organised by the SCLC, SNCC and CORE, went from the spot at which Meredith was shot to Jackson, Mississippi. During the march, the expression 'Black Power' was used for the first time by young activists, who also suggested substituting 'We shall overrun' for the slogan 'We shall overcome'.

Maroons Fugitive slaves who established settlements in the hills of Jamaica, particularly after the island came under English control in 1655. Initially there was little contact between the Maroon settlements and white colonists who were largely confined to the coast. However, following clashes in which colonial forces captured the Maroon base of Nannytown, the Maroons signed treaties with the British authorities in 1738 and 1739 under which they were guaranteed land. In return the Maroons promised to return any further fugitives who fled. A second war between the British and the Maroons was fought in 1795 and many were deported to Nova Scotia and Sierra Leone.

Mason–Dixon Line Originally established as a boundary in 1667 between the English North American colonies of Maryland and Pennsylvania (and named after the surveyors Charles Mason and Jeremiah Dixon), the line came to mark the division between Southern slave states and Northern free states in the early 19th century. The term was first used in this context during Congressional debates over the 1820 Missouri Compromise. The expression 'Dixie' to denote the Confederate states derives from the term.

MIA See Montgomery Improvement Association.

Middle Passage The sea journey across the Atlantic forced on African captives before they were sold as slaves in the Americas and the Caribbean islands. From the mid 15th to the mid 19th century an estimated 11.7 million slaves were transported across the Atlantic. Of these, 9.8 million survived the journey, with 3.9 million going to Brazil, 3.8 million to the non-Hispanic Caribbean, 1.6 million to the Spanish territories and half a million to the United States. In the 17th century, 380,000 slaves were transported, 6 million in the 18th century (with the trade reaching a peak in the last quarter) and over three million in the 19th century. Most Western European nations participated in the trade, with Portugal, Britain and France predominating. Chained in cramped and airless conditions, denied adequate food and water, the victims suffered physically from sea sickness, typhoid, measles, yellow fever or smallpox, as well as the psychological torment of captivity. The average annual death rate on voyages ranged from 10% to 20%. The time of the journey fell from three months in the 17th century to a month in the mid 19th century.

Missouri Compromise Legislation passed in the United States in 1820–21 which attempted to overcome the crisis of extending slavery. Under the Compromise, Missouri was admitted to the Union as a slave state while, as a balance, Maine entered as a free state. Slavery was prohibited in the territory known as the Louisiana Purchase (bought from France in 1803) north of 36°30'. An attempt by Missouri to insert a clause in its state constitution banning the entry of free blacks was resisted by Congress. The agreement, despite resentment among abolitionists in the North and the slave states of the South, remained effective until its repeal under the 1854 Kansas–Nebraska Act.

Montgomery Bus Boycott The refusal of the black population of Montgomery, Alabama, to use segregated public transport following the arrest of NAACP activist Rosa Parks (born 1913) for resisting an attempt to force her to give up her seat to a white passenger. The boycott, which began in December 1955 and ended with a Supreme Court decision in December 1956 ruling segregation to be illegal, brought Martin Luther King Jr (1929–68) into prominence as the voice of black civil rights in the United States.

Montgomery Improvement Association (MIA) An organisation established in Montgomery, Alabama, in December 1955 during a boycott of the bus system. The MIA was formed under the presidency of Martin Luther King Jr (1929–68) to campaign for wider integration in the city. King declared that the MIA's objective was to improve race relations, 'We are not just trying to improve the Negro of Montgomery but the whole of Montgomery.'

Morant Bay Rebellion A rising in the British Caribbean colony of Jamaica in 1865 in protest against the imposition of new taxes and the unpopularity of local magistrates. Four hundred people from the area around Morant Bay stormed the court house in October to release a prisoner and were confronted by the militia. The protestors killed 15 members of the militia and magistrates and over the next three days attacked plantations and killed three owners. The rising was ruthlessly put down on the orders of the British governor, Edward Eyre, and a thousand black homes were destroyed, 439 people killed and 600 sentenced to floggings. The leader of the original demonstration, George Gordon – one of ten black members of a 47-strong House of Assembly – was court martialled and hanged. In Britain, Eyre was acquitted on charges of using excessive methods.

Moyne Commission A Royal Commission under Lord Moyne which was appointed by the British government in 1938 to investigate conditions in the Caribbean colonies following serious disturbances on many of the islands, Moyne's report in 1939 (not made wholly public until 1944) attacked the colonial administration for its economic failures and its incompetence in education, health, housing and industrial relations. The Colonial Development and Welfare Act 1941 allocated funds to improve conditions in the region and provided for reforms to allow greater popular participation in the preparation for universal adult suffrage and representative government.

NAACP See National Association for the Advancement of Colored People.

National Association for the Advancement of Colored People (NAACP) For many years the leading organisation working against racial discrimination and for integration in the United States, the NAACP was formed as a multi-racial non-violent campaigning body on 12 February 1909, the anniversary of Lincoln's birthday. The leading black figure at the movement's foundation was W. E. B. Du Bois (1868–1963), who became director of research and editor of *The Crisis*, and the NAACP came increasingly under black control. The NAACP had an early success with the US Supreme Court decision on *Guinn* v *United States* outlawing 'grandfather clauses' which denied black people voting rights. In the 1920s and 1930s the NAACP campaigned for legislation to combat lynching and for the integration of the labour movement. A NAACP Legal Defense and Education Fund established in 1939 separated from the parent body in 1957. A major success for the NAACP came with the 1954 US Supreme Court decision on *Brown* v *Board of Education of Topeka* which overthrew the segregationist doctrine of 'separate but equal'. The NAACP played a leading role in campaigns leading to the Civil Rights Acts of 1957 and 1964 and the Voting Rights Act of 1965. As the civil rights campaign intensified in the 1950s and 1960s, NAACP membership reached almost half a million and the movement's slogan 'Free by '63' dominated the 1963 March on Washington for Jobs and Freedom. There were, however, demands for greater militancy and the NAACP faced competition from the Congress of Racial Equality, the Southern Christian Leadership Conference and the Student Nonviolent Coordinating Committee. The NAACP remained committed to legal change and led the campaign for the imposition of economic sanctions on the South African apartheid regime in 1986.

National Association of Colored Women Established in Washington DC in July 1896 by the black civil rights activist Mary Church Terrell (1863–1954) to co-ordinate local black women's clubs. The Association was formed in response to intensifying segregation by whites in women's clubs which, until the 1890s, had admitted black members. The Association also hoped to confront increasingly negative portrayals of black women in newspapers.

National Negro Business League An organisation established in August 1900 at a Boston conference attended by 400 delegates from 34 states and convened by the black activist Booker T. Washington (1856–1915). The League was intended to further Washington's advocacy of black achievement rather than political agitation to secure civil rights and encouraged the development of black business. By 1907 the League had 320 branches throughout the United States.

National Negro Convention movement A series of conventions held by black Americans from 1830 to 1864, initially to discuss a proposal for a mass migration to Canada to escape oppression in the United States. A ten day National Negro Convention meeting in Philadelphia in September 1830, with 40 delegates from nine states, established an American Society of Free People of Color. The Society, which supported emigration for free black Americans with children, also favoured attempts to improve black conditions in the United States. Over the next 30 years, while regular national conventions continued to be held, there was also a growth in the number of local and state conventions.

National Urban League The League was established in New York City in 1911 as the National League on Urban Conditions Among Negroes to co-ordinate the activities of a number of groups (including the Committee for Improving the Industrial Conditions of Negroes in New York, the National League for the Protection of Colored Women and the Committee on Urban Conditions Among Negroes) working among black migrants from the Southern states on employment, housing and health issues. The League remains in existence and works for equal economic and political opportunity for all racial minority groups in the United States.

Nation of Islam Black Muslim movement in the United States which emerged in 1933 from a schism in the Moorish Science Temple, established in 1913. Led by Elijah Muhammad (1897–1975), the Nation saw Islam as the black religion and argued that the corruption inherent in white civilisation could only be avoided by economic independence and black separatism through which black people would find 'freedom from contempt'. The Nation's encouragement of separatism placed it out of step with the civil rights campaigns of the 1950s and 1960s but support grew as disappointment mounted with the movement's achievements. In the 1950s and 1960s the movement's leading spokesman was Malcolm X (born Malcolm Little in 1925) until he left in 1964. In 1975 Elijah Muhammad was succeeded as leader of what had become a prosperous organisation by his son Warith who moved to more orthodox Islam and renamed the movement the World Community of al-Islam. The movement divided as Louis Farrakhan (born Louis Walcott in 1933) attempted to re-assert the original programme, reformed the Nation of Islam in 1981 and established its journal *The Final Call*. Farrakhan – increasingly influential as a black American leader – organised a successful Million Man March on Washington DC in 1995.

Nat Turner Revolt A slave rebellion in Virginia in 1831 led by Nat Turner (1800–31). Turner declared while preaching on the eve of the rising that it was necessary to 'take up Christ's struggle for the liberation of the oppressed' and encouraged killing children on the grounds that 'nits breed lice'. On 22 August Turner and eight supporters attacked slave owners' houses, seizing weapons and horses and going on to kill whites in further attacks. The rebels were intercepted by the state militia on their way to seize Jerusalem, the county seat. Turner escaped but was eventually captured and executed. A total of 60 whites died in the rising, 55 slaves were executed and a further 200 murdered. In the ensuing panic throughout the Southern states, religious meetings addressed by blacks were banned.

Negro boçal (Port. 'black mouth') A newly imported African slave in Brazil who had not been exposed to Portuguese culture and was unable to speak any of the language.

Negro de ganho (Port. 'profitable black') A slave in Brazil who was allowed by his or her master to work or to be employed by others. The slave was obliged to pay a portion of earnings to the owner.

New Orleans Riot Part of a pattern of white violence directed against freed slaves in the South, the 1866 riot encouraged Northern support for the Reconstruction policy. In July whites killed 35 blacks and injured over a hundred with no interference from the authorities. In response to this and other similar incidents, Radical Republicans went on to win a majority in Congress for Reconstruction in the November elections.

New York Draft Riots A week of rioting in 1863 – during the 1861–65 American Civil War – which began as a protest against conscription into the Union Army but developed into racial clashes. Violence turned against black citizens because they were ineligible to be drafted into the army and whites feared they would take their jobs. Over a thousand people, mainly black, were killed and injured and over a million dollars worth of property damaged. A black orphanage was among the buildings burnt down.

New York Conspiracy Tension was high in Britain's North American colonies following a 1739 slave rebellion in South Carolina and in March 1741 Fort George in New York was destroyed in a fire. When an English servant informed the authorities that this was part of a black conspiracy, hundreds of whites fled New York in panic. There were accusations that Catholic priests were involved in the conspiracy on behalf of Spanish interests. In ensuing militia attacks on black people, 15 were burned alive, eight were hanged and 71 transported out of the area. The authorities later admitted there was no evidence of a conspiracy.

New York Revolt A slave rebellion in April 1712 in the British North American colony of New York in which 15 whites were killed and many injured before the rising was crushed by the militia. Over 20 slaves were executed for their participation while a further six committed suicide after capture. Fears aroused by the rising encouraged attempts to prevent the growth of numbers of slaves in the northern colonies. Pennsylvania imposed a high duty on imports in August 1712 and Massachusetts banned all slave imports in 1713. In New York itself legislation was introduced imposing a stricter regime on slaves.

Niagara Movement Black American organisation established in 1905 at Niagara Falls, Canada, by William Monroe Trotter (1872–1934) and W. E. B. Du Bois (1868–1963) to combat white discrimination in the United States. The Movement rejected the conservative view of Booker T. Washington (1856–1915) that black Americans should not confront white racism directly and campaigned against educational segregation, the 'Jim Crow' laws and the violation of voting rights. The Movement won little support, despite building 30 branches, and in 1909 merged with the National Negro Conference to form the multi-racial National Association for the Advancement of Colored People (NAACP), with a similar programme of anti-discrimination activity.

North Star Black American newspaper founded by the abolitionist activist Frederick Douglass (c1817–95) in December 1847 and published in different forms until 1863 with funds and a press provided by British abolitionists. The paper's masthead proclaimed, 'Right is of no sex; truth is of no color; God is the Father of us all – and all are brethren.' Douglass established the *North Star* to further what he saw as the need for a more prominent black role in the abolitionist movement and his action led to a break with the white abolitionist William Lloyd Garrison (1805–79). The *North Star* merged with the Liberty Party's newspaper in 1851 and was then renamed the *Frederick Douglass Paper.*

Nossa Senhora do Rosario (Port. 'Our Lady of the Rosary') The patron saint of slaves in Brazil.

Palmares The most prominent of the fugitive slave settlements (also known as *quilimbos*) established in Brazil. Construction of the settlement began in 1605 in the province of Alagoas and Palmares was soon described as 'Black Troy'. Palmares became a magnet not only for fugitive slaves but also for mulattos and even dissident whites, including priests, and at one point its population reached an estimated 20,000. The settlement was attacked by Portuguese forces throughout its existence and was finally broken up by a 9,000-strong army in 1695.

Peça (Port. 'piece') Term used in the Portuguese slave trade to denote a slave of a particular weight.

Pecúlio (Port. 'personal possessions') The personal property of a slave in Brazil, ownership of which was officially acknowledged by the Rio Branco Law which came into effect on 26 September 1871.

Plantocracy An expression first used in England in the late 18th century to describe owners of plantations in the British West Indies, reflecting the wealth to be made from sugar cultivated by slaves. The word was later used to refer to the British colonial authorities in the Caribbean.

Plessy v Ferguson The United States Supreme Court decision of May 1896 which, through the doctrine of 'separate but equal', institutionalised racial segregation into the 20th century. Homer Plessy had refused to ride in a designated black railway carriage in Louisiana and was charged under a state law requiring 'equal but separate' facilities for blacks and whites. When the case eventually reached the Supreme Court, the court ruled that the object of the Fourteenth Amendment to the Constitution in 1868 had been 'undoubtedly to enforce the absolute equality of the two races before the law, but, in the nature of things, it could not have been intended to abolish distinctions based upon color, or to enforce social, as distinguished from political, equality, or a commingling of the two races upon terms unsatisfactory to either. Laws permitting, and even requiring, their separation... do not necessarily imply the inferiority of either race to the other.'

Prohibition on Importation of Slaves Act The Act of 1807 which outlawed importing slaves into the United States. Section 1 of the Act declared, 'That from and after the first day of January, one thousand eight hundred and eight, it shall not be lawful to import or bring into the United States or the territories thereof from any foreign kingdom, place, or country, any negro, mulatto, or person of colour, as a slave, or to be held to service or labour.' The legislation provided for fines, imprisonment and confiscation of vessels equipped for slave trading.

Prosser Rebellion The first major slave revolt in the United States, led in 1800 by Gabriel Prosser (c1775–1800), a slave in Virginia. Prosser's plan was to kill all whites (except Quakers because of their involvement in the abolitionist movement), seize Richmond and call on the state's 300,000 slaves to rebel. Although the rising was betrayed, a thousand slaves gathered in torrential rain. The state governor declared martial law and despatched 650 troops to capture the slaves. Prosser and over 30 others were hanged for the part they played in the rebellion.

Quakers The Quakers, or the Society of Friends, were established in England by George Fox (1624–91) as a radical Protestant sect and its members played a central part in the abolitionist campaign in both Britain and the United States. In 1671 Fox called on Quakers who owned slaves to free them after a period of labour and in 1688 members of the sect in the English North American colony of Pennsylvania declared slavery to be contrary to the teachings of Christianity. Despite this, many Quakers continued to hold slaves and to participate in the slave trade. In Britain in 1776 Quakers were ordered to free slaves they held and in 1783 to cease involvement in the slave trade. Quakers presented an unsuccessful petition against the slave trade to Parliament in 1783. In 1787 the majority of committee members of the newly established Society for Effecting the Abolition of the Slave Trade were Quakers. In North America, Quakers trading in slaves were excluded from membership in 1755 and ownership of slaves was forbidden in 1773. Quakers remained prominent among anti-slavery activists in both Britain and the United States in the 19th century.

Queiroz Law Legislation ending the slave trade to Brazil enacted in 1850 after British warships had entered Brazilian territorial waters to intercept slave traders. In the two years immediately preceding passage of the law, 150,000 slaves were imported into the country. The internal slave trade was allowed to continue and the legislation on the import of slaves was largely evaded. Slavery itself in Brazil was not abolished until 1888.

Quilombo A word, meaning 'village' or 'union', derived from an African language and used to describe fugitive slave settlements built away from centres of European occupations. A *quilombo* provided not only a haven from slavery but also a base in which to preserve African cultural traditions. Settlements of this type were constructed on the northern and coastal areas of Colombia and Venezuela, in Central America, the Caribbean and in the interior of Brazil. The best known of the settlements, Palmares in Brazil (which at its height had an estimated 20,000 inhabitants), came into prominence in the early 17th century and survived a number of attacks until falling to Portuguese forces in 1695. Quilombo Grande, a settlement in the Minas Gerais region of Brazil with a population of a thousand, was destroyed in 1759.

Recaptives Captured Africans released from slave ships off the coast of West Africa by Royal Navy vessels following the British abolition of the slave trade in 1807. Between 1807 and 1850 over 40,000 slaves were freed and settled by the British in Sierra Leone.

Reconstruction The period of rebuilding in the Southern United States that followed the 1861–65 Civil War. Reconstruction was intended to rebuild the Southern states economically and politically, while at the same time integrating the freed slaves by extending and protecting their civil rights. The Freedmen's Bureau worked from 1865 to 1872 to provide economic and educational aid to former slaves and to homeless whites. In addition, the federal government passed legislation to protect black rights, the Fourteenth Amendment to the Constitution providing recognition as citizens and the Fifteenth Amendment guaranteeing the right to vote. The opening of political activity to black citizens in the Southern states (and their alliance with white Republicans) undermined the discriminatory Black Codes brought in by state legislatures in 1865–66 and two black Americans were elected to the Senate and 20 to the House of Representatives. But, as Northern concern faded, Federal troops withdrew from the South in 1877. With the re-emergence of white Democrat power in Southern state governments, the gains made by blacks under Reconstruction were systematically undermined.

'Red Summer' The description by an NAACP leader of the period from April–October 1918 when there were race riots in 25 cities throughout the United States, including Chicago, Philadelphia and Washington DC. Over this period, 79 black people were lynched, 11 burned alive and over a thousand seriously injured.

Reparations See Black Manifesto.

Representative Government Associations Political organisations established throughout the British Caribbean in 1918, largely by World War One veterans, to agitate for elected representation on the governing legislative councils and for a federation of the Caribbean colonies. The first association had been formed by T. A. Marryshow (1887–1958) in Grenada in 1913.

Rio Branco Law Legislation (also known as the 'law of free birth') passed on

28 September 1871 introducing reforms to slavery in Brazil. The law was enacted under José Maria da Silva Branco, Viscount do Rio Branco (the prime minister from 1871–73) and Joaquim Nabucoo de Aruajo, who went on to establish the Brazilian Anti-Slavery Society in 1880. Among the most important sections were those granting freedom to the children of slave women born on or after that date (although owners could require them to work until they reached the age of 21) and recognising the right of slaves to have personal property.

Roça (Port. 'clearing') A patch of land granted to slaves in Brazil on which to raise a crop for sale or personal consumption. The practice was not uncommon in most European colonies in the Caribbean and South America, although in the 18th century codes governing slaves' lives removed many of the privileges of this kind.

Royal African Company A company founded under Royal Charter in 1672 with a monopoly in the slave trade to English colonies in the Caribbean and North America. In return for its monopoly the Company had to establish 17 forts or factories on the African coast. By 1680, the Royal African Company – which included the Duke of York, Prince Rupert and most members of the Royal Family, together with the liberal philosopher John Locke among its shareholders – was transporting an average of 5,000 slaves a year. But as complaints from English merchants excluded from the profitable trade intensified, the government ended the monopoly in 1698. Between 1672 and 1713, the Company purchased 125,000 slaves on the African coast, lost a fifth crossing the Atlantic and sold 100,000 on to Caribbean planters.

Royal French Guinea Company The Company was granted a concession by Spain in 1702 to transport a total of 48,000 slaves over a ten year period to Spanish America. The slaves were carried by the Company to Martinique and Saint Domingue for onward transportation but the Company went bankrupt in 1710.

Saaiva-Cotegipe Law Legislation passed in Brazil on 28 September 1885 freeing all slaves aged 60 or over. However, slaves released under this law were obliged to work for their former owners without pay for five years or until they reached the age of 65.

SCLC See Southern Christian Leadership Conference.

Scottsboro Case One of the most significant racial trials in the United States which followed accusations in March 1931 that nine black youths had raped two white women in Scottsboro, Alabama. A rushed trial before an all-white jury, at which eight of the nine were sentenced to death, prompted a campaign to secure a rehearing. The campaign intensified when one of the women withdrew her allegations. However, all-white juries found the youths guilty at trials in 1933 and 1936. In 1937 four were released and the remaining five served long sentences, the last remaining in prison until 1950. Later examination concluded all nine had been victims of racist justice.

'Seasoning' A period during which slaves newly arrived from Africa were initiated into the labour and discipline their owners would require and tested for their ability to survive disease. Many slaves bound for North America were 'seasoned' in the Caribbean plantations before being passed on. It has been estimated that nearly half of all new slaves died within three years during the process.

Segregation Separation of people, primarily in the use of public facilities, employment, education and housing, usually accompanied by a denial of political rights to the excluded group. Segregation often becomes self-per-petuating, with stereotypes developing as the dominant group believes its privileges derive from some inherent superiority and those who are excluded take on a sense of inferiority. The most notable forms of racial discrimination are represented by the 'Jim Crow' laws in the United States in the 19th and 20th centuries (underpinned judicially by the 1896 *Plessy* v. *Fergusson* case) and by apartheid in South Africa. The civil rights campaigns in the United States in the 1950s and 1960s achieved desegregation legislation, but *de facto* segregation remains. In addition, poor blacks are economically relatively worse off than whites and middle-class blacks than in the 1930s. Similarly, the abolition of formal legislative apartheid in South Africa in the 1990s did not mean an immediate end to differences in economic status and opportunity between the races.

Senzala (Port. 'slave quarters') Buildings in which slaves were housed on plantations in Brazil.

Sharpeville Massacre During a protest against the South African apartheid pass laws in March 1960, 69 unarmed demonstrators were killed by police in the black township of Sharpeville, near Johannesburg. The massacre, which aroused international protests, brought the country close to civil war. The government responded by banning the African National Congress (ANC) and the Pan-Africanist Congress and the ANC's armed wing, Umkhonto we Sizwe (Spear of the Nation) was formed shortly afterwards.

Ship revolts Resistance by slaves which took place on the vessels transporting them to America and the Caribbean. Among notable revolts were those which took place on the *Tiger* in 1702, when 40 slaves and two crew were killed, on the *Adventure* in 1753, when the ship was seized and run aground by slaves, and among the most successful were those on the *Little George* (1730), the *Jolly Bachelor* (1740) and the *Amistad* (1839) when slaves being carried from Cuba to the United States captured the ship.

Slave narratives Over 6,000 works describing the experience of slavery written by former slaves (or ghost written for them) were published between 1700 and 1945. Autobiographies written by former slaves in the United States, many of whom went on to become abolitionist activists, include Frederick Douglass, *My Bondage and My Freedom* (1855), Josiah Henson, *Truth Stranger than Fiction* (1850), Leonard Black, *The Life and Sufferings of Leonard Black, a*

Fugitive from Slavery (1847), Henry Bibb, *Narrative of the Life and Adventures of Henry Bibb, an American Slave* (1849) and Harriet A. Jacobs, *Incidents in the Life of a Slave Girl* (1861). One of the few personal accounts by an African of slavery and the slave trade is Olaudah Equiano, *The Interesting Narrative of the Life of Olaudah Equiano, or Gustavas Vassa, the African*, first published in England in 1789.

SNCC See Student Nonviolent Co-ordinating Committee.

Society for Effecting the Abolition of the Slave Trade The Society was formed in Britain in April 1787 by Granville Sharp (1735–1813), William Wilberforce (1759–1833), Thomas Clarkson (1760–1846) and Josiah Wedgwood (1730–95) and developed from an abolition organisation formed by the London Quaker Committee for Sufferings; nine of the Society's 12-strong founding committee were Quakers. Sharp, who became the Society's secretary, proposed campaigning for the abolition of slavery but fellow committee members saw the slave trade as a more realist target. The Society's initial work involved lobbying government (with Wilberforce as a Member of Parliament prominent in this) and gathering information (with Clarkson as a full-time researcher and propagandist). The Society's seal – a kneeling black slave in chains with his hands lifted skywards and the motto 'Am I Not a Man and a Brother?' – was designed by Wedgwood. Women were active in the Society's activities but were excluded from the leadership. Although support had now broadened to members of the Church of England (particularly Wilberforce and Clarkson), the Quaker system of regular meetings provided an effective framework for spreading organisation outside London. There was a significant movement in the North, particularly Manchester which gathered 11,000 signatures (two thirds of the adult male population) for a petition to Parliament within six months. In its first 18 months, the Society spent over £1,000 and circulated 15,000 copies of a pamphlet by Clarkson on the slave trade, *A Summary View of the Slave Trade and of the Probable Consequences of its Abolition*. From 1788–92, the Society's campaign dominated British politics but its progress came to a halt in the wake of the war with France that followed the revolution. The Society renewed its activities after British conquests in the Caribbean divided planter opinion on the slavery question. Following legislation against British participation in the slave trade in 1806 (effective in 1807), the Society was succeeded by the African Institution and then, in 1823, as the campaign against slavery itself intensified, the Society for the Mitigation and Gradual Abolition of Slavery Throughout the British Dominions.

Society for the Mitigation and Gradual Abolition of Slavery Throughout the British Dominions The Society – often described as the Anti-Slavery Society – was formed in 1823 by Thomas Fowell Buxton, William Wilberforce, Thomas Clarkson and Henry Brougham, and initially aimed at reforming rather than abolishing slavery entirely. With Wilberforce's retirement as an MP in 1825, Buxton took on his role as the voice of anti-slavery in Parliament. As with the campaign against the slave trade, women were prominent in agitation and in 1824 Elizabeth Heyrick produced a pamphlet – *Immediate not Gradual Abolition* – criticising the Society's male leadership. In 1830 women's organisations demanded that the Society took up a programme for complete abolition but the Society restricted itself for the moment to an appeal for immediate freedom for the newborn children of slaves. In 1831 the Agency Committee seceded from the Society to press for immediate abolition, although the two bodies co-operated in agitation. The campaign culminated in the passage of the Abolition of Slavery Act in 1833 (following the presentation of 5,000 petitions with 1,500,000 signatures) and the emancipation of slaves in most British possessions, albeit with a system of apprenticeship that sought to protect the interests of Caribbean plantation owners.

Society of Friends See Quakers.

Société Française pour l'abolition de l'esclavage (French Society for the Abolition of Slavery) Established in 1834, with Victor Schoelcher (1804–93) as a prominent figure. Although it received financial assistance from British anti-slavery activists, the Society was largely secular and acted with less evangelical zealousness than its counterparts in Britain and the United States. However, Roman Catholics were encouraged to support the Society by the Archbishop of Paris in 1847. The Society presented the first major legislation to abolish slavery to the National Assembly in 1838 but was thwarted by the slave owners' representatives. A number of further attempts failed until 1848 when Schoelcher proposed legislation which succeeded in securing an end to slavery in the French colonies, with compensation for the former owners.

Somerset Case A case which had the effect of making slavery in England impossible and which publicised the campaign to end slavery in Britain's colonies. In 1729 a court decision had confirmed that slaves brought to England and Ireland from the Caribbean remained slaves. In 1771, the abolitionist activist Granville Sharp (1735–1813) took up the case of James Somerset, a slave brought by his owner to England from Virginia. Somerset's lawyers argued that as there was no law allowing slavery in England then Somerset could not then be forcibly returned to Virginia. The case was heard by Lord Chief Justice William Mansfield (1705–93). Mansfield, who himself owned a slave, was reluctant to hear the case and delayed it for three terms. Giving his decision in June 1772, Mansfield ruled that Somerset could not be returned as a slave to Virginia. 'Whatever the inconveniences, therefore, may follow from a decision, I cannot say this case is allowed or approved by the law of England; and therefore the black must be discharged.' The ruling had the effect of undermining the legitimacy of slavery in England and eventually restored liberty to the estimated 15,000 slaves living in the country. Mansfield freed his own slave in 1782.

Southern Christian Leadership Conference (SCLC) An organisation of black churches and ministers founded in 1957 under the leadership of Martin Luther King Jr (1929–68), the SCLC formed the core of the American civil rights movement of the 1950s and 1960s, advocating non-violent civil disobedience rather than the purely legal stance of the National Association for the Advancement of Colored People (NAACP). Among prominent SCLC activists were Ralph Abernathy (1926–90), Ella Baker (1903–86) and Jesse Jackson (born 1941). The SCLC organised or participated in protest campaigns in Albany, Georgia, in 1961 and Birmingham, Alabama, in 1963, in the 1963 march on Washington, and the 1965 Selma to Montgomery march. From 1965, the organisation widened its agenda to include economic as well as civil rights issues but came under criticism from sections of the influencial Baptist church for its confrontational tactics while being attacked by Black Power supporters for its pacifism. Abernathy succeeded King as head of the SCLC in 1968 and led the largely unsuccessful Poor People's Campaign. The organisation remained in existence but declined in influence.

South Sea Company Chartered in Britain in 1711 to participate in the Spanish trade, the Company's main activity was shipping slaves from Africa to Spain's territories in the Caribbean and America. The Company shipped almost 5,000 slaves a year but profits from the slave trade proved a disappointment, partly because of a tax imposed on its activities under the terms of the Treaty of Utrecht in 1713. The British government invested in the Company in the hope of using the proceeds to pay off the National Debt. The appointment of King George I as the Company's governor encouraged a confidence in the Company's value and stability. The bursting of the 'bubble' in 1720 led to large losses among the country's financial elite.

Springfield Riots Racial disturbances in 1908 near the Illinois birthplace of Abraham Lincoln (the President who issued the proclamation freeing the slaves) that prompted black and white liberals to form what became the National Association for the Advancement of Colored People (NAACP). The riots followed tension over the use of black workers as strike breakers. Following a wrongful accusation of rape against a black man, white mobs rampaged through black areas, killing eight people and forcing over 2,000 to flee. Four whites were killed but none was ever charged over their part in the disturbances.

Stono Rebellion A slave revolt in the British North American colony of South Carolina in 1739 led by Jemmy, an Angolan. Eighty slaves seized weapons and attempted to flee to the Spanish colony in Florida. Spain and Britain were at war and the Spanish had offered fugitive slaves their freedom. The rebels were overtaken by whites and in the fighting 44 slaves and 21 whites were killed. A further 30 slaves were executed in the aftermath. The colony then introduced a 'Negro Act' which limited the rights of slaves to grow food, earn money, assemble and to learn to read and write.

Student Nonviolent Co-ordinating Committee (SNCC) Civil rights organisation formed by black and white students in North Carolina in 1960 to co-ordinate non-violent direct action against segregation in the United States. The SNCC played an important part in the 1961 Freedom Rides and in voter registration campaigns in the South in 1964 and 1965. In the mid 1960s, as dissatisfaction with slow progress towards civil rights increased and with the rise of Black Power stressing self-reliance and a willingness to use violence in self defence, the SNCC under the leadership of Stokely Carmichael (born 1941) and then of H. Rap Brown (born 1943) severed its alliance with white liberalism and developed co-operation with the Black Panther Party. The SNCC was the first civil rights organisation to oppose United States involvement in the war in Vietnam in 1966. Carmichael left the SNCC in 1967 and in 1969 Brown renamed the organisation the Student National Co-ordinating Committee. In 1970, with Brown facing arrest for incitement to riot, the organisation was disbanded.

Tacky's Rebellion A slave rising on two plantations in Jamaica in 1760 led by Tacky, a Cotomantee chief from Guinea. Over a hundred slaves newly imported from the Gold Coast killed 60 whites. The rebels broke into a fort at Port Maria and captured weapons and were then joined by supporters from neighbouring plantations. The majority of the force surrendered when the militia was deployed against them but Tacky and 25 others fled to the hills, were they were killed by Maroons. In the aftermath of the rebellion, 400 slaves were murdered and 600 deported to Honduras.

Talented tenth An expression first used by Alexander Crummell (1819–97) in his opening address to the American Negro Academy in 1897, encapsulating his view that the future of black Americans depended on creating an educated elite. The expression was developed by W. E. B. Du Bois (1868–1963) in *Dusk of Dawn: An Essay Towards an Autobiography of a Race Concept* in which he wrote, 'I believed in the higher education of the Talented tenth who through their knowledge of modern culture could guide the American Negro into a higher civilisation. I know that without this the Negro would have to accept white leadership.'

Thirteenth Amendment The 1865 amendment to the United States Constitution which abolished slavery. The first section of the amendment declared, 'Neither slavery nor involuntary servitude, except as a punishment for crime whereof the party shall have been duly convicted, shall exist within the United States, or any place subject to their jurisdiction.'

Tordesillas, Treaty of An agreement between Spain and Portugal on the division of the Americas, underpinned by bulls issued by the Spanish-born Pope Alexander VI. A line of demarcation was set 320 miles west of the Cape Verde Islands. Spain was given exclusive rights to all territories west of the line while Portugal was allocated territories to the east. Neither power was to occupy land already owned by a Christian ruler.

Tumbeiro (Port. 'parasite') A slave ship operating from the Portuguese colonies in West Africa. The word was also used to describe a slave hunter operating in Africa itself.

Tuskegee Institute The Tuskegee Normal and Industrial Institute, established in Alabama in 1881 by the black American activist Booker T. Washington (1856–1915). The institute was intended to provide education to black Americans to lay the basis for an economically independent black population. This accorded with Washington's view that black civil rights could be more effectively achieved through economic and cultural advance than political agitation. The institute gave rise to the expression the 'Tuskegee machine', Washington's attempt to dominate discussion of black civil rights.

Twenty Fourth Amendment The 1964 amendment to the United States Constitution which abolished payment of a poll tax as a condition of voting in Federal elections, an imposition made in some Southern states to deny black Americans the right to participate in elections. Section 1 of the amendment declared, 'The right of citizens of the United States to vote in any primary or other election for President or Vice President... shall not be denied or abridged by the United States or any State by reason of failure to pay any poll tax or other tax.'

Uncle Tom's Cabin A novel dealing graphically with the subject of slavery written by Harriet Beecher Stowe (1811–96) and first serialised in 1851–52 in the Washington paper of the American and Foreign Anti-Slavery Society, the *National Era*, and then produced in book form in 1852. The work, which sold 500,000 copies in five years, had an immediate impact on opinion in the Northern states but Stowe was accused of exaggeration by supporters of slavery. In response, she produced *A Key to Uncle Tom's Cabin* in 1853 with background documentation. The success of *Uncle Tom's Cabin* propelled Stowe into prominence as an anti-slavery lecturer in the United States and Europe. She produced a further novel on the theme of slavery, *Dred: A Tale of the Great Dismal Swamp* in 1856. Lincoln is said to have described Stowe on meeting her at the White House in 1862 as 'the little lady who made this big war'. The nature of the novel's main character has led some militants to refer to more moderate blacks as 'Uncle Toms'.

Underground Railroad Means of escape – neither underground, nor a railroad – for thousands of slaves from the Southern United States to the North and Canada which operated from the end of the 18th century to 1862. It was given the title of the 'Underground Railroad' in 1831. Assisted by free blacks and white abolitionists (known as 'conductors') with food and clothing, slaves moved by night and hid in safe locations (called 'stations') by day. The most used routes ran through Ohio, Indiana and western Pennsylvania to Canada or through southern Pennsylvania to New England and Quebec. Among prominent organisers were Levi Coffin (1798–1877), a Quaker who helped over 3,000 slaves escape and was called the 'president' of the Railroad, and Harriet Tubman (1823–1913), an escaped slave known as the 'Black Moses', who returned to the South 19 times to lead over 250 slaves to liberty.

Voting Rights Act, 1965 This United States legislation attempted to strengthen the effectiveness of previous legislation intended to protect the right of black Americans to vote. Section 2 of the Act declared, 'No voting qualification or

217

prerequisite to voting, or standard, practice, or procedure shall be imposed by any State or political subdivision to deny or abridge the right of any citizen of the United States to vote on account of race or color.' Within three years over half of black Americans of voting age had registered in each Southern state.

Watts Riots The worst racial disturbances in the history of the United States, which took place from 11–21 August 1865 in the two square miles black Watts section of Los Angeles, California. The events were triggered by a clash between black youths and the police but their background lay in unemployment, police racism and the disproportionate impact of the developing war in Vietnam on black conscripts. Over a third of the Watts population were estimated to have taken part in the rioting in which 34 people were killed, over a thousand seriously injured and almost 4,000 arrested. The National Guard were employed to restore order. President Lyndon Johnson recognised that there were 'legitimate grievances' but declared they did not excuse violence. Martin Luther King Jr criticised the effect such events might have on the progress of the civil rights movement.

'Weeping time', the A contemporary description of the largest single slave sale in the United States. The sale was held at a racetrack in Savannah, Georgia, in March 1859. In two days, 436 men, women and children were sold for a total of $303,850. The highest price paid for an individual slave was $1,750 and the lowest $250. The price for a slave family – a woman and her five adult children – was $6,180. The slaves were the property of Pierce Butler (1806–67), whose former partner, Frances Kemble (1809–93), was an abolitionist.

Whitney's cotton gin The invention in 1793 by Eli Whitney of the cotton gin (an engine which separated seeds from the cotton plant) encouraged an increase in cotton cultivation in the United States, leading to a demand for slave labour in the Southern states (particularly female labour as harvesting was seen as a 'sensitive' activity) and an expansion in cotton mills in the Northern states and in England. The demand for slaves increased as 'King Cotton' moved into the 'New South' of Alabama, Louisiana, Mississippi and Texas, with annual cotton production rising from 140,000 pounds in 1791 to 35 million pounds in two decades. In 1803, cotton overtook tobacco as the main export crop of the United States. As a result of the demand for labour encouraged by the cotton gin's effectiveness, the numbers of slaves in the Southern states rose from 694,000 in 1790 to 3,950,528 in 1860. Ten years before the outbreak of the American Civil War in 1861 almost two thirds of plantation slaves were engaged in cotton production, with an average of 35 slaves on each plantation.

Wilmot Proviso An amendment introduced in the House of Representatives by Pennsylvania Democrat David Wilmot shortly after the outbreak of the 1846–48 war between the United States and Mexico. Wilmot sought to ensure that slavery should be outlawed in any territories acquired from Mexico

(California and New Mexico were seized in 1848). The amendment was accepted by the House of Representatives but rejected by the Senate, opening an argument between the Northern and Southern states that found a temporary culmination in the Compromise of 1850.

Wood Report A report on conditions in the British Caribbean colonies presented by junior Colonial Minister Edward Ward (later Lord Halifax) in 1922 following a three month investigation. The British government was responding to growing demands for political reform. Wood – who confined his enquiries largely to white officials, businessmen and merchants and who neglected to meet civil rights and political activists – recommended a limited expansion in the franchise and representative government through the local legislatures.

Yorke–Talbot Decision A ruling by Solicitor-General Yorke and Attorney-General Talbot in 1729 that holding slaves in Britain was legal and that slave owners had the right to forcibly return slaves brought to Britain from the Caribbean. The previous legal position of slaves in Britain had been unclear and there had appeared to be no basis for slavery under common law. The Yorke–Talbot decision was reversed in the Somerset case of 1772.

Zong case An influential case which demonstrated the cruelty of slave trading to British public opinion. The *Zong*, a British slave ship, was sailing from Africa to Jamaica in January 1783 when it was struck by an epidemic. As insurance covered only slaves who were lost at sea and not those who died from sickness brought on by bad conditions, the commander of the *Zong*, Captain Collingwood, ordered 133 slaves to be thrown overboard. Thirty-six who resisted were shackled together before being cast into the sea. When the owners' claim to compensation was resisted by the insurers, the owners went to court where Lord Chief Justice Mansfield (of Somerset case fame) ruled in their favour in *Gregson* v *Gilbert* in 1783. The incident and the case had a dramatic effect on public opinion. However, attempts by Granville Sharp (1735–1813) and other abolitionists to have those responsible for the deaths brought to trial failed.

BIBLIOGRAPHIES

This bibliography provides an introduction to the main areas covered in this *Companion* but, given the wealth of material that is now being produced, is not exhaustive. A reader with a deeper interest in specific aspects will want to consult the bibliographies in each of the suggested works. Unless otherwise stated, the place of publication is London.

The slave trade

General studies of the slave trade include Herbert Klein, *The Atlantic Slave Trade* (Cambridge, 1999), Hugh Thomas, *The Slave Trade: The History of the Atlantic Slave Trade, 1440–1870* (1997), James Rawley, *The Transatlantic Slave Trade: A History* (New York, 1981) and Herbert Klein, *The Middle Passage: Comparative Studies in the Atlantic Slave Trade* (Princeton, 1978). For a useful view of the early period, see John Thornton, *Africa and the Africans in the Making of the Atlantic World, 1400–1800* (Cambridge, 1992) and for the broader African background, Patrick Manning, *Slavery and African Life: Occidental, Oriental, and African Slave Traders* (Cambridge, 1990). See also James Searing, *West African Slavery and Atlantic Commerce* (Cambridge, 1993).

For calculations of the numbers involved, see Philip D. Curtin, *The Atlantic Slave Trade: A Census* (Madison, 1969) and Stanley L. Engerman and Eugene D. Genovese (eds), *Race and Slavery in the Western Hemisphere: Quantitative Studies* (Princeton, 1975). More recent accounting includes David Richardson, 'Slave Exports from West and West-Central Africa, 1700–1810: New Estimates of Volume and Distribution', *Journal of African History* 30 (1989), David Eltis and David Richardson, 'Routes to Slavery and the Numbers Game' and David Eltis and David Richardson, 'West Africa and the Transatlantic Slave Trade: New Evidence of Long-run Trends', both in *Slavery and Abolition* 18: 1 (1997).

On the broader effects of the trade see Joseph E. Inikori and Stanley L. Engerman (eds), *The Atlantic Slave Trade: Effects on Economies, Societies, and Peoples in Africa, the Americas, and Europe* (Durham, North Carolina, 1992). For the direct effect on Africa, see Robin Law, *The Slave Coast of West Africa, 1550–1750: The Impact of the Atlantic Slave Trade on an African Society* (Oxford, 1991), Paul Lovejoy, 'The Impact of the Atlantic Slave Trade on Africa', *Journal of African History* 30 (1989) and Henry Gemery and Jan Hogendom, 'The Economic Costs of West African Participation in the Atlantic Slave Trade', in Gemery and Hogendom (eds), *The Uncommon Market: Essays in the Economic History of the Atlantic Slave Trade* (New York, 1979). See also, David Eltis and David Richardson, *Routes to Slavery: Direction, Ethnicity and Mortality in the Transatlantic Slave Trade* (1997) and Herbert Klein and Stanley L. Engerman, 'Trends in Slave Mortality in the Atlantic Slave Trade', *Slavery and Abolition* 18: 1 (1997). For the trade during the period of its abolition, see David Eltis, 'The Export of Slaves from Africa, 1821–1843', *Journal of Economic History* 37 (1977).

On the traders themselves, see Joseph C. Miller, *Way of Death: Merchant*

Capitalism and the Angolan Slave Trade, 1730–1830 (Madison, 1988), Trevor Burnham, 'Who Bought Slaves in Early America? Purchasers of Slaves from the Royal African Company in Jamaica, 1674–1708', *Slavery and Abolition* 17: 2 (1996) and Michael Tadman, *Speculators and Slaves: Masters, Traders, and Slaves in the Old South* (Madison, 1989). For the story of John Newton, a slave trader who became an abolitionist, see Bernard Martin and Mark Spurrell (eds), *The Journal of a Slave Trader, 1750–1754* (1962).

The major slave trading powers are examined in Johannes Postma, *The Dutch in the Atlantic Slave Trade, 1600–1815* (Cambridge, 1990), Robert L. Stein, *The French Slave Trade in the Eighteenth Century: An Old Regime Business* (Madison, 1979) and Robert Conrad, *World of Sorrow: The African Slave Trade to Brazil* (1986). For Britain, see Colin Palmer, *Human Cargoes: The British Slave Trade to Spanish America, 1700–1739* (Urbana, 1981), James Walvin, *Black Ivory: A History of British Slavery* (1994). On Spain, Murdo MacLeod, 'Spain and America: The Atlantic Trade 1492–1720', in Leslie Bethell (ed.), *The Cambridge History of Latin America* (Cambridge, 1984). Denmark's Caribbean involvement is covered in Svend Pedersen, 'The Scope and Structure of the Danish Slave Trade', *Scandinavian History Review* 19 (1971).

On the broader economic benefits for the countries involved in the slave trade, see Elizabeth Fox-Genovese and Eugene Genovese, *Fruits of Merchant Capital: Slavery and Bourgeois Property in the Rise and Expansion of Capitalism* (Oxford, 1983) and David Richardson, 'The Slave Trade, Sugar and British Economic Growth, 1748 to 1776', in Barbara Solow and Stanley L. Engerman (eds), *British Capitalism and Caribbean Slavery* (Cambridge, 1987). Eli Faber, 'Jews, Slaves, and the Slave Trade: Setting the Record Straight' (1998) and Richard Gray, 'The Papacy and the Atlantic Slave Trade', *Past and Present* 115 (1987) consider two other aspects of the trade.

Slavery

For the broad background to slavery see M. I. Finley, *Ancient Slavery and Modern Ideology* (Harmondsworth, 1983), David Brion Davis, *The Problem of Slavery in Western Culture* (Oxford, 1988) and David Brion Davis, *Slavery and Human Progress* (Oxford, 1984). Orlando Patterson, *Slavery and Social Death: A Comparative Study* (Cambridge, 1982) is wide-ranging. An important study to consult is Robin Blackburn, *The Making of New World Slavery: From the Baroque to the Modern, 1492–1800* (1997). There is a discussion of the academic approaches taken in P. J. Parish, *Slavery: History and Historians* (1989). On pre-existing slavery in Africa, see Patrick Manning, *Slavery and African Life: Occidental, Oriental and African Slave Trades* (Cambridge, 1990) and Paul Lovejoy, *Transformations in Slavery: History of Slavery in Africa* (Cambridge, 1983).

Recent major studies of slavery in the Americas include David Eltis, *The Rise of African Slavery in the Americas* (Cambridge, 2000), Paul Lovejoy and Nicholas Rogers (eds), *Unfree Labour in the Development of the Atlantic World*

(1994) and Barbara Solow, *Slavery and the Rise of the Atlantic System* (Cambridge, 1991). See also Philip D. Curtin, *The Rise and Fall of the Plantation Complex: Essays in Atlantic History* (New York, 1994).

On slavery in the country which had the largest number of slaves, Brazil, see Robert Conrad, *Children of God's Fire: A Documentary History of Black Slavery in Brazil* (University Park, Pennsylvania, 1995) and A. Russell Wood, *The Black Man in Slavery and Freedom in Colonial Brazil* (1982). For particular aspects, see Stuart Schwartz, *Sugar Plantations in the Formation of Brazilian Society: Bahia, 1550–1835* (Cambridge, 1985) and Stanley Stein, *Vassouras: A Brazilian Coffee County, 1850–1900* (Princeton, 1985). See also Laird W. Bergad, *Slavery and the Demographic and Economic History of Minas Gerais, Brazil, 1720–1888* (Cambridge, 2000). Carl Delger, *Neither Black nor White: Slavery and Race Relations in Brazil and the United States* (New York, 1971) provides a useful comparative study.

For slavery in Spanish America, see Rolanda Mellafe, *Negro Slavery in Latin America* (1975) and Robert Toplin (ed.), *Slavery and Race Relations in Latin America* (1974). Slavery in one country is considered in Frederick Bowser, *The African Slave in Colonial Peru, 1524–1650* (Stanford, 1974) and in Central America in Nigel O. Bolland, 'Colonization and Slavery in Central America', in Paul Lovejoy and Nicholas Rogers (eds), *Unfree Labour in the Development of the Atlantic World* (1994).

On Cuba, the Spanish territory with the largest slave population over the longest period, see Herbert S. Klein, *Slavery in the Americas: A Comparative Study of Virginia and Cuba* (Chicago, 1967), and Manuel Moreno Fraginals, Frank Moya Pons and Stanley L. Engerman (eds) *Between Slavery and Free Labor: The Spanish-Speaking Caribbean in the Nineteenth Century* (Baltimore, 1985). On 19th century slavery in the Spanish colony see Laird Bergad, Fe Iglesias Garcia and Maria del Carmen Barcia, *The Cuban Slave Market, 1790–1880* (New York, 1995) and Franklin W. Knight, *Slave Society in Cuba During the Nineteenth Century* (Madison, 1970). For slavery in another significant Spanish Caribbean colony, see Francisco Scarano, *Sugar and Slavery in Puerto Rico: The Plantation Economy of Ponce, 1800–1850* (Madison, 1984). See also Herbert Klein, *African Slavery in Latin America and the Caribbean* (Oxford, 1986).

The broader studies on slavery in the British Caribbean are Michael Craton, *Empire, Enslavement and Freedom in the Caribbean* (Oxford, 1997), Barbara Solow and Stanley L. Engerman (eds), *British Capitalism and Caribbean Slavery* (Cambridge, 1987), Hilary Beckles and Verene Stephens, *Caribbean Slave Society and Economy* (1991). For the final phase, see John Ward, *British West Indian Slavery, 1750–1834: The Process of Amelioration* (Oxford, 1988).

For why the slaves were there, see Arthur Stinchcombe, *Sugar Island Slavery in the Age of Enlightenment: The Political Economy of the Caribbean World* (Chichester, 1995), Richard Dunn, *Sugar and Slaves: The Rise of the Planter Class in the English West Indies, 1624–1713* (Chapel Hill, 1972), Richard Sheridan, *Sugar and Slavery: An Economic History of the British West Indies, 1623–1775* (1974) and J. R. Ward, 'The Profitability of Sugar Plantations in the British

West Indies: 1650–1834', *Economic History Review*, 2nd series, 21: 2 (1978). See also J. R. Ward, 'A Planter and His Slaves in Eighteenth Century Jamaica', in T. C. Smouth (ed.), *The Search for Wealth and Stability* (1979).

On specific Caribbean islands, see Michael Craton, *Searching for the Invisible Man: Slaves and Plantation Life in Jamaica* (Cambridge, Mass., 1978), Barry W. Higman, *Slave Population and Economy in Jamaica, 1807–1834* (Cambridge, 1976), Gail Saunders, *Slavery in the Bahamas, 1648–1838* (Nassau, 1985), Virginia Bernhard, *Slaves and Slaveholders in Bermuda, 1616–1782* (1999) and Elsa Goveia, *Slave Society in the British Leeward Islands at the End of the Eighteenth Century* (New Haven, 1965).

The Dutch were, for a long period, dominant in the slavery business. Their involvement in slavery is well covered in Pieter Emmer, *The Dutch in the Atlantic economy, 1580–1880: Trade, Slavery and Emancipation* (Aldershot, 1998), and Pieter Emmer, 'The Dutch and the Making of the Second Atlantic System', in Barbara Solow (ed.), *Slavery and the Rise of the Atlantic System* (Cambridge, 1991). Danish Caribbean slavery is examined in George Tyson, 'On the Periphery of the Peripheries: The Cotton Plantations of St. Croix, Danish West Indies, 1735–1815', *Journal of Caribbean History* 26 (1992).

Information on slavery in France and the French Caribbean can be found in Clarence Munford, *The Black Ordeal of Slavery and Slave Trading in the French West Indies* (Lewiston, 1991), Sue Peabody, *'There are no slaves in France': The Political Culture of Race and Slavery in the Ancien Regime* (Oxford, 1996), Robert Stein, *The French Sugar Business in the Eighteenth Century* (1988) and David Geggus, 'Slave Society in the Sugar Plantation Zones of Saint Domingue and the Revolution of 1791–93', *Slavery and Abolition* 20: 2 (1999).

On slavery in British North America, see Oscar Reiss, *Blacks in Colonial America* (1997) and Betty Wood, *The Origins of American Slavery: Freedom and Bondage in the English Colonies* (New York, 1997). Examinations of the contradictions between the American colonists' desire for liberty alongside slavery include Duncan MacLeod, *Slavery, Race and the American Revolution* (Cambridge, 1974), Staughton Lynd, *Class Struggle, Slavery and the United States Constitution* (New York, 1967) and Edmund Morgan, 'Slavery and Freedom: The American Paradox', *Journal of American History* 59: 1 (1972).

There is a vast amount of material on slavery in the United States and only a small selection can be included here. For general coverage, see Duncan Clarke, *Slaves and Slavery* (1999), Peter Kolchin, *American Slavery, 1619–1877* (1995), and Robert William Fogel and Stanley L. Engerman (eds), *Without Consent or Contract: The Rise and Fall of American Slavery* (1992). For useful documents, see Willie Lee Rose, *A Documentary History of Slavery in North America* (New York, 1976) and Michael Mullin, *American Negro Slavery: A Documentary History* (New York, 1976).

S. M. Elkins, *Slavery: A Problem in American Institutional and Intellectual Life* (Chicago, 1959) still makes interesting points, as does David Brion Davis, *The Problem of Slavery in the Age of Revolution, 1770–1823* (Oxford, 1975). See also, James C. Morgan, *Slavery in the United States: Four Views* (1985), and John Ashworth, *Slavery, Capitalism and Politics in the Antebellum Republic* (Cambridge,

1995). For the legal aspect, see Andrew Fede, *People Without Rights: An Interpretation of the Fundamentals of the Law of Slavery in the United States South* (1992) and on politics, William J. Cooper, *The South and the Politics of Slavery, 1828–1856* (1980).

For more information on the Southern states, see Kenneth M. Stampp, *The Peculiar Institution: Slavery in the Ante-bellum South* (New York, 1956), Eugene D. Genovese, *In Red and Black: Marxian Explorations in Southern and Afro-American History* (New York, 1971), John W. Blassingame, *The Slave Community: Plantation Life in the Antebellum South* (Oxford, 1978) and Leslie Owens, *This Species of Property: Slave Life and Culture in the Old South* (Oxford, 1977). Richard C. Wade, *Slavery in the Cities: The South 1820–1860* (Oxford, 1964) and Robert S. Starobin, *Industrial Slavery in the Old South* (Oxford, 1970) cover another aspect. See also, Barbara Fields, 'Slavery, Race and Ideology in the United States of America', *New Left Review* 181 (1990). On slave lives in the United States see Paul Finkleman, *The Culture and Community of Slavery* (1989) and Charles T. Davis and Henry Louis Gates, *The Slave's Narrative* (Oxford, 1985). For the other end of the question, see James Oakes, *The Ruling Race: A History of American Slaveholders* (New York, 1982) and Larry Tise, *Proslavery: A History of the Defense of Slavery in America, 1701–1840* (Athens, 1987) and, for the attitudes behind this view, Winthrop Jordan, *The White Man's Burden: Historical Origins of Racism in the United States* (Oxford, 1974).

For a discussion on the broader economic impact of slavery, see Elizabeth Fox-Genovese and Eugene Genovese, *Fruits of Merchant Capital: Slavery and Bourgeois Property in the Rise and Expansion of Capitalism* (Oxford, 1983). One of the earliest studies of the economics of slavery in the United States, which remains useful, is Ulrich B. Phillips, *American Negro Slavery: A Survey of the Supply, Employment, and Control of Negro Labor as Determined by the Plantation Regime* (New York, 1918). Also of interest are Robert Fogel and Stanley L. Engerman, *Time on the Cross: The Economics of American Negro Slavery* (Boston, 1989), Eugene Genovese, *The Political Economy of Slavery: Studies in the Economy and Society of the Slave South* (New York, 1965) and Gavin Wright, *The Political Economy of the Cotton South: Households, Markets and Wealth in the Nineteenth Century* (New York, 1978). A more recent study, Daniel H. Usner, 'Frontier Exchange and Cotton Production: The Slave Economy in Mississippi, 1798–1836', *Slavery and Abolition* 20: 1 (1999), considers a specific state. Gavin Wright, *Old South, New South: Revolutions in the Southern Economy since the Civil War* (New York, 1986) examines the economic impact of emancipation.

On the economic value of slavery in the British Caribbean, see Richard Sheridan, *Sugar and Slavery: An Economic History of the British West Indies, 1623–1775* (1974) and David Richardson, 'The Slave Trade, Sugar and British Economic Growth, 1748 to 1776', in Barbara Solow and Stanley Engerman (eds), *British Capitalism and Caribbean Slavery* (Cambridge, 1987). For South America, see Rolando Mellafe, *Negro Slavery in Latin America* (1975).

For a view of the lives led by slaves, see John Thornton, *Africa and Africans in the Making of the Atlantic World 1400–1800* (Cambridge, 1998) and Ira Berlin and Philip D. Morgan (eds), *Cultivation and Culture: Labor and the Shaping of*

Slave Life in the Americas (1993). On aspects of slave life in the United States, see Eugene Genovese, *Roll, Jordan, Roll: The World the Slaves Made* (New York, 1974), Brenda E. Stevenson, *Life in Black and White: Family and Community in the Slave South* (Oxford, 1996) and John W. Blassingame, *The Slave Community: Plantation Life in the Antebellum South* (Oxford, 1972). There is a description of the element of independence allowed in Ira Berlin and Philip Morgan, *The Slaves' Economy: Independent Production by Slaves in the Americas* (1991). There is an informative study of labour in Richard Dunn, '"Dreadful Idlers" in the Cane Fields: The Slave Labor Pattern on a Jamaican Sugar Estate, 1762–1831', in Barbara Solow and Stanley Engerman, *British Capitalism and Caribbean Slavery* (Cambridge, 1987). For experiences in Brazil, see Mary Karasch, *Slave Life in Rio de Janeiro, 1808–1850* (Princeton, 1987) and Katia de Quieró Mattoso, *To Be a Slave in Brazil* (New Brunswick, 1986).

On the importance of religion in slave life, see Albert Raboteau, *Slave Religion: The Invisible Institution in the Antebellum South* (Oxford, 1978). For slave life in one important area, see David Geggus, 'Slave Society in the Sugar Plantation Zones of Saint Domingue and the Revolution of 1791–93', *Slavery and Abolition* 20: 2 (1999). Herbert Gutman, *The Black Family in Slavery and Freedom, 1750–1925* (New York, 1976) gives a comparative view of black life.

A central component of slaves' lives was their owners. For a useful study of slave-owning in the United States see J. Oakes, *The Ruling Race: A History of American Slaveholders* (1982). Ownership involved the related concepts of the morality of the institution itself and the laws governing it. On morality, see David Brion Davis, *The Problem of Slavery in Western Culture* (1966) and Eugene Genovese, *The Slaveholder's Dilemma: Freedom and Progress in Southern Conservative Thought 1820–1860* (1992). On the systems of law that underpinned slavery, Alan Watson, *Slave Law in the Americas* (Athens, 1989) provides a valuable overview while Thomas D. Morris, *Southern Slavery and the Law, 1619–1800* (Chapel Hill, 1996), Mark Tushnet, *The American Law of Slavery, 1810–1860* (Princeton, 1981) and Philip Schwarz, *Slave laws in Virginia* (1996) concentrate on colonial North America and the United States. The subject is also considered in Rolando Mellafe, *Negro Slavery in Latin America* (1975), Carl Delger, *Neither Black Nor White: Slavery and Race Relations in Brazil and the United States* (1971) and Herbert Klein, *Slavery in the Americas: A Comparative Study of Virginia and Cuba* (Chicago, 1967). For the Caribbean, see Elsa Goveia, *The West Indian Slave Laws of the Eighteenth Century* (1970).

There are a number of useful studies of the lives of women under slavery. The American experience is well covered in Patricia Morton (ed.), *Discovering the Women in Slavery: Emancipating Perspectives on the American Past* (1996), Elizabeth Fox-Genovese, *Within the Plantation Household: Black and White Women of the Old South* (Chapel Hill, 1988), Deborah Gray White, *Ar'n't I a Woman? Female Slaves in the Plantation South* (New York, 1985). See also Carol Shammas, 'Black Women's Work and the Evolution of Plantation Society in Virginia', *Labor History* 26: 1 (1985). On the longer term impact in the United States, see Jacqueline Jones, *Labor of Love, Labor of Sorrow: Black Women and the Family from Slavery to the Present* (New York, 1985).

For women's lives in the Caribbean, see particularly Verene Shepherd, *Engendering History: Caribbean Women in Historical Perspective* (Kingston, Jamaica, 1995), Barbara Bush, *Slave Women in Caribbean Society, 1650–1838* (1990), Marrietta Morrissey, *Slave Women in the New World: Gender Stratification in the Caribbean* (Lawrence, 1989) and Hilary Beckles, *Centring Woman: Gender Relations in Caribbean Slave Society* (Oxford, 1999). Mary Turner's article, 'The 10 o'clock Flog: Women, Work and Labour Law in the British Caribbean', *Slavery and Abolition* 20: 1 (1999), and Barbara Bush-Slimani, 'Hard Labour: Women, Childbirth and Resistance in British Caribbean Slave Societies', *History Workshop* (Autumn 1993) are also interesting.

Resistance to slavery

There has been a growing interest in the resistance to slavery, which ranged from flight to full-scale rebellion. For an overview see F. O. Best (ed.), *Black Resistance Movements in the United States and Africa, 1800–1993: Oppression and Retaliation* (Lampeter, 1995) and Eugene Genovese, *From Rebellion to Revolution: The Afro-American Slave Revolts in the Making of the Modern World* (1979). On revolt at the source, see William MacGowan, 'African Resistance to the Atlantic Slave Trade in West Africa', *Slavery and Abolition* 11: 1 (1990). For the continuing struggle, see Michael Mullin, *Africa in America: Slave Acculturation and Resistance in the American South and British Caribbean, 1736–1831* (Urbana, 1992) and Oruno Laro, 'Resistance to Slavery: From Africa to Black America', in V. Tuden (ed.), *Comparative Perspectives on Slavery in the New World Plantation Societies* (New York, 1977).

On the organisation of fugitive slaves see Gad Heuman (ed.), *Out of the House of Bondage: Runaways, Resistance and Maroonage in Africa and the New World* (1986) and R. Price (ed.), *Maroon Societies: Rebel Slave Communities in the Americas* (Baltimore, 1979). There is a useful study of a long-lasting maroon settlement in R. K. Kent, 'Palmares: An African State in Brazil', *Journal of African History* 6 (1965).

For examples of resistance in specific areas of the United States see N. T. Jones, *Born a Child of Freedom, Yet a Slave: Mechanisms of Control and Strategies of Resistance in Ante-bellum South Carolina* (Hanover, 1990), J. Sidbury, *Ploughshares into Swords: Race, Rebellion, and Identity in Gabriel's Virginia, 1730–1810* (Cambridge, 1997) and G. Mullin, *Flight and Rebellion: Slave Resistance in Eighteenth-Century Virginia* (Oxford, 1972). On an early action, see Thomas Davis, *Rumor of Revolt: The 'Great Negro Plot' in Colonial New York* (1985). E. Pearson, ' "A Countryside Full of Flames": A Reconsideration of the Stono Rebellion and Slave Rebellions in Early Nineteenth-Century South Carolina Low Country', *Slavery and Abolition* 17: 2 (1996) is also informative.

On resistance in the British Caribbean see Michael Craton, *Testing the Chains: Resistance to Slavery in the British West Indies* (1982) and, for examples in particular areas, Hilary Beckles, *Black Rebellions* (Bridgetown, 1984) and V. Bernham, 'Bids for Freedom: Slave Resistance and Rebellion Plots in

Bermuda, 1656–1761', *Slavery and Abolition* 17: 3 (1996). On later resistance, see Michael Craton, 'Proto-Peasant Revolt? The Late Slave Rebellions in the British West Indies', *Past and Present* 85, (1979). For the slave revolution in Haiti see C. E. Fick, *The Making of Haiti: The Saint Domingue Revolution From Below* (Knoxville, 1990). C. L. R. James, *The Black Jacobins: Toussaint L'Ouverture and the San Domingo Revolution* (1980) remains interesting. The best-known ship revolt and its repercussions is well covered in H. Jones, *Mutiny on the Amistad: the Saga of a Slave Revolt and its Impact on American Abolition, Law, and Diplomacy* (Oxford, 1987).

Emancipation

Major studies of the ending of slavery are Robin Blackburn, *The Overthrow of Colonial Slavery 1776–1848* (1988) and Thomas Bender (ed.), *The Antislavery Debate: Capitalism and Abolition in Historical Perspective* (Berkeley, 1991). On the end of the slave trade, see David Eltis and James Walvin (eds), *The Abolition of the Atlantic Slave Trade: Origins and Effects in Europe, Africa and the Americas* (Madison, 1981). Among more recent works are Seymour Drescher, *From Slavery to Freedom: Comparative studies in the Rise and Fall of Atlantic slavery* (Basingstoke, 1999) and Sylvia R. Frey and Betty Wood (eds), *From Slavery to Emancipation in the Atlantic World* (1999).

For the course of the campaign in Britain against the slave trade, see J. R. Oldfield, *Popular Politics and British Anti-slavery: The Mobilisation of Public Opinion against the Slave Trade, 1787–1807* (Manchester, 1998) and Judi Jennings, *The Business of Abolishing the British Slave Trade 1783–1807* (1997). On the main imperatives and effects, Seymour Drescher, *Econocide: British Slavery in the Era of Abolition* (1977), Seymour Drescher, *Capitalism and Anti-Slavery: British Mobilisation in Comparative Perspective* (1986), and David Eltis, *Economic Growth and the Ending of the Transatlantic Slave Trade* (Oxford, 1987). On the general anti-slavery campaign see, Michael Craton, James Walvin and David Wright (eds), *Slavery, Abolition and Emancipation: Black Slaves and the British Empire: A Thematic Documentary* (1976).

For the political arguments around British abolitionism, see Edith Hurwitz, *Politics and Public Conscience: Slave Emancipation and the Abolitionist Movement in Britain* (1973), and for the Parliamentary debates, Inhak Gross, 'The Abolition of Negro Slavery and British Parliamentary Politics, 1832–3', *Historical Journal* 23: 5 (1980). There is an interesting discussion of the role of women in Louis Billington and Rosamund Billington, '"A Burning Zeal for Righteousness": Women in the British Anti-Slavery Movement', in Jane Rendall (ed.), *Equal or Different: Women's Politics in Britain, 1800–1914* (Oxford, 1987). Peter J. Kitson and Debbie Lee (eds), *Slavery, Abolition, and Emancipation: Writings in the British Romantic Period* (1999) and David Turley, *The Culture of English Antislavery, 1780–1860* (1991) also provide useful background.

On emancipation and its aftermath in the British-controlled Caribbean see

William A. Green, *British Slave Emancipation: The Sugar Colonies and the Great Experiment, 1830–1865* (Oxford, 1976), Michael Craton, *Empire, Enslavement and Freedom in the Caribbean* (Oxford, 1997), and Jack Hayward, *Out of Slavery: Abolition and After: Legacies of West Indian Slavery* (1985). For one example of the temporary expedient that followed, see Robert S. Shelton, 'A Modified Crime: The Apprenticeship System in St Kitts', *Slavery and Abolition* 16: 3 (1995).

Howard Temperley, *British Antislavery, 1833–1870* (1972) is useful on the international campaign for abolition. For moves towards emancipation by colonial powers other than Britain, see, for Holland, Pieter Emmer, *The Dutch in the Atlantic Economy, 1580–1880: Trade, Slavery and Emancipation* (Aldershot, 1998), Gert Oostindie (ed.), *Fifty Years Later: Antislavery, Capitalism and Modernity in the Dutch Orbit* (Pittsburgh, 1996), and Seymour Drescher, 'The Long Goodbye: Dutch Capitalism and Anti-Slavery in Comparative Perspective', *American Historical Review* 99 (1994). On France, see Lawrence Jennings, *French Reaction to British Slave Emancipation* (1988), Daniel P. Restick, 'The Société des Amis des Noirs and the Abolition of Slavery', *French Historical Studies* 7: 4 (1972). For Denmark, see Hans Christian Johansen, 'The Reality Behind the Demographic Arguments to Abolish the Danish Slave Trade', in David Eltis and James Walvin (eds), *The Abolition of the Atlantic Slave Trade: Origins and Effects in Europe, Africa and the Americas* (Madison, 1981).

Brazil was a major slave centre and one of the last countries to abandon the institution. An important study of abolition is Robert Conrad, *The Destruction of Brazilian Slavery, 1850–1888* (1993). Joaquim Nabuco, *Abolitionism: The Brazilian Antislavery Struggle* (1977) and Celia Azevedo, *Abolitionism in the United States and Brazil: A Comparative Perspective* (1995) are also useful. On international involvement, see Leslie Bethell, *The Abolition of the Brazilian Slave Trade: Britain, Brazil and the Slave Trade Question, 1807–1869* (Cambridge, 1970).

Spain's abandonment of slavery is considered in Christopher Schmidt-Nowara, *Empire and Antislavery: Spain, Cuba, and Puerto Rico, 1833–1874* (1999). The major study of Cuba is Rebecca Scott, *Slave Emancipation in Cuba: The Transition to Free Labor, 1860–1899* (Guildford, 1985). On the ending of the slave trade, see David R. Murray, *Odious Commerce: Britain, Spain and the Abolition of the Cuban Slave Trade* (Cambridge, 1980) and for an interesting examination of the complications of Cuba's colonial status, see David Murray, 'The Slave Trade, Slavery and Cuban Independence', *Slavery and Abolition* 20: 3 (1999). For abolition in other parts of the Americas, see John Lombardi, *The Decline and Abolition of Negro Slavery in Venezuela, 1820–1854* (Westport, 1971) and Peter Blanchard, *Slavery and Abolition in Early Republican Peru* (Wilmington, 1992).

A useful introduction to the abolitionist movement in the United States is Hugh Hawkins (ed.), *The Abolitionists: Means, Ends and Motivations* (Lexington, 1995). For early activity, see Roger Burns (ed.), *Am I Not a Man and a Brother: The Antislavery Crusade of Revolutionary America 1688–1788* (New York, 1977), and for the contradictions of slavery and revolution, David Brion

Davis, *The Problem of Slavery in the Age of Revolution, 1770–1823* (Oxford, 1975), and Staughton Lynd, *Class Struggle, Slavery and the United States Constitution* (New York, 1967). The movement in its final phase is covered in Ronald Walters, *The Antislavery Appeal: American Abolitionism after 1830* (1976). See also, James Brewer Stewart, *Holy Warriors: The Abolitionists and American Slavery* (New York, 1976). On black involvement, see R. J. M. Blackett, *Building on Antislavery Wall: Black Americans in the Atlantic Abolitionist Movement, 1830–1860* (1983) and Benjamin Quarles, *Black Abolitionists* (Oxford, 1969).

The process of emancipation in the United States was gradual, with Northern states leading the way. Joanne Mellish, *Disowning slavery: Gradual Emancipation and 'Race' in New England, 1780–1860* (1998) and Arthur Zilversmit, *The First Emancipation: The Abolition of Slavery in the North* (Chicago, 1967) provide an overview. For individual states, see Patience Essah, *A House Divided: Slavery and Emancipation in Delaware, 1638–1865* (Charlottesville, 1996), Shane White, *Somewhat More Independent: The End of Slavery in New York City, 1770–1810* (1991), Gary Nash, *Freedom by Degrees: Emancipation in Pennsylvania and its Aftermath* (Oxford, 1991). For an examination of the granting of liberty to individual slaves by their owners, see Robert Olwell, 'Becoming Free: Manumission and the Genesis of a Free Black Community in South Carolina, 1740–90', *Slavery and Abolition* 17: 1 (1996).

As in Britain, women played a significant part in the campaign against slavery in the United States. For examples of some of the tensions this caused, see Michael Pierson, 'Gender and Party Ideology: The Constitutional Thought of Women and Men in American Anti-Slavery Politics', *Slavery and Abolition* 20: 1 (1999). See also Patricia Morton (ed.), *Discovering the Women in Slavery: Emancipating Perspectives on The American Past* (1996).

For the role of religion in the movement against slavery, see Douglas Strong, *Perfectionist Politics: Abolitionism and the Religious Tensions of American Democracy* (New York, 1999) and John McKivigan, *The War against Proslavery Religion: Abolitionism and the Northern Churches, 1830–1865* (1984). See also, James D. Essig, *The Bonds of Wickedness: American Evangelicals Against Slavery, 1770–1808* (Philadelphia, 1982) and Donald Matthews, *Slavery and Methodism: A Chapter in American Morality, 1780–1845* (Princeton, 1965).

The American Civil War ended slavery in the United States. Roger Ransom, *Conflict and Compromise: The Political Economy of Slavery, Emancipation and the American Civil War* (Cambridge, 1989) and Howard Jones, *Abraham Lincoln and a New Birth of Freedom: the Union and Slavery in the Diplomacy of the Civil War* (1999) both provide a valuable introduction. There are also interesting views of the war in Gary Kynoch, 'Terrible Dilemmas: Black Enlistment in the Union Army during the American Civil War', *Slavery and Abolition* 18: 2 (1997), and Richard Blackett, 'African Americans, the British Working Class and the American Civil War', *Slavery and Abolition* 17: 2 (1996).

On the period of Reconstruction that followed the Civil War, see Eric Foner, *Reconstruction: America's Unfinished Revolution, 1863–1977* (New York, 1988), James Schmidt, *Free to work: Labor Law, Emancipation, and Reconstruction, 1865–1880* (1998), Donald Nieman (ed.), *The Politics of Freedom: African*

Americans and the Political Process during Reconstruction (1994) and James Bond, *No Easy Walk to Freedom: Reconstruction and the Ratification of the Fourteenth Amendment* (1997). On the organisation established by the government to assist emancipated slaves, see Donald Nieman (ed.), *The Freedmen's Bureau and Black Freedom* (1994). On the role of the Radical Republicans, see Herman Betz, *A New Birth of Freedom: The Republican Party and Freedmen's Rights, 1861–66* (1976).

Among interesting studies of the aftermath and consequences of emancipation in the United States, are Frank McGlynn and Seymour Drescher (eds), *The Meaning of Freedom: Economics, Politics and Culture after Slavery* (Pittsburgh, 1992), Amy Stanley, *From Bondage to Contract: Wage Labor, Marriage, and the Market in the Age of Slave Emancipation* (Cambridge, 1998) and Roger Ransom and Richard Sutch, *One Kind of Freedom: The Economic Consequences of Emancipation* (Cambridge, 1977). For a comparison between the United States and the Caribbean, see Frank McGlynn, *The Meaning of Freedom: Economics, Politics and Culture after Slavery* (1992). Specifically on labour in the Southern states, see Donald Nieman (ed.), *From Slavery to Sharecropping: White Land and Black Labor in the Rural South, 1865–1900* (1994), and on the legal system, Donald Nieman (ed.), *Black Southerners and the Law, 1865–1900* (1994).

Civil rights

The issues of emancipation from slavery and civil rights are interlinked. Two useful general works are Ron Field, *African Peoples of the Americas: From Slavery to Civil Rights* (Cambridge, 1995) and, on the economic aspects, Mary Turner (ed.), *From Chattel Slaves to Wage Slaves: The Dynamics of Labour Bargaining in the Americas* (1995). There are also interesting views in Anthony Marx, *Making Race and Nation: A Comparison of South Africa, the United States and Brazil* (Cambridge, 1999).

On the Caribbean, see David Richardson (ed.), *Abolition and its Aftermath: The Historical Context, 1790–1916* (1985), Hilary Beckles and Verene Shepherd, *Caribbean Freedom: Economy and Society from Emancipation to the Present* (1993), Malcolm Cross and Gad Heuman (eds), *Labour in the Caribbean: From Emancipation to Independence* (1988) and Thomas Holt, *The Problem of Freedom: Race, Labor and Politics in Jamaica and Britain, 1832–1938* (1992). Eric Williams, *From Columbus to Castro: The History of Caribbean, 1492–1969* (1970) remains interesting, particularly on the 20th century.

For early developments in individual British colonies, see William Green, *British Slave Emancipation: The Sugar Colonies and the Great Experiment 1830–1865* (Oxford, 1976), Philip James, *Power and Economic Change: The Response to Emancipation in Jamaica and British Guiana, 1840–1865* (1987). Among other useful works are Brian Moore, *Race, Power and Social Segmentation in Colonial Society: Guyana after Slavery, 1838–1891* (1987), Claude Levy, *Emancipation, Sugar and Federalism: Barbados and the West Indies,*

1833–1876 (Gainsville, 1979) and Gail Saunders, *Bahamian Society after Emancipation: Essays in Nineteenth and Early Twentieth Century Bahamian History* (Nassau, 1990).

On early civil rights issues in Cuba, see Rebecca Scott, *Slave Emancipation in Cuba: The Transition to Free Labor, 1860–1899* (Guildford, 1985). For a longer view, see Marianne Masferrer and Carmelo Mesa Lago, 'The Gradual Integration of the Black in Cuba: Under the Colony, the Republic and the Revolution', in Robert Toplin (ed.), *Slavery and Race Relations in Latin America* (Westport, 1974). On Brazil, Kim Butler, *Freedoms Given, Freedoms Won: Afro-Brazilians in Post-abolition São Paulo and Salvador* (1998). On Brazil, see also A. Russell Wood, *The Black Man in Slavery and Freedom in Colonial Brazil* (1982) and France Twine, *Racism in a Racial Democracy: The Maintenance of White Supremacy in Brazil* (New Brunswick, 1998).

A particular issue involves the position of black people living outside slavery. For information on this, see Jane Landers, *Against the Odds: Free Blacks in the Slave Societies of the Americas* (1996) and David W. Cohen and Jack P. Greene (eds), *Neither Slave nor Free: The Freedman of African Descent in the Slave Societies of the New World* (Baltimore, 1972). On the Caribbean see Gad Heuman, *Between Black and White: Race, Politics and the Free Coloreds in Jamaica, 1792–1865* (Westport, 1981) and Jerome Handler, *The Unappropriated People: Freedmen in the Slave Society of Barbados* (Baltimore, 1974). For Latin America, see Frederick P. Bowser, 'The Free Person of Color in Mexico and Lima, 1580–1650', in Stanley Engerman and Eugene Genovese (eds), *Race and Slavery in the Western Hemisphere: Quantitative Studies* (Princeton, 1975). For the United States, see Ira Berlin, *Slaves Without Masters: The Free Negro in the Antebellum South* (Oxford, 1974) and, for a specific area, Paul Lachance, 'The Limits of Privilege: Where Free Persons of Color Stood in the Hierarchy of Wealth in Antebellum New Orleans', *Slavery and Abolition* 17: 1 (1996).

Two useful short studies of the civil rights movement in the United States are Robert Cook, *Sweet Land of Liberty? The African – American Struggle for Civil Rights in the Twentieth Century* (1998) and William T. Martin Riches, *The Civil Rights Movement: Struggle and Resistance* (Basingstoke, 1997). Winthrop Jordan, *The White Man's Burden: Historical Origins of Racism in the United States* (Oxford, 1974) is a valuable background. Among the large number of general studies are Steven Lawson and Tony Lancaster, *Civil Rights in America, 1945–1989* (Basingstoke, 1990), David Garrow, *The Civil Rights Movement in the United States in the 1950s* (New York, 1989), Aldon Morris, *The Origins of the Civil Rights Movement: Black Communities Organising for Change* (1984), Manning Marable, *Race, Reform and Rebellion: The Second Reconstruction in Black America, 1945–1982* (1984), Juan Williams, *Eyes on the Prize: America's Civil Rights Years, 1954–1965* (Harmondsworth, 1987), Peter Levy, *The Civil Rights Movement* (1998) and Michael Weber, *Causes and Consequences of the African American Civil Rights Movement* (1997).

For the civil rights struggle in the United States before emancipation, see Jay Sigler, *Civil Rights in America: 1500 to the Present* (1998). For a more complex examination of pre-Civil War campaigning, see R. J. Young,

Antebellum Black Activists: Race, Gender, and Self (1996) and for a long-term study of a particular area see George Fishman, *The African American Struggle for Freedom and Equality: The Development of a People's Identity, New Jersey, 1624–1850* (1997).

After emancipation, segregation, a refusal by whites to share their everyday lives with blacks, lay at the centre of the discrimination the civil rights movement opposed. The most useful introductions to the subject are Donald Nieman (ed.), *African Americans and The Emergence of Segregation, 1865–1900* (1994), Edward Ayers, *The Promise of the New South* (Oxford, 1992) and Robert Haws, *The Age of Segregation: Race Relations in the South, 1890–1945* (Jackson, 1978). Two classics which remain of interest are C. Vann Woodward, *Origins of the New South, 1877–1913* (1951) and C. Vann Woodward, *The Strange Career of Jim Crow* (Oxford, 1974). For a particular aspect of segregation, see Donald Nieman (ed.), *African Americans and Education in the South, 1865–1900* (1994). There is also a useful summary of the issue, together with a comparison with apartheid, in John W. Cell, *The Highest Stage of White Supremacy: The Origins of Segregation in South Africa and the American South* (Cambridge, 1982).

Further background can be found in Thomas Durant and J. David Knottnerus (eds), *Plantation Society and Race Relations: The Origins of Inequality* (1999). Joel Williamson, *The Crucible of Race: Black–White Relations in the American South Since Emancipation* (Oxford, 1984) and Donald Nieman, *Black Freedom/White Violence* (1994).

On the politics of civil rights, see Steven Lawson, *Running for Freedom: Civil Rights and Black Politics in America since 1941* (1997), Ralphe Bunche, *The Political Status of the Negro in the Age of FDR* (Chicago, 1973), and on one of the most important pieces of legislation, Robert Loevy, *To End All Segregation: The Politics of the Passage of the Civil Rights Act of 1964* (1990). The central part played (or avoided) by successive administrations is well covered in Steven Shull, *American Civil Rights Policy from Truman to Clinton: The Role of Presidential Leadership* (1999) and Kenneth O'Reilly, *Nixon's Piano: Presidents and Racial Politics from Washington to Clinton* (1995). There is an examination of the wider aims of activists in Dona Hamilton and Charles Hamilton, *The Dual Agenda: Race and Social Welfare Policies of Civil Rights Organizations* (Chichester, 1997). On a crucial early argument over the strategy required to secure civil rights, see Thomas Harris, *Analysis of the Clash over the Issues between Booker T. Washington and W. E. B. Du Bois* (1993).

The philosophy behind much civil rights activism of the 1950s and 1960s in the United States is considered in Greg Moses, *Revolution of Conscience: Martin Luther King Jr and The Philosophy of Nonviolence* (1997). On the part King played as the voice of the movement see Taylor Branch, *Parting the Waters: Martin Luther King and the Civil Rights Movement, 1954–63* (1990) and Taylor Branch, *Pillar of Fire: America in the King Years, 1963–65* (1998). James Washington (ed.), *A Testament of Hope: The Essential Writings and Speeches of Martin Luther King Jr* (New York, 1991) provides a useful background. On urban disorders, see Michael Belknap (ed.), *Urban Race Riots* (1991) and, for one of the most dramatic, Gerald Horne, *Fire This Time: The Watts Uprising and the 1960s* (1995).

There are a number of studies of the main movements involved in the civil rights struggle in the United States. A useful general work is Cedric Robinson, *Black Movements in America* (1997). For the National Association for the Advancement of Colored People over the period, see James McPherson, *The Abolitionist Legacy: From Reconstruction to the NAACP* (Chichester, 1995) and Minnie Finch, *The NAACP: Its Fight for Justice* (1981), and for the views of its leading figures, Sondra Wilson (ed.), *In Search of Democracy: The NAACP Writings of James Weldon Johnson, Walter White, and Roy Wilkins* (Oxford, 1999). On the organisation's activity in two major areas, see Mark Tushnet, *The NAACP's Legal Strategy against Segregated Education* (1987) and Robert Zangrando, *The NAACP Crusade against Lynching, 1909–1950* (Philadelphia, 1980).

The Southern Christian Leadership Conference and its dominant figure are well covered in Adam Fairclough, *To Redeem the Soul of America: The Southern Christian Leadership Conference and Martin Luther King Jr* (Athens, 1987). On the Student Nonviolent Coordinating Committee, see Emily Stoper, *The Student Nonviolent Coordinating Committee: The Growth of Radicalism in a Civil Rights Organization* (Brooklyn, 1989) and Clayborne Carson, *In Struggle: SNCC and the Black Awakening of the 1960s* (Cambridge, Mass., 1981). For a description of the activities of the Congress of Racial Equality, see August Meier and Elliott Radick, *CORE: A Study in the Civil Rights Movement* (Oxford, 1973). The National Urban League is examined in Jesse Thomas Moore, *A Search for Equality: The National Urban League, 1810–1961* (University Park, Pennsylvania, 1981).

For the flavour of one aspect of the era, see Bobby Seale, *Seize the Time: The Story of the Black Panthers and Huey Newton* (1970). Women played an important part in the civil rights movement. See, for example, Zita Allen, *Black Women Leaders of the Civil Rights Movement* (1996) and Gayle Hardy, *American Women Civil Rights Activists: Biobibliographies of 68 Leaders, 1825–1992* (1993).

For civil rights campaigns in particular areas of the United States, see Nicolaus Mills, *Like a Holy Crusade: Mississippi, 1964 – The Turning of the Civil Rights Movement in America* (Chicago, 1992). Also in Mississippi, see John Dittmer, *Local People: The Struggle for Civil Rights in Mississippi* (Urbana, 1994). For Louisiana see Adam Fairclough, *Race and Democracy: The Civil Rights Struggle in Louisiana, 1915–1972* (1995). For two crucial campaigns in Alabama, see David Garrow, *The Walking City: The Montgomery Bus Boycott, 1955–1956* (New York, 1989) and David Garrow, *Protest at Selma: Martin Luther King, Jr, and the Voting Rights Act of 1965* (1979). On King's controversial turn to the Northern ghettos, see James Ralph, *Northern Protest: Martin Luther King, Jr., Chicago, and the Civil Rights Movement* (1993). For the desegregating sit-in campaign, see Martin Oppenheimer, *The Sit-In Movement of 1960* (New York, 1989).

The NAACP concentrated in particular on securing black civil rights through court action. A major study of this aspect of the American legal system can be found in Henry Abraham, *Freedom and the Court: Civil Rights and*

Liberties in the United States (Oxford, 1998). The central role of the Supreme Court is examined in John Howard, *The Shifting Wind: The Supreme Court and Civil Rights from Reconstruction to Brown* (1999) and the part played by a leading judicial figure in Mark Tushnet, *Making Civil Rights Law: Thurgood Marshall and the Supreme Court, 1936–1961* (Oxford, 1994). The abuse of the legal system to intimidate civil rights activists is covered by David Garrow, *The FBI and Martin Luther King, Jr: From 'Solo' to Memphis* (New York, 1981), and, over a longer period, Kenneth O'Reilly, *Black Americans: The FBI Files* (New York, 1994).

For contrasting aspects of the white response in the Southern states to civil rights agitation, see Neil McMillen, *The Citizens Council: Organised Resistance to the Second Reconstruction, 1954–64* (Champaign, 1971), David Chappell, *Inside Agitators: White Southerners in the Civil Rights Movement* (1994), and for the longer term effects, James Button, *Blacks and Social Change: Impact of the Civil Rights Movement in Southern Communities* (1989).

Apartheid

There is a wide range of useful material on apartheid in South Africa. For an overview of the country, see J. D. Omer-Cooper, *A History of South Africa* (1994). It is also worth looking at Nigel Worden, *Slavery in Dutch South Africa* (Cambridge, 1985) for the background. Among studies of apartheid itself are Merle Lipton, *Capitalism and Apartheid, 1910–1986* (1986), Brian Lapping, *Apartheid: A History* (1986), Philip Bonner, *Apartheid's Genesis 1935–1962: Contradiction, Continuity and Popular Struggle* (Witwatersrand, 1996), and Max Coleman (ed.), *A Crime against Humanity: Analysing the Repression of the Apartheid State* (Cape Town, 1998). On the role of the church in underpinning the system, see Tracy Kuperus, *State, Civil Society and Apartheid in South Africa: An Examination of Dutch Reformed Church–State Relations* (Basingstoke, 1999) and J. A. Louber, *A Critical Review of Racial Theology in South Africa: The Apartheid Bible* (1990). The latter stages are covered in Robert Scrine, *Adapt or Die: The End of White Politics in South Africa* (1992) and Lindsay Eades, *The End of Apartheid in South Africa* (1999). Some aspects of the opposition can be found in Joyce Kirk, *Making a Voice: African Resistance to Segregation in South Africa* (Oxford, 1998), Stephen Ellis and Tsepo Sechaba, *Comrades against Apartheid: The ANC and the South African Communist Party in Exile* (1992) and Mamphela Ramphele: *Across Boundaries: The Journey of a South African Woman Leader* (1999). The stories of two opponents who symbolised the hope for reconciliation that followed the fall of apartheid can be found in Nelson Mandela, *Long Walk to Freedom* (1995) and F. W. de Klerk, *The Last Trek: A New Beginning* (1999).

MAPS

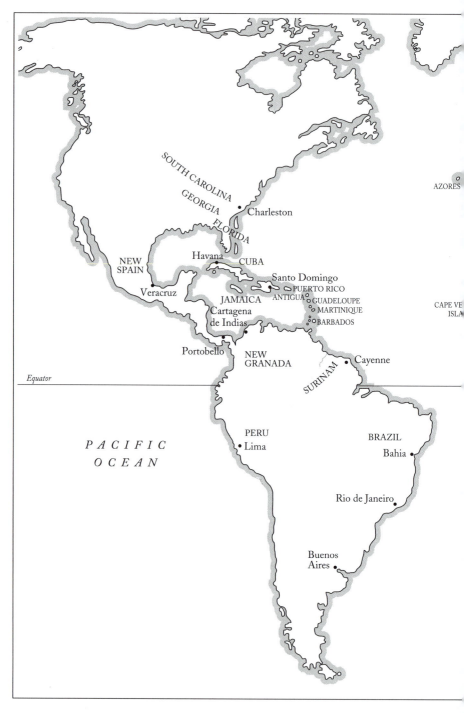

MAP 1

ADEIRA
NARY ISLES

rguin
énégal
oree
Gambia
Sierra Leone

Whydah • Benin
• Calabar
Elmina
PRINCIPE
SÃO TOMÉ   Loango

• Cabinda
• Luanda
• Benguela   Mozambique•

Congo

A T L A N T I C
O C E A N

MADAGASCAR

N

0   1000   2000 miles
0   1500   3000 km

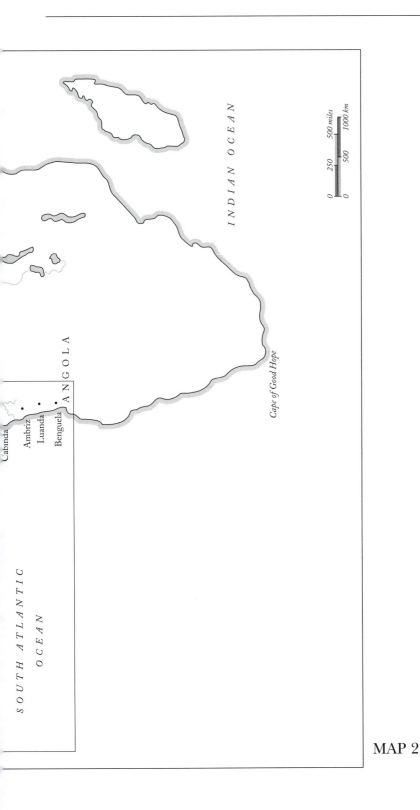

MAP 2

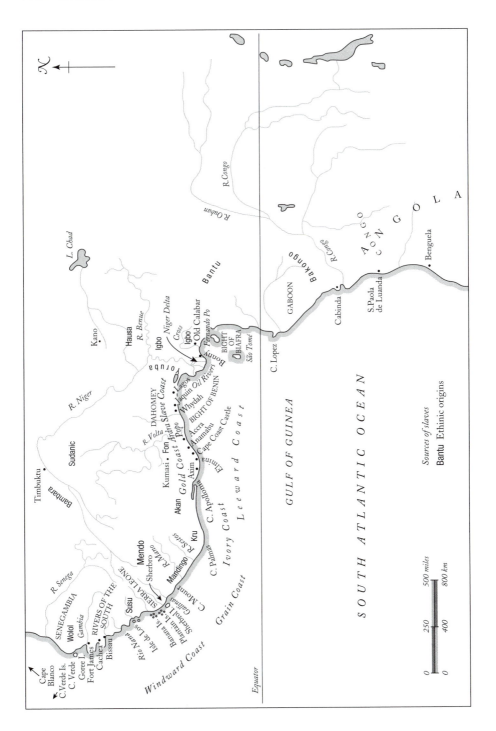

MAP 3

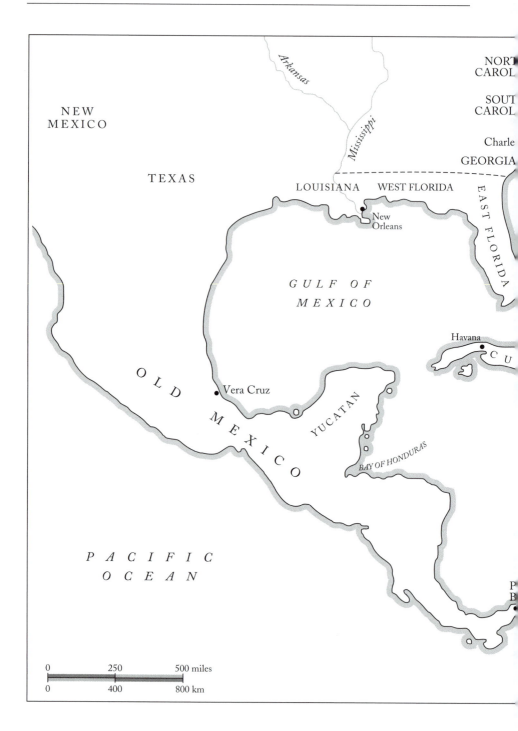

MAP 4

MAP 5

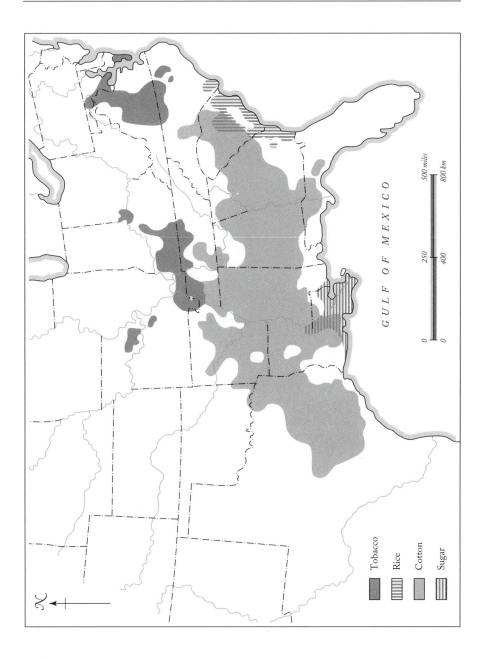

Tobacco
Rice
Cotton
Sugar

GULF OF MEXICO

500 miles
800 km

250
400

0
0

MAP 6

249

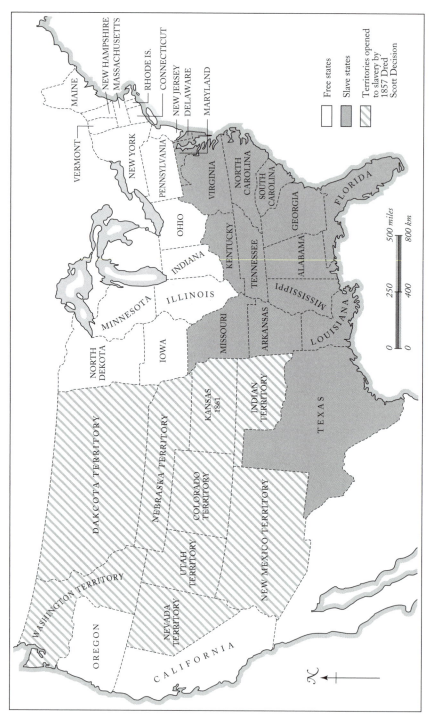

Free states

Slave states

Territories opened to slavery by 1857 Dred Scott Decision

500 miles

800 km

250

400

0

0

MAP 7

INDEX

Where there is a main entry in a group of entries, it is denoted in bold. An entry may appear more than once on a page.

MAR 2 8 2002

DATE DUE

GAYLORD			PRINTED IN U.S.A.